GREY WARS

GREY WARS

A CONTEMPORARY HISTORY OF
U.S. SPECIAL OPERATIONS

N. W. COLLINS

Yale UNIVERSITY PRESS

NEW HAVEN & LONDON

Published with assistance from the Frank M. Turner Publication Fund, the Schoff Fund, and the Louis Stern Memorial Fund.

Yale University Press books may be purchased in quantity for educational, business, or promotional use. For information, please e-mail sales.press@yale.edu (U.S. office) or sales@yaleup.co.uk (U.K. office).

Illustrations by Matt Chase.

Set in Meridien and Futura type by IDS Infotech, Ltd.
Printed in the United States of America.

Library of Congress Control Number: 2020949636
ISBN 978-0-300-19841-6 (hardcover : alk. paper)
ISBN 978-0-300-28006-7 (paperback)

A catalogue record for this book is available from the British Library.

10 9 8 7 6 5 4 3 2 1

Our special operations forces are the worst nightmare of America's worst enemies.

—*President George W. Bush, 2004*

Our special forces are the best of the best . . . it's hard to describe how courageous, how tough, how skilled, how precise they are.

—*President Barack Obama, 2011*

Just the strike part of it can never do more than keep an enemy at bay . . . Americans have got to understand that.

—*General Stanley McChrystal, 2013*

We are a command at war and will remain so for the foreseeable future.

—*General Tony Thomas, 2017*

Warfighting excellence . . . after all, we've been doing this for decades.

—*General Joseph L. Votel, 2019*

CONTENTS

1 First Day at Headquarters   1

2 Commander's Introduction   30

3 The Tour   65

4 More Boots Yet to Come   98

5 America's Superheroes   115

6 Fourteen Minutes of Fame   146

7 Fallen Angel   166

8 Use of the Golden Spear   193

Notes   213

Acknowledgments   291

Index   293

GREY WARS

1

FIRST DAY AT HEADQUARTERS

The fire-breathers are almost always civilians.
—Robert M. Gates, U.S. Secretary of Defense

This is not what war is supposed to look like.[1]

That's my first thought upon arriving at MacDill Air Force Base, Florida, in 2010.

We stop at a red-roofed gatehouse with a single-beamed electric post. The small structure is neither substantial nor imposing. It does not hint of Fortress America—nor would it pass the minimum post-9/11 standards of perimeter security. Its diminutive scale is far out of proportion to the consequential institutions on the other side.

The quiet entrance of this base, with its orange-leafed palms, towering oaks, and rows of citrus trees, set on a 6,000-acre peninsula, has the appearance of an idyllic beach resort.

The disparity is jarring. Small dark lettering at the checkpoint, however, does read "MacDill AFB." So, here it is: the military installation at the center of America's twenty-first-century wars—impelled by an attack on U.S. soil; launched and waged as a new type of global war; and ultimately splintering into a spectrum of regional conflicts.

Inside this fight—neither hot war nor cold peace—the use of U.S. Special Operations may be understood as paradox. The forces are the central instrument of America's military campaign—operating in about 100 countries on any given day—but are often peripheral in national security decision-making. The results are our nation's grey wars: hazy and lethal.

———

At the gatehouse, standing in battle uniform, a courteous young airman offers a warm welcome. Gracious, even deferential, he speaks with a quiet southern cadence, an accent I rarely hear living north of the Mason-Dixon Line. He accepts our paperwork, including a stack of drivers' licenses, and checks each name against his clipboard roster. Within a few minutes, the gate-guard waves our white van through with a smile.

We are here at MacDill for a series of briefings on the 9/11 wars. We will visit the two combatant commands co-located here: U.S. Special Operations Command, or SOCOM, develops forces for global counterterrorism activities, unconventional operations, and crisis missions; and U.S. Central Command, or CENTCOM, organized geographically, directs forces deployed to the Middle East and Central Asia.[2]

For most of us—a group of eighteen, a trip organized by the Council on Foreign Relations, a think tank—this is our first time both at MacDill and on the road together. Several in the cohort have a policy background, some as appointees in the Bush or Clinton administrations, but most now work in the private sector in New York and Washington. Two participants are American expats, traveling long distances, one from Beijing, the head of Intel's China operations, and another from Dubai, an infrastructure financier. I am the one academic, traveling from Columbia University, to undertake research on 9/11 coalition warfare. Two participants are also military veterans, one from Naval Special Warfare, the other an Army reservist, and both know their way around the base.

We are in luck with our trip leader, a U.S. Marine helicopter pilot, who goes by the nickname Bones. Ramrod straight with a buzz cut, he takes personal responsibility for the itinerary, minute by minute. Immediately prior to being awarded a fellowship year at the Council—a sabbatical billet bestowed on a rising military star—he was posted to MacDill for three years, working in SOCOM's future operations division.

For now, though, we are early for our SOCOM meetings. Sitting shotgun, Bones asks if we would like to drive around MacDill before our opening briefing.

"Yep." A quick response from a guy in the second row.

The road widens after the red gate and Tampa's interbay peninsula stretches out before us. Black mangroves rim its edge, tidal mudflats layer its coast, and in the distance, the city's high-rises form a faint wash of blues and whites. As we inch forward, well below the base's posted speed limit of 25 mph, we see a striking outdoor exhibit to our right.

Anchored into the ground is a half-century of artifacts of MacDill's past—World War II and the Cold War. Dignified cabbage palms surround the tactical parts that once fit into America's military theories of containment, deterrence, and mutually assured destruction. On display are a chronology of MacDill's airpower: its Liberators that once patrolled the Gulf of Mexico in search of Nazi U-boats; its B-26s for the bombardment of Hitler's Europe and Emperor Hirohito's Pacific; its KB-50 Superfortress, a post–World War II redesign for the delivery of nuclear bombs; and its Cold War breakthrough, the supersonic Phantom to tangle with Soviet MiGs.[3]

Despite the empty hardscape in the static display, suggesting that its twentieth-century planners expected the visual index of airpower to continue, the exhibit has not been brought up to date. Operations after 1991, from Desert Storm to Joint Endeavor, from Enduring Freedom to New Dawn, are not represented. Including a Predator or a Reaper would show a progression of sorts, of the increased use of aerial vehicles without onboard pilots, but neither is lodged in the concrete here. Displaying an F-35 would show a leap in stealth fighters, but with an average price tag of well into nine figures, even a stripped-down shell would be costly to place. Here is a time capsule of a sort, with its last additions from the Cold War.

We then move alongside a narrow asphalt strip that is filled with early-morning runners, fit and fast. Following their loop around the bay, about a half-mile up that path, we pass a golf course and what looks to be a giant golf ball. It's actually a bit of MacDill's mission that the bright white geodesic dome covers, connectivity from these headquarters to their forces downrange, provided by this AN/GSC-39 satellite terminal and its forty-foot parabolic antenna.

Completing the curve here are MacDill's first buildings, notably its arched steel hangars for a national air defense system initiated in the 1930s and a 10,000-foot runway built in the forties for its long-range atomic bombers, then reinforced in the sixties for its tactical fighter wings. We stop briefly at the base's air-traffic control tower, a ten-story structure that today watches over mostly empty runways. On the flight line are the base's few dedicated aircraft: eight KC-135 Stratotankers, rather clunky aerial gas stations about the size of commercial jetliners; three WP-3D Orions, weather planes also known as hurricane hunters; and two C-37As, the military equivalent of Gulfstream V jets, to transport the base's two four-star commanders.

Both SOCOM and CENTCOM rely heavily on airpower—from the newer CV-22 Osprey, equal parts helicopter and airplane, to the classic four-bladed Black Hawk—but at this time, much is forward deployed in the Middle East as well as on lilypads from Colombia to Djibouti to the Philippines.

The Council's driver then turns down some interior side streets, passing a chapel and a daycare center. I follow along with a detailed base map given to us at the hotel that morning. Its key shows elements of everyday life—a grocery store, a school, banks, gas stations, a library, and the post office. Until you're deployed, you actually never need to leave—a sequestered life if one chooses—and there's much to keep a community here, including a movie theater, beach club, and marina.

For those on orders to CENTCOM or SOCOM, a large gym, track, and pool are available, but otherwise, sustaining even their most basic skills will require travel to training facilities. Neither shoot houses nor obstacle courses, neither jump schools nor diving chambers are at MacDill. This is not the place to improve fast-roping speed or ballistic breaching techniques. Nearly all are here for staff assignments, office duty at headquarters, typically a two- or three-year posting.

We then pass a bowling alley and head into a leafy residential neighborhood with homes of pastel stucco walls and terracotta tile roofs, all with hurricane shutters and raised high on concrete pilings above the flood plain.

"See those two houses in the middle—right next to each other?" Bones points toward a long row of waterfront homes. "Those are for the bosses, one for SOCOM, one for CENTCOM." They're new and nearly identical—side by side, they form mirror images of each other.

That's the center of gravity at MacDill now, Bones explains.[4]

———

The *Washington Post* concludes the same, describing the role of the combatant commands as "the modern-day equivalent of the Roman Empire's pro-consuls—well-funded, semi-autonomous, unconventional centers of U.S. foreign policy."[5]

That characterization is an overstatement, but one that conveys some important truth. Reporting to the secretary of defense, as led and directed by the president, these commands do carry immense and lethal responsibilities. Their resources are substantial, they are routinely deployed as central instruments of national power, and their role is—at times—expansively defined as regional (CENTCOM) or global (SOCOM) first-responders. At the start of the twenty-first century, the extent of four-star foreign policy implementation for the United States is sweeping, an institutional phenomenon only deepened by the trajectory of the 9/11 wars.[6]

That massive infrastructure has long been in the making and often in flux. This overall system is rooted in the new uses of the U.S. military during World War II, outlined in the National Security Act of 1947, amended in 1949, and constructed over almost a half-century of Cold War conflicts. While neither CENTCOM nor SOCOM was present at this creation, both rest their war-fighting capabilities and authorities on that buildup. Each is grounded in the U.S. military's shift to the combatant command as its essential organizing principle. That institutional line reaches back to the forties with the concept of a worldwide command of U.S. forces, carries forward to the seventies with the U.S. policy objective of attacking regional threats, and was then ultimately overhauled in a period of crisis in the late seventies and eighties through Pentagon leadership and congressional intervention. Throughout that era, the concept was one of U.S. geographical domains, of American leaders determining the placement of global boundaries and then assigning U.S. forces accordingly, parsing security problems into regional bundles and area containments.[7]

When President Harry S. Truman and Secretary of Defense Robert P. Patterson launched the initial combatant commands in the forties, they established a Strategic Air Command to serve a global nuclear strike function and then added a system of seven regional domains: Alaskan, Atlantic, Caribbean, European, Far East, Northeast, and Pacific. In the fifties, President Dwight D. Eisenhower and three successive secretaries of defense trimmed those regional areas, eliminating the Northeast Command in its sixth year and the Far East Command at its decade mark. While still underscoring their pivotal function, Eisenhower declared, "Separate ground, sea, and air warfare is gone forever," and future wars would demand "one single concentrated effort."[8]

President John Kennedy and Secretary of Defense Robert McNamara followed with their own review. Judging the U.S. combatant structure to be lacking in Central and South America, in 1963, they designated a new Southern Command based at the Panama Canal for increased U.S. military activities. In this new area of responsibility, as well as the "whole southern half of the globe," Kennedy directed the expansion of special forces and unconventional warfare units to counter subversive actors who would stand in the way of any nation's drive for freedom. Kennedy, elevating the role of the Army's special forces and investing in the Navy's sea, air, and land teams, stated that these capabilities would be necessary in a fight increasingly marked by irregular warfare, paramilitary options, and guerrilla tactics.[9]

Two years later, in 1965, underscoring the need for American forces to stop a second satellite state of the Soviet Union "off our shores," President Lyndon B. Johnson stepped up operations still more: "We don't propose to sit here in our rocking chair with our hands folded and let the Communists set up any government in the Western Hemisphere." Even during a period of post–Vietnam War reductions, this formation remained both central to, and malleable within, the U.S. national security establishment. In 1975, President Gerald Ford and Secretary of Defense James Schlesinger eliminated the Alaskan Command as part of rolling cutbacks, while expanding the maritime range of the Pacific Command, and all the while preserving the overarching responsibilities of these headquarters to command and control the global deployment of U.S. forces.[10]

When Secretary of Defense Donald Rumsfeld arrived at the Pentagon—on his first tour from 1975 to 1977—he presided over the implementation of that revised command plan and further initiated work on areas it did not address, including the role of U.S. military force as an arbiter of "the difficult problem of terrorism" and the relative priority of the Middle East and Africa in Pentagon planning. U.S. policy leaders shared his apprehension of insufficient attention to different forms of international violence, such as an emerging virulent form of Islamic nationalism and its regional implications. In December 1978, when National Security Adviser Zbigniew Brzezinski gave his current assessment to President Jimmy Carter, he visualized "our greatest vulnerability" as an arc, a curving line "stretching from Chittagong through Islamabad to Aden." Former Secretary of State Henry Kissinger, in an interview a month later, pointed to a similar geography, drawing a line from Afghanistan to Angola as the site of "enormous unreadiness . . . enormous uncertainty."[11]

It was only after the Islamist upheavals in 1979, however, that counterterrorism as a military capability, and the Middle East as its originating region, emerged as two priorities in U.S. policymaking. By 1980, in then-classified directives, the White House shifted specific resources away from Europe and Asia to bolster efforts in the Middle East, especially as they pertained to energy resources, including the establishment of "a politically-oriented, quick intervention capability in the Persian Gulf." In his last State of the Union address, President Carter laid out the new overarching framework, a sort of Monroe Doctrine for the Middle East, declaring that "An attempt by any outside force to gain control of the Persian Gulf region will be regarded as an assault on the vital interests of the United States of America, and such an assault will be repelled by any means necessary, including military force."[12]

Those changes to U.S. organizing principles were interwoven with further international conflicts in the late seventies, including in southwest Asia—Russia invaded Afghanistan in December 1978, overthrowing the Kabul government, executing its deposed leader, and beginning a decade-long occupation—and southeast Asia—China invaded Vietnam in February 1979, following Vietnam's takeover of Cambodia.

At the height of this cascading sequence of events, with reemerging Cold War hostilities, Kissinger observed that the United States was "oscillating between incompatible views of the world" and that this, in and of itself, posed "a grave danger."[13]

Interposed into this geopolitical instability was the growing recognition among U.S. leaders that the U.S. military was positioned neither to confront nor to contain this type of multifront fight spanning the Middle East and Asia.

Even its most basic Cold War infrastructure was showing strain, including a technical glitch that nearly escalated the use of nuclear force—one small example but indicative of a broader systemic challenge. America's North American Aerospace Defense Command (NORAD) computers, a network established in the fifties to give warning of impending nuclear attack, gave false alerts in 1979 and 1980 to the entire defense chain of nuclear command. Twice at MacDill Air Force Base and other nodes in the system, officers received the alarm that Soviet nuclear missiles had launched from both land bases and submarines, therefore putting a counterattack into motion. American and Canadian fighter jets scrambled in response to the apparent surprise attack and remained aloft for several minutes until the correction came. No nuclear strike was indeed imminent.

This type of infrastructure at MacDill and elsewhere in the nuclear alert system, though, would not be applicable in the emerging Islamist fight.

The year 1979 presented the problem in sharp relief with high-profile U.S. political captives—and deeply divergent U.S. views on how to act and respond to the threat. Specifically, it started and ended with U.S. citizens held hostage in Afghanistan and Iran, with no means of U.S. governmental rescue. America's first major confrontation with this type of security problem revealed a country unprepared.

A global population observed the American uncertainty—confront or contain, respond or combat—and recognized its sharp contrast with other Western societies, including France, Germany, Israel, and the United Kingdom—already the targets of hostage plots and well advanced in their counterterrorism strategies, countermeasures, and specialized rescue teams.

In the United States, however, the notion that hostage-taking could exist on a scale sufficient to require a military intervention—and that it was more than an episodic act of violent political spectacle—was not widely accepted.

That reversed by the end of 1979. With American hostages being paraded down foreign streets, U.S. political leadership ordered military forces to the Middle East to end the standoff and to rescue its citizens.[14]

Shifting the U.S. military posture gained urgency in the aftermath of these failures, and this included accounting for crises emanating from the so-named Third World conflicts and revolutionary Islamic movements. The Middle East became a high U.S. regional priority—a site of military investment even at the expense of longstanding arrangements in Western Europe and Japan.

Hostage-rescue capabilities—and the broader proxy fights in the Persian Gulf, the Mediterranean basin, and the Horn of Africa—gave impetus to the designation of a U.S. counterterrorism command in 1980 and the formation of two new unified combatant commands in the ensuing decade. The new structure co-located at MacDill Air Force Base represented a major institutional development in U.S. defense policy.[15]

———

In Iran, during a New Year's celebration 1978, when President Carter raised a crystal glass to Shah Mohammad Reza Pahlavi and Empress Farah Pahlavi in the gilded ballroom of the Niavaran Palace, such unease was not yet evident. To the contrary, Carter's toast to the Pahlavi royal family went beyond the pleasantries of holiday celebration to state America's stance unequivocally on the Islamic revolutions roiling the Middle East: "Iran, because of the great leadership of the Shah, is an island of stability in one of the more troubled areas of the world . . . And there is no leader with whom I have a deeper sense of personal gratitude and personal friendship." Journalists and television crews then followed the Carters from the white portico, soaring 6,000 feet above south Tehran, to the nearby and nearly as opulent Saadabad Palace, where America's first couple slept that night. The next morning,

Carter and the U.S. delegation reviewed details of its military assistance and weapons sales to Iran—including hundreds of F-14 Tomcats and F-16 Falcons—and then departed for India, Saudi Arabia, and Egypt, before returning to Europe by week's end.[16]

Eleven months later, on November 13, 1978, in an hour-long interview that PBS aired nationally, President Carter, two months after hosting Middle East peace talks between Israel and Palestine at Camp David, reaffirmed support for the shah as "a friend, a loyal ally," continuing U.S. support for this ruler.

That reiteration, however, came after a year of deadly repression by the shah's forces of Iranian civic protests, a period when more than five million Iranians took to the streets to demonstrate their counter-convictions and -beliefs. Photographers captured images of street slaughters, and when those rolls of film reached a global audience through mass newspaper and magazine circulation, they evoked fierce condemnations of the shah's government.

French philosopher and writer Michel Foucault, on assignment for the Italian newspaper *Corriere della Sera* to Iran twice that year, had sent dispatches to his European readers about witnessing a "political edifice . . . irreparably cracked from top to bottom" and demonstrators standing "bare-handed in front of armed soldiers." He reported the lifeless forms and bloody bodies of protesters, killed under the "treads of the tanks . . . [with] the methodical coldness of a firing squad."[17]

Two days, in particular, stood out for their brutality. September 8, 1978—later referred to as Black Friday—registered international alarm when the shah's security forces gunned down demonstrators in Jaleh Square. "From the other end . . . a cannonade of gunfire. This is not a fight; this is a massacre," reported another journalist. November 4, 1978—later the date of national remembrance—generated a heightened sense of urgency and unity after police forces circled the University of Tehran, killing students in a fusillade of rifle fire through the iron gates. One student described their ardor as inextinguishable. We must proceed, he explained: "The injustices of the society are no longer endurable." Disparate groups of opposition, emboldened rather than deterred by the violent crackdown, previously without a shared agenda, now had one cemented: Down with the shah. The new revolutionaries stayed on the streets, united in seeking the end of the Pahlavi dynasty.

The United States was not among those that condemned the Iranian government crackdowns. This further heightened the concerns of demonstrators that America would carry on propping up the shah regardless of violent repression, a view that ultimately underpinned the highest-profile U.S. hostage crisis in history.

Iran's protesters responded to America's rejection of their cause at the gates of the U.S. embassy in Tehran. On Christmas Eve 1978, they made one short-lived intrusion into the embassy grounds. Their shouts and rallying denounced America's support of, and complicity in, the quarter-century of the shah's rule dating from the CIA-supported coup in 1953. Protests at the U.S. embassy grew in both ferocity and magnitude that winter, focusing on America's continuing role in Iran, including with its provisional and fragmented national government, and on its offers to the Pahlavi family of exile in the United States.

The shah rejected that American offer of exile, traveling first to Egypt on January 16, 1979, and then to Morocco a week later, apparently on the belief that his political return to Tehran was more likely if he remained in the region, a stance that reignited street protests in Iran.

In that same month, Ayatollah Ruhollah Khomeini, the Iranian cleric then living in the French village of Neauphle-le-Château, exiled by the shah in the sixties, offered a way forward, popular to some, controversial and unacceptable to others. From France, immediately following the shah's departure, Khomeini called on the Iranian people to stage a mass march to protest the "illegal" government of the shah—a million responded in Tehran on the appointed day. The parliamentary leadership reacted, too, placing tanks on the runways of the capital's Mehrabad Airport to block Khomeini and his followers from returning on January 26. That temporary impediment, however, ended after a few days.

On February 1, 1979, Khomeini tried again, boarding an Air France Boeing 747 near Paris to return to Iran, the end of his fourteen years of exile in Iraq and France. Joining him for the six-hour flight to Tehran were approximately fifty Iranian companions as well as more than 100 journalists covering the return. The euphoric reception of the Grand Ayatollah—thousands greeted him upon his arrival at the airport, and millions more out on the streets—exceeded stated expectations and gave particular weight to Khomeini's offer. The Ayatollah and his followers set up a sort of government in waiting, taking over a school building in Tehran for both living and working.

Ten days later, on February 11, the Ayatollah publicly elaborated the principles of this new Islamic state to his supporters. He underscored the necessity of expelling most foreigners to create the Republic—especially the Americans, he declared, who had repeatedly shown a heavy hand in Iranian state affairs and did not practice the peaceful principles of Islam. Three days later, on February 14, on what came to be known wryly as the St. Valentine's Day Open House, revolutionaries applied physical pressure alongside that edict. Arriving in three vehicles with machine guns, they stopped at the wrought-iron gates of the twenty-acre U.S. embassy compound. Then, joined by a few hundred more on foot, they climbed over the embassy's red brick walls, exchanged fire with U.S. Marine guards, and seized the main building. They killed one Iranian employee on the spot, took one Marine away to a prison for a week, and held staff—including the U.S. ambassador—as hostages. That same day, when an Iranian deputy foreign minister of the provisional government showed up with soldiers to scatter them, the Iranian revolutionaries left—but the new ministry forces, in turn, did not.

The Islamic revolutionary action may have achieved its greatest prominence in Tehran, but this was not isolated to Iran.

Over 1,000 miles away, in Kabul, on that same day, the staff of the U.S. embassy also faced a crisis. For the U.S. ambassador in Afghanistan, Spike Dubs, this Valentine's Day 1979 proved to be fatal. Dubs began that Wednesday as he had so many others, climbing into the back seat of a beige Oldsmobile, small U.S. flags on the car hood's edge marking its official status, carrying a day-old U.S. newspaper to skim en route from residence to embassy. This time, though, as the driver later recalled, idling at a red light a few miles in, they were stopped by men dressed as police officers and diverted to the Hotel Kabul. At the cavernous government-owned hotel in the city's center, witnesses later recalled seeing one foreigner in a business suit—described by a close colleague as "all ears and feet, with a largish head that looked like it had been bald forever"—and three men in police uniforms who crossed the lobby and took the stairs to the second floor.[18]

The first U.S. embassy official to arrive at the hostage scene at the Hotel Kabul on that morning, the deputy chief of mission, found the lobby already crowded with uniformed Afghan officers—and the head of security from the Soviet embassy in discussions with one—who, in turn, informed him that Ambassador Dubs had been taken by "terrorists." Three hours of hostage negotiations ensued, with the U.S. deputy chief of mission talking to Dubs through the door of a hotel room, with Soviet officers providing guidance and weapons to the Afghan forces. Meanwhile, embassy officials sent cables to the U.S. secretary of state, the U.S. secretary of defense, and ultimately, the White House. Phone lines in Kabul only reached as far as Pakistan on a good day, so interventions from Washington were limited to their typing into tape, to what they passed via the diplomatic cable system. Washington's objections, to the taking of the U.S. ambassador, were furious but moot.

At the end of the third hour of the standoff, Afghan snipers fired their AK-47s into the hostage room from an adjacent balcony, and Afghan commandos stormed the hotel suite. "The shooting was quite long . . . 40 to 50 seconds," estimated a U.S. special agent, crouched in the second-floor corridor. He then described a pause, followed by a short burst inside the room. When the colleagues of Ambassador Dubs were allowed to enter, they found him slumped in a chair, bound, and riddled with bullet holes. A later autopsy at Walter Reed Army Medical Center in Washington, DC, showed it was not the balcony fusillade that killed the ambassador, but rather four bullets fired into his head at "extremely close range."[19]

The U.S. intelligence community soon interpreted the killing of the U.S. ambassador as instigated by the new Afghan leadership and at least tacitly supported by Soviet officials on the ground. They deemed this a blunt ratcheting up of the Afghan proxy fights—and a blinking-red alert of the need for the United States not only to reevaluate foreign policies toward terror but also, on a pragmatic level, to upgrade diplomatic security measures and to develop international hostage-rescue capabilities.

Among those working in the U.S. embassy in Tehran, the professional opinions were mixed on how to categorize the brief intrusions and hostage-taking that they had experienced in December 1978 and February 1979—and how to determine the most effective response.[20]

To one seasoned diplomat inside who had anticipated the incursion for four months, none of these moves was unexpected. He had pushed warnings at nearly every staff meeting, in discussions with Iranian officials, and in cables back to senior leadership in Washington. Another practiced diplomat was far from cheery about the new atmosphere after February 14: teenaged Iranian forces carrying M1s camp in the garden, "shooting over the heads of our Marine guards as they would do their morning run inside the compound." The older Iranian guardsmen, carrying Israeli Uzi machine guns, had made a business of charging extra fees to the hundreds of locals lined up each morning to purchase U.S. visas.

Both embassy officials chronicled the year as a time of nightly gunfire, with even an occasional grenade lobbed into the compound. A meager set of precautions—office filing cabinets blocking doors and sandbags stacked in front of windows—offered them little comfort. Nothing came close to resembling a capability by the United States for rescue. Instead, if a special operation were to be needed to rescue these Americans, the U.S. embassy was to rely wholly on Iranian forces per U.S. State Department instructions.

When later asked if the U.S. embassy in Tehran should have been closed, further hardened, or scaled back, none of the embassy staff expressed support. One noted with irony: "Prescient political analyst that I am . . . I argued that if you close down the embassy every time there is a demonstration in Tehran, you might as well close it down permanently . . . you get kind of blasé about these after a while."[21]

From February 1979, with the U.S. embassy occupied by armed Iranian guards around the clock, Washington recalled its ambassador and left a skeletal staff in place of about 100 people under the chargé d'affaires, down from a few thousand. The Iranian forces, under orders from Prime Minister Mehdi Bazargan to protect the U.S. embassy from violent extremist followers of Khomeini, did maintain a sort of peace—even the largest demonstration in the first months, of about 40,000 people on Easter, stayed on the streets outside and did not escalate into crowd violence. For the first half of this year, street protests focused on the return of the shah to stand trial for high crimes against Iran. The United States responded, in part, by rescinding its offer to the shah to find refuge in America, a small step to improve fragile and frayed relations with Iran's new government.

It was in the autumn, though, that the posture of the U.S. embassy in Tehran underwent a major shift. On October 22, 1979, a dramatic change in U.S. policy was communicated to the embassy by cable, directing the chargé d'affaires to "advise the

Iranian government" that the United States had reversed its decision and was now permitting the shah to come to the United States. On the day of the announcement, the shah traveled on a private Gulfstream jet from Mexico—where he had briefly settled after stops in Egypt, Morocco, and the Bahamas during his peripatetic year—to New York.

The embassy staff, dumbfounded and with no good options, assessed "the risk to American lives at that time was serious, apparent, and exigent." Stunned staff members recorded their distress—"I could not believe what I was reading," wrote one. The willingness of the United States at that juncture to interact at all with the exiled king was unfathomable to one official, who had predicted that "no one would be dumb enough to allow it." One junior CIA officer in Tehran stated: "Manifestly, the entry of the shah would no doubt unleash severe and potentially uncontrollable repercussions." The mood had completely soured during his tour here, he explained. "On the streets of Tehran, I [once] reveled in it all." Now, repression was widespread, he explained, including some of his CIA colleagues having just been taken hostage at another location in Iran. The impact of the inflammatory act, he expected, would come quickly.[22]

A week later, on the morning of November 4, thousands gathered at Tehran University, marking the one-year memorial of the students killed by the shah's forces. Staff of the U.S. embassy reviewed their plans for the day of commemoration, with a few questioning the leadership's decision to have staff stay at work at all. Washington had responded with public silence to the amplified extradition demands from Tehran—the deposed shah stayed put in the United States.

The Grand Ayatollah further intensified his rhetoric, going beyond a call for the permanent closure of the embassy, and now expanding the edict to the expulsion of all Americans from Iran.

With no return of the shah imminent, widespread frustration with U.S. actions inside Iran, and Khomeini's growing consolidation of authority, a few hundred young revolutionaries walked the short distance from Tehran University to the U.S. embassy on that Sunday and scaled its walls and stormed its gates. Declaring an end to American meddling in Iran, they remained, taking hostages to force American compliance with Khomeini's decree, agreeing to release the U.S. embassy staff only upon the extradition of the shah.

In the United States, the stalwart news anchor Walter Cronkite, then in his forty-fourth year as a journalist, voted "the most trusted man in America" in a 1970s poll and then in his tenth year with the highest-rated news program, reached the nation each night. At the dinner hour, Cronkite provided an update on the embassy hostage standoff in Iran including footage of blindfolded Americans paraded down the streets of Tehran before angry crowds. Starting on the fiftieth night of the hostage situation, the one-year mark since the shah fled, Cronkite added a day count to his trademark signoff of "That's the way it is," a sort of numerical accountability that continued to draw America's attention to its citizens held overseas.[23]

Two weeks after this takeover of the embassy in Tehran, yet another hostage crisis drew the world's attention. On November 21, 1979, an extraordinary report, later shown to be false, came out of Saudi Arabia: American and Israeli troops had entered the Grand Mosque in the holy city of Mecca. That was soon updated with the announcement that as a result of a foreign troop invasion, more than 100,000 Muslims had been taken hostage during the dawn prayer. Word spread rapidly, including an alert of the rumor broadcast globally on Voice of America, and tens of thousands in the Islamic world took to the streets in protest. On Iranian radio, Khomeini reported a further development from Saudi Arabia that more than 200 Muslims on pilgrimage had been killed in the U.S. attack, and that many more were suffering from critical wounds.[24]

Members of a group led by a local Saudi then living in Medina, Juhayman al Uteybi, a Bedouin preacher with a small but devoted militant following, disputed reports of U.S. and Israeli troops, identifying themselves as the occupiers of the holy site in Saudi Arabia. Standing at the gold-and-black silk drapes of the Kabaa, the cubic stone structure at the center of Islam's most sacred mosque, they announced that they had been the ones who shut down Mecca's gates. Al Uteybi gave a succinct explanation: they were awaiting the arrival of the Savior, al-Mahdi.

However, Khomeini's declaration about America, given from Iran, still resonated widely. Thousands of miles away, in Islamabad, Pakistan, a few hundred students from Quidi-Azam University, upon hearing the information, gathered outside the adjacent U.S. embassy's twelve-foot-high walls of cyclone fencing. By the late afternoon, the protest swelled to several thousand protesters flowing in from the nearby city of Rawalpindi. They overran the newly built compound, firing at the steel doors and into the windows covered by metal bars, a siege that continued until nightfall. The embassy staff took refuge in a security vault on the top floor—a Marine guard on the roof was shot while they took cover. The group attack ultimately ended with the brick-and-cement building set aflame with gasoline. Staff who had been holding out in the vault, but with no apparent rescue forthcoming, survived by climbing through a steel hatch to the roof to escape the fire then engulfing the building.

The deputy chief of mission in Pakistan later described the night: "this is not the greatest disaster we've ever had now, but . . . [as] far as I'm aware, it's still the only incident of an entire embassy being destroyed—I mean everything."[25]

In Mecca, though, it took another two weeks for Saudi Arabia to eliminate the hostage-takers from both the mosque and the labyrinth underneath of about 1,000 rooms. The bin Laden family, who had completed major construction projects in Mecca, assisted the Saudi Kingdom's assault on the hostage-takers with blueprints and layouts. Saudi Arabia made the highly controversial decision to call on Western military advisers to join them in the counterassault, and combined tactics included armored tanks and poisoned gas.[26]

One of the younger bin Laden sons—Usama—was then completing college, and he expressed shock at the kingdom's decision to use major force of any kind to clear Mecca of al Uteybi and his followers—the sixty-seven captured men were soon beheaded by sword in public squares in eight Saudi cities for their role in the seizure. Usama expressed further duress at the role of Westerners in the Saudi kingdom's operations, given their little regard for the sacred space. Foreign tactics, he stated, had caused the utter desecration of these buildings, far greater damage than if local forces had managed the operation, he argued.[27]

Meanwhile, it was day 30 of the U.S. embassy hostage crisis in Tehran, and the United States watched, powerless.[28]

In the Pentagon, from the start, in a twenty-four-hour cycle of teams, planners worked on hostage rescue plans for the Americans in Iran.

This was a U.S. special operation built in crisis—there was no U.S. counterterrorism command in 1979, but there were newly created counterterrorism forces. Five months in, having exhausted other options to pressure Iran for the release of the embassy staffers, including financial measures of halting oil imports and freezing Iranian accounts in U.S. banks, President Carter ordered the Pentagon to proceed with its best military option. U.S. forces would fly helicopters into downtown Tehran, a city of five million people, retake the U.S. embassy, and carry out the fifty-plus captives by air.

The joint task force, commanded by General James B. Vaught, devised a two-night operation drawing on diverse elements from across the armed services, including Army special operators, Navy and Air Force pilots, Air Force combat controllers, and a Marine helicopter unit. Each unit trained in its own environment, including the Army's forces in North Carolina; helicopter crews in Yuma, Arizona; Air Force crews in Florida; and Army personnel in Europe. Elements routinely trained together at joint tasks at Hurlburt Field, Fort Bragg, and Yuma Proving Ground, among other locations. The advance work would include creating a temporary airstrip for six C-130 Hercules to land on the first night, carried out by the lead Air Force combatant controller, who had flown in on a CIA-piloted Twin Otter three weeks earlier. Eight rescue helicopters, launching from the U.S.S. *Nimitz* at dusk, would meet at that airstrip before heading to a second staging area, close to Tehran, to hide for a day. As the plan laid out, the Army forces would move forward in trucks to the capital, hiding in a warehouse for one night, before emerging on the second night to retake the embassy, while at the same time extracting U.S. diplomats being held at the nearby Iranian Foreign Ministry. The C-130 gunships would provide support overhead, while the hostages would be brought to an adjacent soccer stadium for airlift. A Ranger force would seize the nearby Manzariyeh airfield to complete the transport of Americans out of Iran.[29]

On the night of April 24, 1980, they launched. The C-130s arrived first in the sands of Iran—about five miles out, they activated the buried lights, creating a glowing diamond, ninety feet wide by 300 feet long—and they then waited for the helicopters to reach that preliminary landing site, labeled Desert One. Of the pilots who flew RH-53D helos from the Persian Gulf—six of eight made it, but one then had an indicator of blade integrity failure, leaving five, falling below the threshold requirement to proceed.

The U.S. special operation did not make it past this first stage—in a sense, it was over before it began. Upon receiving updates from the ground commanders, President Carter concurred with the plan for such an event: to abort for twenty-four hours, for the forces to return to base and to reengage the following night. In readying for that departure, one RH-53D helicopter collided with a parked C-130 aircraft, one holding troops and massive fuel bladders. The result was a fiery crash.

The remaining forces escaped the chaos of the fire and exploding munitions—but they left eight dead men behind. When Iranian television crews reached the site, they broadcast the burned bodies of the eight U.S. service members alongside their still-smoldering equipment and charred diagrams and plans. Networks around the world picked up and rebroadcast the footage to their local audiences, alongside new images they received from Tehran of the U.S. embassy captives on display, then put the footage on replay for another few hundred days.

Several political leaders asked in the immediate aftermath of the RH-53 to C-130 inferno at Desert One: How many special operations can you afford to fail?

The short answer: None like this.

Therefore, with a no-fail mindset, the units returned to multiple training locations, rehearsing for a second attempt, expanding their exercises to large-scale rehearsals and upgrading their technology, notably in air capabilities. While the call did not come up for a second rescue attempt, these investments provided the foundation upon which U.S. capabilities for crisis missions would soon be built.

Nine months later, in January 1981, in a significant diplomatic agreement to end the hostage standoff, the United States agreed to unfreeze billions in Iranian assets. The formal terms of the Algiers Accords concluded on January 19, 1981, the last day of the Carter Administration. The next day, news anchor Walter Cronkite reported to the American public that "a day that began as the 444th day . . . ended as the first day of freedom for the American hostages in Iran."

The standoff had ended at a day and time of Iran's choosing, moments after the inauguration of Ronald Reagan as America's fortieth President.[30]

High-profile U.S. hostages such as these proved to be a unique asset, far more useful than the quickly killed hostage in Afghanistan, Ambassador Dubs, or the hundreds of thousands of unnamed worshippers in Mecca. That is perhaps an unsurprising observation in hindsight, but it was not then well appreciated by either Khomeini or the American public. Only as the weeks unfolded did Khomeini's government come to value the standoff as a way to draw and to energize followers. Challenging the United States as "the Great Satan"—an epithet that stuck—the Iranians diminished their enemy with each passing day. Khomeini had praised his dedicated followers for their conquest of this den of spies, pointing to the weakness of their American enemy: "the talk about, 'in case of military intervention' is nonsense . . . It is impossible for them to do so."

In Washington, there was widespread agreement with the military assessment of the Grand Ayatollah: America did not have the extant capability to carry out a U.S. special operation to rescue its government representatives and citizens overseas—and had been unable to build that type of special operation force on the fly.

These struggles and failures would soon spark major investments in U.S. counterterrorism capabilities—and a new form of U.S. Special Operations Forces. In the eighties, the terms would be set by which the U.S. military would confront Middle East conflicts and terrorist threats for decades to come.[31]

Or, some would argue, without end.

———

Nearing the time of our first meeting at MacDill, Bones turns to our van driver to offer further directions—just past the Surf's Edge Club, the unmarked road on the right will lead to SOCOM.

Bones then calls our attention to the two agendas for the entirety of the trip, one from each Command. CENTCOM's agenda sets out its priorities throughout the greater Middle East and south-central Asia, an expansive outlook, one that emphasizes U.S. civilian-military strategies. Their documents detail the surge of 30,000 forces then deploying to Afghanistan for eighteen months—reaching a total U.S. force of more than 100,000 in 2010—as preparation for a new effort to reverse the Taliban's momentum among the local Afghan population. Labeling it as an adaptation of their Iraq model from a few years prior, CENTCOM presents a program of "concurrent bottom-up and top-down initiatives" which they assert will establish conditions for both stability and prosperity while at the same time continuing its "direct action" against "numerous violent extremist organizations."

For the other half of the agenda, at SOCOM, the information is scant, just a short list of names, titles, and topics such as "training special operators" and "offering an approach of preventive and low-visibility actions."

In advance of the trip, a retired naval officer tells me to expect polished and glossy presentations at CENTCOM, adding that they will seek to burnish their histories of the Afghanistan and Iraq Wars, promote a big-tent approach, and show extensive metrics as evidence of their effectiveness. He cautions an entirely different reception at SOCOM—not to expect too much of a welcome: they will act as if we should not be let in the door, and will wonder the whole time when we will leave.

They are decidedly different cultures, and he will be spot-on about CENTCOM and somewhat near the mark about SOCOM and its Rangers, Air Commandos, Night Stalkers, Green Berets,

SEALs, and other special operators. A few will display their skepticism of our visit. Many will project quiet professionalism—self-containment, reticence, and a penchant for anonymity. Some, though, turn out not to be as tight-lipped as the stereo-type—or ethos—of shadow warriors would suggest.

A year from now, the SOCOM culture will markedly shift, albe-it briefly. The operation against Usama bin Laden will be the reason, the end of a twenty-two-year counterterrorism hunt by the United States and other nations, by way of Afghanistan, Bosnia, Indonesia, Iran, Iraq, Pakistan, the Philippines, Saudi Arabia, Somalia, Sudan, and Yemen, among others. Paparazzi will stand outside MacDill's gates with their long-lens cameras slung around their necks, striv-ing for photos and pushing for the names of raid insiders.

For now, though, during this spring visit in 2010, the base is calm and placid.[32]

We reach another security gate, with no signage, and wait.

Tucked away in the middle of MacDill, marked off by con-crete barriers, this is SOCOM.

No physical aspect of this structure invites contact, and it had not been on the original Council on Foreign Relations plan. At the request of Bones, and with the commander's approval, SOCOM had been added to the start of the itinerary. Had we not already committed to spend the day inside U.S. Special Operations Command, we may well have skipped over this beige box—but then we would have missed out on its consequential dissonance in the 9/11 wars. Their fights are not large-scale wars of annihila-tion, of steel on steel. Instead, their grey wars are marked by protracted and persistent struggles, without a beginning and an end, without a victor and a vanquished.

2

COMMANDER'S INTRODUCTION

The public recognition is for our ability to put the habeas
grabus on a terrorist in the middle of the night.
—Admiral Eric Olson

Behind another gate and largely out of sight, SOCOM is
housed in a long cement building with tiny darkened windows.

On that first day, awaiting us against that plain and even austere
backdrop is its commander, Eric Olson, alone, on the front steps.
Wearing a service working uniform, its sleeves rolled to a three-inch
band, cuff right-side out—he welcomes us each individually.

After quick introductions, we turn to follow Admiral Olson,
but before we can go inside the building, we hit another layer of

physical security, an odd double-locked and backward ingress. An airman, in a raised guardsman box on the inside, looks squarely at us, and we awkwardly wait until a set of glass doors swing outward.

After a pause, we file through, and the commander leads us around the enclosure, stopping our group in front of a large oil painting that hangs under an angled pin spotlight, as if on museum display. The formal portrait depicts a silver-haired, somber man in profile, wearing the uniform of a U.S. Army general, stars on his shoulders, ribbons on his chest, and most notably, the Medal of Honor.

After a moment, and without a word about this picture of William J. Donovan, founder of the Office of Strategic Services (OSS) during World War II, Admiral Olson turns to the right, and our group funnels down a long corridor.

Fluorescent-lit, harsh and dreary, this hall is empty except for one row of small black-and-white photos that Bones points to as a typical inventory of an operator: a shortened M4 carbine with flash suppressor; a variety of pistols including Glock, Sig Sauer, Heckler & Koch; a Barrett rifle with cylindrical muzzle brake; and a sniper rifle that looks like a brick with a barrel, too bulky to be an easy carry.

When we reach the only door here that is ajar, Olson leads us through, into a small meeting room where our group takes unassigned seats at a long laminate table. Standing near one end of it, his opening puts us at ease.[1]

————

"I don't like giving PowerPoint briefings, and I know you don't like getting them." Skipping the formal welcome and stereotypical

Department of Defense presentation—slides crammed with met-rics or bullet points without verbs—he initiates a conversation about SOCOM's big-picture issues. In rapid succession, he sets forth a number of proliferating difficulties, including a U.S. over-reliance on military force and an uneven transition from known adversaries to elusive enemies.[2]

Turning to a nighttime map of the world projected onto the front wall, an image produced by NASA from overlapping satel-lite images, the commander illustrates the geopolitical frame-work that SOCOM now employs. He points to the lit areas, the industrialized countries, with the illumination marking their connectivity, energy levels, and technological use.

"During the Cold War, we focused on those electric spaces," he explains, noting the traditional industrial power centers that were lit at night. In those scenarios, battle readiness aligned to global confrontation with the Soviet Union, to the prospect of war between two nuclear superpowers, to the peril that human-ity could be erased in several flashes of light. War plans focused largely on equivalent threats among nations, from assaults by large standing forces to attacks by nuclear missiles—and some measure of cold comfort was to be found in counting tanks, sub-marines, and a wide range of known targets.

Pointing to the unlit portions of the image, the commander offers a comparison: "these dark areas of the world [are] where we think our national security objectives are most at risk."

What was once a low geographic priority for SOCOM, a so-called Third World country or backwater but potentially the site of a proxy campaign, the Command has judged since 9/11 to be a central part of the fight. It is within the ambit of such large swaths of unfamiliar territory that SOCOM attempts to track organizations and individuals. It's a medley with increasingly lethal capabilities, digital disruption tools, and global reach.[3]

In SOCOM's strategic outlook as presented, here are isolated regions largely untouched by infrastructure and transportation systems—places without regular access to electricity or high-speed communications—but which they cannot ignore. The vast terrain hides forces destructive to the United States, SOCOM stresses, areas where enemies can most easily hide. Such territories, which they designate as ungoverned spaces and safe havens, form an analytical category for SOCOM, one which further contains specific sites to be targeted, disrupted, or eliminated by U.S. Special Operations Forces.

"The primary threat to U.S. national security lies in the numerous transnational threats . . . that continue to increase exponentially," the admiral continues, "most sponsored or originated from nonstate actors rather than traditional nation states."

If most U.S. security professionals concurred with SOCOM's assessment of America's strategic risk—shifting away from a model of U.S. military readiness for two large-scale conventional wars and toward its priority of the "dark areas" above all, that is, the nuances of today's operational environment characterized more by asymmetric and irregular warfare—then SOCOM's mission would be straightforward. But they do not. Lit, unlit, or otherwise, no U.S. global or grand strategy is widely agreed upon—but a tilt toward competition with advanced and industrialized spheres does predominate.

In the Annual Threat Assessment of the U.S. intelligence community, then being presented to Congress, the director of the

Office of National Intelligence emphasized the far-reaching impact of cyber threats above all, describing the attacks and vulnerabilities as the most severe threat that the country is facing. In that same hearing, the director of the Defense Intelligence Agency, while recognizing ongoing combat operations in several theaters as part of a U.S. global counterterrorism strategy, pointed to the need to address simultaneously, and not lose sight of, the risk posed by other nations that are growing their "abilities to challenge our qualitative military superiority in other regions."[4]

At this time, the chairman of the Joint Chiefs of Staff, the nation's top military adviser, pointed to America's unsustainable financial trajectory as his greatest concern. "Debt," Admiral Mike Mullen asserted, is the "single biggest threat to our national security." His successors, Martin E. Dempsey and Joseph F. Dunford, Jr., would soon hew to the more common practice among U.S. military leaders of naming an adversarial nation or two when queried about strategic risks. General Dempsey placed Russia and China first among global threats: "The world in which we live, and the security which we seek, and the actions which we conduct, are always conducted strategically within the context of what effect it will have on the two heavyweights, that is Russia and China." Dunford, in testimony before Congress, replied singularly and unequivocally, "Russia presents the greatest threat to our national security," not only aiming the lens on the lit areas of NASA's map of the world, but also establishing a conceptual link with three generations of Cold Warriors who focused on the existential threat from the Soviet Union.[5]

For the U.S. Department of Defense and U.S. national security professionals across departments and branches, SOCOM's request for further advanced counterterrorism capabilities was no longer incontrovertible. Rather, after so many years of fighting the global war on terror, the calls for rebalancing military priorities were growing louder. The shock of September 11, 2001, overturned military planning for a decade, shifting leadership, talent, and resources away from traditional missions centered around nations and regions, and toward fighting terrorist individuals and organizations. But whether that would continue after a period of laser focus on counterterrorism seemed uncertain—and whether a potential rebalancing could indeed incorporate the post-9/11 capabilities also remained unknown.

In closing out the first session at SOCOM, Admiral Olson underscores the importance of broadening U.S. geostrategic priorities. Pointing to central Africa and southeast Asia on the map, and emphasizing the deficits in U.S. attention to the "unlit areas" and misunderstandings of their relational power and connectivity, he leaves us with a visual to contemplate: "Maybe these places aren't so 'dark' after all."

The commander knows such shifts in military priorities—and estimations and judgments. Over a career of thirty-three years, he has been awarded more than forty medals and ribbons, including the Silver Star for his actions during the Battle of Mogadishu, Somalia, in October 1993, colloquially known by its shorthand, "Black Hawk Down."

That fight in Somalia—similar to the development of Operation Eagle Claw (Iran, 1980)—evinces a complete cycle in policymaker use of U.S. Special Operations Forces, with crisis as catalyst, with tactical setbacks (perceived or actual) leading to short-term strategic reluctance to deploy, and, ultimately, long-term reinvestments in these advanced capabilities for national missions.

———

"A slaughter," a U.S. journalist pronounced the morning of July 12, 1993, in the Somali capital of Mogadishu. Keith B. Richburg, then in his third year as the Africa bureau chief for the *Washington Post*, later remembered that day as the start of his disillusionment in Somalia.[6]

"A video taken just after the attack showed the mangled bodies literally blown apart in the attack—the religious leaders, the elders, even the women in their colorful wrap dresses." The Red Cross reported fifty-four dead and 174 injured in the attack.[7]

Measured against the dire and brutal circumstances of the rest of Richburg's beat—the Sudanese civil war between Khartoum's central government and southern Christian separatists; the Liberian fight between a provisional government set up by West African nations and a military faction under rebel leader Charles Taylor; the implosion of Zaire in the wake of dictator Mobutu Sese Seko—as well as his reporting of Somalia's everyday violence for nearly two years, that's a remarkable statement. Even well before July 12, the brutality of Somalia—and the meagre responses he received from Americans back home—had become his odd kind of normalcy. Eighteen months earlier, Richburg had already raised the alarm with bleak accounts of the streets of Mogadishu and the desperation of hungry families. He heard back: "Somalia has ceased to exist . . . And right now, nobody cares," explained one U.S. government official.[8]

The *Post* journalist chronicled the unraveling of the coastal capital anyway—including its anemic food supply, its bare, tin-roofed shelters, and its rusted harbor on the warm and salty Indian Ocean. Attacks on relief workers receiving food from cargo shifts at the country's two major ports, in Mogadishu and Kismaayo, had forced a change to delivery by rowboats south of the capital, offloading crates to small docks and then trucking the food back up to the capital. On the basic hardware of the two groups fighting for urban territory, Richburg conveyed the market rates in Mogadishu's bustling gun bazaar—M16 assault rifles on offer for $75, or the preferred AK-47 at a going rate of about $100. Writing from the city's Ben Adir Hospital of a "quiet day" in its triage, he recounted the lost fingers of a child from a grenade, others hit by shrapnel, and two children covered in burns from an explosion. Of those Somalis who were leaving Mogadishu, the *Post* followed their trails to the Kenyan border, to the makeshift tent cities then struggling to provide water and food to an influx of a few hundred thousand refugees. Even there, airdrops of supplies proved precarious, still more often than not ending up in the hands of an individual thug or a well-armed group, who in turn set out to sell their wares in their ragtag convoys. Brandishing bazookas and machine guns to hold onto their prize, they moved their stacks of fifty-gallon sacks of rice and cornmeal, among other stolen charity staples, to the next broker in the supply chain.

The *Post* at one point tried a different tack, to weave the detachment of outsiders into the chronicle. The story was shifted from an analysis of fratricidal bloodshed on the Horn of Africa into a drizzly weather metaphor. Perhaps that would make the events—bizarrely but effectively—more relatable to their audience: "People here talk of the shelling . . . like people elsewhere might discuss the rain: not too heavy today, but likely to pick up again tomorrow." After more than a year of such journalism, American readers could perhaps be numb to such horror stories far from their own life, geographically and conceptually, but even quick glances at the headlines would demonstrate the grim pattern. These harsh stories documented not aberrations but rather the collective plight and systematic plunder of a nation and its region—one that Americans were notified of and then kept apprised of in 1992.

On December 4, 1992, President George H. W. Bush announced a major stepping-up by the United States and allies. In a daytime address to the nation, the president declared, "Only the United States has the global reach to place a large security force on the ground in such a distant place quickly and efficiently and thus save thousands of innocents from death. We will not, however, be acting alone. I expect forces from about a dozen countries to join us in this mission."[9]

U.S. forces sent the previous August, in a CENTCOM Joint Task Force led by a brigadier general of the U.S. Marine Corps, made use of C-5 Galaxy and C-141 Starlifter cargo planes as well as smaller C-130 Hercules turboprop transports and KC-10 Extender aircraft. However, it was not until this December surge of overwhelming force to establish security that the international community truly focused its attention on Somalia. The United States moved forward with the deployment of 28,000 troops into Somalia, under the leadership of CENTCOM, with a first phase of over 1,000 U.S. forces landing on Mogadishu's beach on December 9, 1992. Remarkably, the American media turned out as well, including TV anchors from the major networks, Tom

Brokaw (NBC), Ted Koppel (ABC), and Dan Rather (CBS)—as they previously had gone forward during the Persian Gulf War in 1991—awaiting the arrival of U.S. forces to secure the Mogadishu seaport, airport, and then overland roads.

The stated U.S. objective was to ensure the safe distribution of relief supplies—food, water, medicine—and complete that short-term security mission before January 20, 1993, the end of President Bush's administration. At such point, as it was planned, the U.S. forces would turn responsibility over to U.N. peacekeeping leaders, who would ensure the safety of a large humanitarian mission and stability operations for its duration. U.S. assumptions rested on a belief that local populations would rally to support international relief organizations; that U.S. technological advantages and logistics expertise would defeat efforts by warring clans to derail and to profit from food distribution; and, most significant, that as the leader of a new world order, as its only superpower, ending starvation in this small country in East Africa was both its inherent responsibility and a manageable undertaking.

U.S. Ambassador Smith Hempstone, writing on December 1, 1992, from his post in Kenya, in the week before the U.S. forces reached the Mogadishu shoreline, rejected that idea out of hand, dismissing both the notion that America knows what's best and also ought to deliver that themselves: "We ought to have learned by now that these situations are easier to get into than get out of . . . [and not] the quick fix so beloved of Americans." His cable laid it out flatly: "The one 'beneficial' effect a major American intrusion is likely to have [is] to reunite the Somali nation against the invaders, the outsiders . . . who may have fed their children but also have killed their young men." Concluding, in reference to the chaos of Lebanon in the eighties, the ambassador offered: "If you liked Beirut, you'll love Mogadishu."[10]

The U.S. deputy chief of mission in Somalia from 1993 to 1994, Stevenson McIlvaine, a U.S. Army veteran with twenty-five years in the Foreign Service, primarily in Africa, believed an intervention in Somalia would be no easy effort: "The logistics were daunting. This was a country in civil war. You couldn't find any airport. We managed to get some food in, but . . . you couldn't keep anybody on the ground safe without some sort of security . . . we organized a humanitarian relief effort, flying out of Mombasa, Kenya, C-130s onto Somali airstrips to unload food. But here, too, as soon as the food was unloaded, the gunmen rode in on their technicals, which are jeeps with machine guns mounted in the back, and stole the food." International relief organizations were then estimating that half of Somalia's population was in the hunger zone.[11]

The premise of the U.N. mission included a belief that its unified task force—with units from thirty-two countries, including large components from Australia, Belgium, Canada, France, Germany, Italy, Malaysia, Morocco, Pakistan, the United Kingdom, and the United States, totaling 37,000 armed services personnel at its height—would readily establish a nationwide ceasefire. According to their mandate, they would create a new police force for enduring stability and hold nationwide democratic elections within two years. In early 1993, the U.N. stepped up the charge to use "all necessary means . . . to end the violence against international relief efforts."[12]

They concentrated the existing resources on securing the capital and increasing offensive measures, most notably conducting raids and airstrikes against weapons facilities and compounds. In January 1993, the first month of the new policy, U.S. forces used Cobra helicopter gunships and accompanying M1 tanks to seize depot buildings in Mogadishu, taking the tanks and artillery they found stored behind their walls. U.S. soldiers sealed off a one-square-kilometer perimeter around the open gun bazaar at the Bakara Market to confiscate its inventory of mortar rounds, rocket-propelled grenades, and even armored personnel carriers.

Despite the major shows of U.S. force, though, and thousands of multinational forces in the capital, aid workers from the Red Cross, Save the Children, and UNICEF, among others, were still routinely attacked by local factions.

The brutal street fight and shelling war continued unabated in Mogadishu between the Somali National Alliance and the United Somali Congress, despite foreign efforts to stop the "artillery duel." General Mohamed Farrah Aidid, in particular, who led the Alliance and effectively controlled a southern swath of battered Mogadishu, found the U.S. and U.N. presence to be a threat to his sense of order—that is, to his Alliance's territorial gains won in the civil war.

By late March 1993, the U.N. Security Council broadened the effort again, from creating order to building a nation, adopting an astonishingly broad—and ambiguous—resolution not only for the "consolidation, expansion, and maintenance of a secure environment," but also for "the rehabilitation of the political institutions and economy of Somalia." This would be "an unprecedented enterprise aimed at nothing less than the restoration of an entire country," explained the U.S. Ambassador to the

United Nations. Such steps would include a "coercive disarmament" program and a new national government.[13]

Somalia's situation—in myriad forms—deteriorated rapidly as the mission shifted from international peacekeeping toward a new venture of peace enforcement. Neither the Somali National Alliance nor the United Somali Congress concurred with the U.N.'s plan to remake its country. The appeal of the two major Somali political parties seemed to grow in direct proportion to their rejection of U.N. mandates, characterizing the international solutions as the hubris of outsiders seeking to recolonize Somalia, foreign aggressors who sought to impose their ways. All the while, U.S. military forces were being drawn down rapidly, and future forces from other nations had been called to fill their places in the U.N. peacekeeping force, but most countries had not sent their soldiers forward.

On June 5, 1993, the Somali National Alliance conducted its first major retaliation, launching five near-simultaneous ambushes on U.N. forces across Mogadishu. They attacked the blue-helmeted peacekeepers, all of whom came from a single Pakistani brigade, while they conducted both their enforcement operations—a routine inspection of weapon depots—and their humanitarian aid— distributing food, water, and basic supplies. Aidid's supporters killed twenty-four Pakistani soldiers, including several unloading food from a truck, and then mutilated some of their bodies for street display. Other corpses were dragged by rope through main streets and alleyways, and still others were broken into body parts, sold out of roadside wheelbarrows as macabre keepsakes.[14]

"That [June 5] incident stunned everyone. It was incredible that General Aidid would have the nerve to mount an attack against the United Nations forces and so quickly after [their] arrival," one American official observed. And the violence begat more. The U.N. Security Council expressed grave alarm and authorized punitive actions. Airstrikes commenced on Aidid's enclave, an area no longer considered merely, though euphemistically, a "pocket of tension" but declared as the location of enemy forces under a ruthless warlord.

The attack marked a shift in the Alliance's targeting of U.N. forces, which led to high casualties of forces from Pakistan, Morocco, and Nigeria, followed by Italy and Malaysia.

To a senior American diplomat then working in Mogadishu, with deep Africa experience, the attack should have been expected. He characterized it as "a political statement that 'We will not countenance this interference. If there is going to be feeding in my territory, I'll do it' . . . Aidid was beginning to see this mission as a threat to his chances of taking over Somalia."

In a direct response to the June 5 attack on the U.N. peacekeepers, the United States sent over an Air Force Special Operations Squadron with four AC-130 gunships to conduct operations. Over five nights of sorties in June, they knocked out Aidid's headquarters compound in south Mogadishu; the Somalia National Alliances weapon storage facilities and its vehicle compounds; and Aidid's Radio Mogadishu station. Further U.S. reinforcements soon followed, including eight Army Bell AH-1 Cobra helicopters and sixty M-113 armored personnel carriers.

Jonathan T. Howe, a retired U.S. Navy admiral and the newly appointed special representative to the U.N. Secretary General for Somalia, proposed a $25,000 bounty for Aidid's capture and also requested U.S. Special Operations Forces to be sent for his apprehension—that last request was initially turned down.

In mid-July, having stepped up its capture operations, and as part of its operational turn toward manhunting, the U.N. incursion went much further in targeting Aidid. The U.S. forces struck a building in a dense urban district and conducted the attack without warning, breaking from its past practices of alerting residents over loudspeakers to clear an area. Seventeen U.S. helicopters surrounded a structure that the forces had targeted as a stronghold of Aidid's leadership. With antitank missiles and cannons fired from helicopters, they destroyed the compound and killed elders of Aidid's clan, the Habr Gidr—but missed Aidid.

"We knew what we were hitting. It was well planned," explained Howe.

A U.N. spokesman confirmed that seventeen helicopters in all, four of which were U.S. Cobra helicopter gunships, had fired sixteen TOW missiles and more than 2,000 rounds of 20-millimeter cannon fire.

The operation, though, was immediately questioned by U.S. officials in Somalia as both disproportionate in force and destabilizing, thereby undermining its very mission. A retired U.S. Army colonel, then serving as a foreign service officer in Somalia, wrote the next day, "This UNOSOM [United Nations Operation in Somalia] military operation raises important legal and human rights issues from a UN perspective. The issue boils down to whether the Security Council Resolution's directive [following the killing of the Pakistanis] authorizing UNOSOM to 'take all necessary measures' against those responsible for attacks on UNOSOM forces meant for UNOSOM to use lethal force . . . did the Security Council allow that persons suspected to be respon-sible for attacks against UNOSOM forces . . . have an opportunity to be detained by UNOSOM forces[?]"[15]

Richburg is more blunt about what he described as the slaughter of July 12, 1993: "It was, to anyone's knowledge, the United Nations' first ever officially authorized assassination."

In practice, the forces were under U.S. command, but in loose terms, the conflation is straightforward to grasp.

An officer assigned to the unit from the 10th Mountain Division's 1st Battalion, 22nd Infantry, ordered to conduct the helicopter assault, later explained their surprise at both the change to combat operations and the choice to escalate that day with the gunship attack. The officer described how the "battalion prepared for and deployed to . . . be [on] a humanitarian mission in Somalia" after coming off their deployment to Homestead, Florida, in the wake of Hurricane Andrew. Initially, they were assigned an area—Shabele Valley—to cordon, to search, and to protect. After the killing of U.N. peacekeepers on June 5, the officer's battalion was informed that their mission would shift from humanitarian relief to combat operations—and ultimately to an attack on the house of Abdi Hasan Awale, the interior min-ister of Aidid, on July 12.

Public responses and personal reactions to the Abdi House assault were swift.

Crowds of Mogadishu residents retaliated, including beating three Reuters journalists and one Associated Press photographer to death that day. A colleague of theirs later wrote, "It is not like in Sarajevo, where death comes from a bullet or a mortar shell. Death in Somalia is more personal . . . vicious and vengeful . . .

[the journalists] were chased down by a crowd of men and women, dragged out of cars as they tried to escape and stoned to death. Their bodies were mutilated."[16]

Richburg's reaction was visceral. "Four of my friends were beaten to death by a Somali mob outside of a packed house that had just been blown to bits, along with everyone inside, by American helicopter gunships." In Nairobi for the weekend when he heard the report, Richburg had been spending most of his days in Mogadishu, in the *Post*'s office he had set up there, and these journalists were in his immediate circle.

"We're not supposed to be here," one soldier said at the time. He complained of being used as a police officer, given the task of arresting Aidid as part of a manhunt strategy. "This whole notion of arresting [him] was a false one from the beginning . . . of surrounding buildings and detaining people and issuing wanted posters—militaries just don't operate that way. We're trained for traditional combat. We make our living blowing things up and killing people."[17]

A senior civilian official expressed a similar concern at the miscasting of the mission, of the apparent objective they had been given to reduce the overall murder rates in Somalia: "The military is a blunt instrument . . . [this] is a police action."[18]

Robert B. Oakley, U.S. ambassador to Somalia in the early eighties, who returned to Somalia as a special envoy for President Bush in the early nineties and returned again for President Clinton in 1993, put that expression of disconnect in context. He noted that the overarching U.S. policy goals were well intentioned but highly idealistic and not supported by necessary resources. Moreover, he observed, street violence escalated while the U.N. Security Council approved increasingly broad and assertive mandates. The Pentagon leadership had already drawn down U.S. troops and assets after the first phase of securing routes for humanitarian aid.

Meanwhile, Howe pressed for U.S. Special Operations Forces and a Marine Expeditionary Unit to take over the manhunt for Aidid. The secretary of defense, the chairman of the Joint Chiefs of Staff, and the CENTCOM commander—Les Aspin, U.S. Army General Colin Powell, and U.S. Marine General Joseph P. Hoar—initially rejected that request, preferring to "marginalize" rather than focus on, and thereby elevate, Aidid.

Three weeks later, on August 8, 1993, four U.S. military personnel were killed in their Humvee, torn through by a remotely detonated land mine on a busy Mogadishu street. On August 19, four U.S. soldiers were wounded in a similar attack, and another six U.S. soldiers were injured on August 22. On September 9, U.S. helicopters fired into a crowd of Somalis, killing many.

Then, on September 25, in a harbinger of a larger clash soon to follow, militias aligned with Aidid sent a barrage of rocket-propelled grenades into the air. While the skies had already been filled with targets for months—one observer likened the crisscrossing helicopters to dragonflies darting over a pond, and another described the helos as a big, white taxi service—the Alliance fired their newly adjusted anti-armor weapons and got the takedown they wanted. Even though unguided, their cheap but reliable RPG-7s, when changed to explode by duration rather than on impact, gave them a new tactic of airbursts to try. At approximately 2:00 a.m. that Saturday night, a U.S. Army helicopter hovering at rooftop level in search of mortar launches, was hit at close range, a blast that caused the helicopter's fatal spin.

Three U.S. Army soldiers died in the crash.

An Army captain, looking back, describes how he overlooked the specter: "I rashly believed . . . that we were relatively impervious to groundfire. I maintained this belief even after the following week," referring to the September 25 downing.[19]

On the ground on that Saturday, the only Western journalist then in Mogadishu, Paul Watson, a reporter for the *Toronto Star*, reached the site. Passing the flaming tires cordoning the area, a sort of alarm system for locals, Watson described the slow burn of the long rotor blades, the orange-red of the helicopter's embers, and his anguish observing the cheering, the dancing, and the prize-claiming. One woman "swung a piece of stringy, scorched flesh from a stick in front of my face. Another rushed up to show me a human tooth wrapped in a small piece of dirt-smeared paper . . . They claimed their best trophy, the headless torso of one of the soldiers killed in the crash, had been dragged off for display in Bakara Market . . . charging money for a peek."[20]

Aidid, hitting foreign forces, gilded his leadership of local militia in these days. Combined with fifteen weeks of eluding capture, the Alliance commander poised himself for victory in the capital and, he hoped, a change from fugitive warrior to presidential authority over Somalia.

Many years later, an al-Qaeda trainer described their support of Aidid's forces, one part of the broader mission of Usama bin Laden to bring fighting capabilities to Muslims fighting infidels. The trainer was one of a group flown in from Sudan, where bin

Laden was then based, to strengthen the militia's capabilities, and he had been tasked with targeting U.S. helicopters then routinely flying low over the capital. First, he said, we measure the standard distance that a U.S. helicopter hovers over a target when they drop a guy by rope; then, we aim for the Black Hawk's rear-assembly. Get enough shrapnel in the gearbox and the sleek charcoal-black attack helicopters will fall out of the sky—or so he said he would hope.[21]

Eight days later, on a U.S. operation to snatch Aidid and his top advisers, eighteen members of a U.S. Special Operations task force were killed in a protracted firefight in south Mogadishu. A surviving pilot later remembered a degree of normalcy on October 3, 1993, even confidence beforehand, describing a calm start of that day at their compound on the western end of the Mogadishu airport. They hung out at an abandoned hangar, he explained, surrounded by sandbagged revetments, and alongside U.N. contingents from Egypt, New Zealand, Romania, and Russia, among others.

"Some of the guys were out there on the ramp playing volleyball; just an ordinary Sunday," one of the U.S. pilots recalled about the start of the period later memorialized in a book and a film, *Black Hawk Down*.[22]

This new U.S. Special Operations task force had arrived just six weeks earlier, in late August, to undertake Operation Gothic Serpent, an escalation in the manhunt of Aidid. After a rapid survey of the environment, the task force commander requested general purpose forces and additional capabilities. Those requests, including for AC-130 gunships and armored vehicles, were denied. Between August 26 and October 3, the task force undertook seven combat missions in Mogadishu—separate from U.N. or multinational force structures.[23]

The U.S. policy team in-country watched the ground conditions deteriorate rapidly. The deputy chief of mission in the U.S. embassy in Mogadishu expressed frustration at being excluded from operational planning: "What we were not consulted on was this Ranger force, where they should go, what they should do. They came in, set themselves up at the airport, attached a liaison officer to work with us, but made it clear that . . . they would only tell us about missions after they happened."

Even if there had been a consult in advance, or additional U.S. military capabilities, it will forever be unknown if that would have had a material impact on what took place next.

Also unmissable was the harsh irony for the U.S. pilots selected for the deployment—the Night Stalkers, so named to match their function. These Army special operators—with a creed that leaves little ambiguity about their intended use, "My only true ally is the night and the element of surprise"—had neither when ordered on what was deemed a routine raid in the midafternoon of October 3, one they were expected to complete in under an hour.

A fire support officer explained the planning: "Based upon previous missions, we had determined that the SNA [Somali National Alliance] could not react effectively if we stuck to about one hour on the ground . . . We also concluded that we could strike anywhere in Mogadishu and complete our mission successfully."

By the end of October 3, five U.S. helicopters had been hit by RPGs, with one crashing three blocks from a targeted building and a second shot down as pilots delivered a rescue team to the first crash site. Two ground vehicles were destroyed, others so damaged as to be immovable. The fight ended eighteen hours later, after a U.N. relief column with Pakistani tanks in the lead and Malaysian armored personnel carriers rolling forward, in a convoy totaling more than sixty vehicles, with U.S. helicopters overhead, reached the trapped U.S. operators, then made it out of the city and returned to U.N. bases. A number of the tactical objectives of the operation were achieved, but the broad strategic costs would soon be high.

The Toronto journalist, Watson, got to the crash sites on Monday, October 4. Unlike previous occasions, the reporter grabbed his 35mm Nikon camera, feeling an imperative to gather visual evidence, he later explained. Watson, then living and reporting through weeks of street shelling, feared that words alone from Somalia could no longer rise above the international din. Whether it was too easy for his Canadian readership to dismiss his reports as "mere" descriptions of tribal warfare, or to skip over them when the fervent violence grew too grim to follow or fathom, Watson didn't know. Whatever the reason, neither the mutilation of AP and Reuters journalists in mid-July nor the dismemberment of U.S. soldiers in late September had received the scrutiny or care that Watson believed such attacks had warranted.

On that Monday, he captured an image tragically familiar to him—but new to others—of a U.S. soldier's body being dragged through the streets of Mogadishu. Several U.S. media outlets declined to show the picture, citing its graphic and brutal content. The few that did show it circulated an altered or partial image. *Time* magazine covered over the dead soldier's exposed scrotum with digital editing, and the AP ran a more tightly framed version of the image. The photograph, even though mediated by its conduit, broke through and had immediate impact. Delivered in its delimited form, the picture still functioned as an explicit symbol of the ghastly stasis of Mogadishu.

On October 5, as global attention continued to intensify on the events in Mogadishu, Ambassador Oakley returned to Somalia to seek to free the injured U.S. pilot taken captive from the second helicopter crash. The then two-time presidential envoy to Somalia left no doubt as to the uncertainty of his task and of relying on Aidid's forces for its outcome—"I treat[ed] him [Aidid] as if he were a vial of nitroglycerine that could go off in my hands." Aidid, after receiving assurances from America of the retreat of U.S. and Coalition forces, paid a ransom to take custody of the hostage and then released the pilot as a "goodwill gesture."[24]

Two days later, the United States announced a reversal in its Somalia policy, effectively ending its role in both the U.N. humanitarian mission and its national intervention in Somalia's violent conflicts. The White House set a six-month deadline for withdrawal of most U.S. forces from the region and immediately ordered an end to all U.S. Special Operations manhunts in Somalia, as well as to any use of American force in-country with the sole exception of an act of self-defense.

In the three weeks following the raid, nearly every U.S. public assumption about the value and purpose of the country's mission in Somalia had been overturned, including the premise that congressional leaders would sustain the operations until their successful conclusion. On November 11, 1993, Congress followed with a formal prohibition: an amendment to the National

Defense Appropriations Act to end the use of funds on U.S. military operations in Somalia by early spring. By mid-December, Secretary of Defense Les Aspin resigned under pressure, a decision that others tied to failures in Somalia.[25]

The retired Army colonel who had previously questioned the legality of the July 12 assault returned to Mogadishu in late October to work on the White House exit strategy. The National Security Council plan for the area as then described was: "We would wash our hands of Somalia. Blackhawk Down was a military and political embarrassment to the United States. Two helicopters shot down by Aidid's militia. The warlords were beating our most experienced and talented special operations troops. So the U.S. would back out of this mess."[26]

As U.S. Marine General Anthony Zinni later recalled, "I think everybody thought we were there to do a very limited humanitarian effort. When it became nation-building and hunting warlords, then casualties associated with that mission were not understood. It was not what the American people felt that they had signed up to."[27]

A U.S. Army special operator later pointed out, though: "The American 'people' didn't sign up for anything."

————

For the rest of the 1990s, U.S. civilian decision-makers largely avoided the overt use of U.S. Special Operations Forces for manhunting or raids.[28]

Chairman of the Joint Chiefs of Staff Colin Powell, later secretary of state, acknowledged the major shift in the use of U.S. Special Operations Forces after Somalia, while also expressing astonishment.[29] He noted that eighteen deaths in a firefight during the Vietnam War would not have merited even a head-line, much less a reversal of U.S. foreign policy.[30]

Robert M. Gates, who retired from the CIA in 1993 and later was named secretary of defense, described the Mogadishu operation as an important reminder that the undertaking of any raid involves a high level of uncertainty. The phrase "Black Hawk Down" is still enough to conjure a violent memory among some U.S. national security professionals, and a shorthand way to underscore the potential for even small-scale military actions to go horribly wrong. That may seem like an unnecessary warning, Gates stated, but if you have lived through Operation Eagle Claw's end at Desert One (Iran, 1980) and Operation Gothic Serpent (Somalia, 1993), the fears and risks are hard to shake.

A former undersecretary of defense for policy explained the shift in 1993, "The attitude was: 'Don't let these SOF [Special Operations Forces] guys go through the door because they're dangerous . . . They are going to do something to embarrass the country.'"[31]

Some U.S. policy leaders followed such concerns with a broad rejection of the use of U.S. Special Operations Forces for manhunting and other forms of direct action. Some expressed criticism of specific tactics, dismissing them as less than honorable, a kind of dirty fighting—furtive and surreptitious. The "black ops" of these forces carried extreme and even unacceptable risk, they asserted. Critics contrasted them to the more controlled methods of the established, general purpose forces (or general forces). Some publicly remarked that such operators did not represent an elite, or the best of the best, but an eccentric group of "cowboys" to be barely tolerated. "Door-kickers" and "assassins" were some of their other labels.[32]

Back then, one operator explains, some military leaders eyed Special Operations Forces warily—as "snake-eaters" or "just a bunch of knuckledraggers." Some outright rejected them as wannabe rivals rather than peers. The forces were treated as peripheral and odd—"the problem children, the red-headed stepchild." In that earlier era, one also came across a sort of resentment of specialized forces, as if they were a false elite appearing to be a superior group. The label "special" occasionally caused friction with general purpose forces. To paraphrase an old line by U.S. Army Chief of Staff General George Decker, when dismissing the need for Army Special Forces, or Green Berets: "Any good soldier can handle guerrillas."[33]

Some military leaders who believed that special operations did serve a necessary and important function inside the U.S. military, and tolerated their risk profiles, still described the forces as shadow warriors, operating near the edges of legitimate and lawful action. It was best to separate them from the large U.S. military units and the overarching defense infrastructure, and to deploy them in isolated small units. In this way, apart from conventional or general purpose forces, they could focus on clandestine missions and operate as a sort of ghost militia, evolving into different forms of fighting and tactics.[34]

The official historian of U.S. Central Command in the 1990s, after completing an oral history project of retiring leaders, summarized the general attitude of senior military officers who had not served in U.S. Special Operations Forces: "Ninety-nine percent of the time . . . whenever you involve special operations you run a risk, but you have the advantage that special operations can get stuff done that nobody else can even talk about or will talk about."[35]

That more constrained use, as advocated by some senior U.S. military leaders, fit U.S. civilian policy toward military operations of that period. On the rare occasions of U.S. direct deployments to combat zones, such as in the Balkan Wars, the rules of engagement were kept narrow. U.S. special operators were sent forward to conduct largely shrouded manhunts for Persons Indicted for War Crimes, or PIFWCs, as they were known. Operators were ordered to conduct "bloodless arrests"—to apprehend these individuals, but to do so in a way that did not risk a body bag.[36]

A few U.S. leaders, though, thought there was no place for such forces, even in a limited way. Special operations, they asserted, emphasized the wrong kind of war-fighting—irregular and unconventional. Even the concept of Special Operations Forces itself, they asserted—if defined as unorthodox and apart—contradicted standard U.S. military doctrine requiring unity of force. Special Operations Forces, in this argument, were dismissed not simply as ineffective, but also irrelevant and counterproductive. A few leaders proposed their elimination altogether.[37]

Pointing to the Persian Gulf War of two years earlier, some U.S. civilian and military leaders offered a way forward. In that fight, Operation Desert Storm, U.S. and Coalition forces conducted an operational strategy of bombardment to restore an international boundary between Iraq and Kuwait. The United States, in its largest deployment since the Vietnam War, sent more than 500,000 personnel to roll back Iraq's forced annexation of its oil-rich neighbor. That buildup lasted six months, but the period of combat was brief, with five weeks of aerial campaigns followed by a ground assault. In that last stage, dubbed the 100-Hour War to refer to the speed from ground attack to cease-fire, the force was overwhelming and the military victory was decisive.[38]

Here, they argued, was the American way to fight and the future of war.

They were wrong.

———

Usama bin Laden said that he also learned a lot about Americans from Somalia 1993, and that it shaped his judgment of U.S. forces for the remainder of the 1990s. When "one American was dragged in the streets of Mogadishu you left; the extent of your nation's impotence . . . became very clear."[39]

Describing the events of October 1993 as having met al-Qaeda's supreme objective—to drive the infidels out of Muslim lands—bin Laden labeled the Somalia fight as al-Qaeda's first jihadist battlefield victory over the Americans and its success as a demonstration to the world that a global jihad against the West would advance. He, along with four others identifying themselves as the World Islamic Front, followed with their edict that "the ruling to kill the Americans and their allies—civilians and military—is an individual duty for every Muslim." He described several justifications for the decree, including the ways in which the Arabian Peninsula is being stormed, "the crusader armies spreading in it like locusts, eating its riches . . . All these crimes and sins committed by the Americans are a clear declaration of war on Allah, his messenger, and Muslims." Bin Laden claimed to receive holy guidance: "fight and slay the pagans wherever ye find them."[40]

In this period, U.S. intelligence officials were tracking bin Laden. Former special operator Billy Waugh, then on contract with the CIA, trailed the Saudi in his exile in Khartoum, following his white Mercedes 300, plate number 0990, and tracked some of his support—trainers and weapons—to Somalian factions. Bin Laden was also one name on a larger surveillance list that Waugh handled in Sudan between February 1991 and July 1992. "Keep an eye on him," Waugh was told by the chief of station, "We don't know what he's up to . . . we think he's harboring some of these outfits called al Qaeda." In 1993, CIA officer Gina Bennett pointed to the threat of bin Laden as a major private donor to Islamists, examining his "religious zeal and financial largess . . . funnel[ing] support to . . . places as diverse as Yemen and the US."[41]

In 1996, the Republic of the Sudan offered to share its round-the-clock surveillance information with Saudi Arabia and the United States or, if preferred, to give custody of the "Wandering Mujahideen" to the kingdom. Neither offer was embraced.

On August 7, 1998, al-Qaeda followers undertook their highest-visibility attack to date. Near-simultaneous truck explosions killed 224 people—and wounded more than 4,000—at the U.S. embassies in Kenya and Tanzania, the first mass-casualty attack publicly attributed to bin Laden and his partner jihadists. In an interview broadcast on al-Jazeera from an unspecified location in Afghanistan, bin Laden further explained his outlook.

America could—and would—be defeated through episodic violence. Even small-scale terrorist acts could culminate in victory.

Somewhat paradoxically, in that same year, the leadership of the U.S. national security community advanced a similar perspective. In what later proved to be tragic foresight that terrorist acts could profoundly alter the United States, the intelligence community declared that "Usama Bin Ladin poses a continuing, serious, and imminent threat of violence and death to United States persons and interests . . . this threat [is] unprecedented in geographic scope and potential risk."[42]

Three months later, U.S. Attorney Mary Jo White of the Southern District of New York released a 238-count indictment against bin Laden, alleging crimes dating back nine years. Notable were its charges relating to attacks on U.S. embassies in East Africa, which the indictment called "the most heinous acts of violence ever committed against American diplomatic posts": the near-simultaneous explosions of a Nissan Atlas refrigerator truck at the U.S. embassy's gates in Dar es Salaam and the plowing of a Toyota Dyna into the U.S. embassy's courtyard and main building in Nairobi. Both vehicles were packed with TNT, made more potent with aluminum powder.[43]

Two years later, the FBI briefed seventy open investigations pertaining to bin Laden and reported "patterns of suspicious activity in this country consistent with preparations for hijackings or other types of attacks, including surveillance of federal buildings in New York." In August 2001, CIA officer Barbara Sude stated the threat bluntly in her "For the President Only" memo titled "Bin Laden Determined to Strike in U.S."[44]

One month later, less than twenty-four hours after the plane attacks on New York and Washington, the matter converted from a judicial action to a manhunt of massive proportions. On the morning of September 12, 2001, President George W. Bush gave the order to Secretary of Defense Donald Rumsfeld and Director of Central Intelligence George Tenet to "get bin Laden first."

In the immediate aftermath of Usama bin Laden's attack on the United States on September 11, 2001, much did change—including a different way of, and far more broad approach to, dispensing violence. The sites and magnitude of the September 11 attacks impelled that transformation. In less than a week's time, the legal foundation, the Authorization for the Use of Military Force, was set in place: "That the President is authorized to use all necessary and appropriate force against those nations, organizations, or persons he determines . . . in order to prevent any future acts of international terrorism against the United States."[45]

President Bush, when he formally declared the Global War on Terror on September 20, 2001, before a joint session of Congress and the nation, explained the expansiveness and urgent priority of the new war. Speaking from the rostrum of the House of Representatives, with more than eighty million Americans tuned in, President Bush boldly stated the mission: "Our war on terror will not end until every terrorist group of global reach has been found, stopped and defeated."

In late September 2001, President Bush selected U.S. Special Operations Forces to take the military lead in America's initial response. From 2001, special operators—along with other personnel from across the U.S. government—followed the

CIA into Afghanistan, the most visible site of the fight's beginnings, a campaign of unconventional warfare for the purpose of counterterrorism.[46]

Indeed, it was the lack of options and readiness that propelled special operators forward, by a process of elimination, not distinct selection. That became apparent within hours after the attacks, explained Cofer Black, then director of the CIA's Counterterrorism Center, about the requirement for a swift use of force in Afghanistan. Black noted that it would have taken months to move any large formation of conventional forces into the remote mountainous terrain. Bush approved the swift paramilitary plan and later described the rapid deployment of these teams comprised of CIA and U.S. Special Operations personnel as a "turning point in my thinking."[47]

In that literally overnight shift, core capabilities of U.S. Special Operations Forces—counterterrorism and unconventional warfare—rose to be the nation's stated priority. These forces, also previously responsible for a catch-all U.S. defense category of "everything else," found its skills now singularly focused on the 9/11 military campaigns—a mission that quickly expanded well beyond an unconventional warfare campaign in Afghanistan to countering terrorist groups of "global reach" to then nearly any terrorist cell, regardless of scale or place, as well as nonstate armed groups with diverse methods and aims.

Mike Vickers, in testimony before the U.S. House Armed Services Committee, prior to being confirmed as assistant secretary of defense for special operations and low-intensity conflict, summarized a proposed understanding of the new use of U.S. Special Operations Forces within the U.S. Department of Defense

(DoD): "SOF will really be the main DoD instrument, not necessarily the main U.S. Government instrument in all cases, but the main DoD instrument in the longer term Global War on Terror."[48]

The special operator had become neither an extreme nor a luxury choice, but the expedient and widely used instrument of the U.S. military. The use and significance of special operators were now entirely different in the U.S. national security establishment and its armed forces.

Moreover, combating terrorism in Afghanistan and elsewhere, conducted under new conditions and with new authorities, was not only the urgent task of SOCOM, but the essential priority across the whole of the U.S. national security establishment, including the Office of the President, the U.S. Department of Defense, and CENTCOM, SOCOM's MacDill partner.

In this shift, U.S. counterterrorism measures were assigned a new meaning. Some called it a "blank check" that justified nearly any U.S. military action, and others described it as a permanent framework for a forever war. In this significant change in meaning, counterterrorism activities by the U.S. government were given a new and expansive—and literal—label: war.[49]

———

Back inside SOCOM's Donovan Room in 2010, returning to a discussion of the dark areas of the map, but moving from the laminate table to the front of the room, the commander shifts to his current concerns about America's strategic reliance on singular tactics by U.S. special operators.

"More than anything else now, the public recognition is for our ability to put the habeas grabus on a terrorist in the middle of the night," Olson says to our group. He is referring to raids, a fighting method in use for literally thousands of years and basically unchanged.

By this time, a decade into the global war on terror, policymakers had come to routinely praise U.S. special operators for their raids, describing them as the world's premier lethal global counterterrorism force: America's finest warriors; the force of choice; and the hallmark of U.S. national security in the twenty-first century.[50]

SOCOM and its component commands were being credited with changing from an ad hoc approach to a method that was technologically and mechanically enhanced, highly disciplined, and even strict in its execution. No longer apart from the U.S. national security establishment, such forces had become, by presidential order and congressional approval, interconnected and interdependent across the breadth of federal departments, agencies, and units—as well as with the equivalent functions in allied partners.[51]

The commander has accepted the conventional wisdom on tactical sophistication, but he questions the extent of the strategic effectiveness of these pivotal chapters.[52]

In the "9-1-1 fights," Olson's preferred label for the post-9/11 military campaigns, "the night raid is a core tactic in the overall strategy of high-value targeting . . . At a tactical level, the raid is now routine, and after years of practice, we carry out these operations with near-zero defect," he asserts.

Walking back to the table and appearing to pause for emphasis in front of our group, he cautions: "I have a concern: We rely too heavily on this approach to win the fight." He goes on to explain that the surprise element is largely gone. The bad guys are much better at evading it.

In addition, the impact of such operations is unknown or, worse, suggestive of no positive impact at all: "We say that the most dangerous job in the world is the Number Three of al-Qaeda—we eliminate the man each time, but he regenerates quickly from their pipeline . . . Given these factors—and others which we will discuss—I believe we should reduce our use of this tactic."

Instead of promoting or trumpeting raids, the Command's most visible activity, he questions its centrality to—and effectiveness in—the mission. That he challenges the future utility of the Command's capture/kill raids—which dominate nights in the nearly decade-long combat zones—draws in our visiting group from the Council. When he takes that unexpected turn, challenging what seems to be settled practice, describing the method as less valuable than well-known public and formal claims by some U.S. national security leaders, the words carry a leaden weight.[53]

"We have an alternative," the commander continues, "and if you'll allow me to share some ideas, I can save you reading 750 pages of top-secret material."

With that, he turns to an aide and directs him to lead us on a tour of SOCOM's facilities. "I'll rejoin you in a few hours—we'll discuss some of our alternatives to targeting . . . our options."

We file out of the Donovan Room, through a few corridors, with the only differentiation being the framed photographs.

3

THE TOUR

War is not composed of the tactics of targetry.

—General James N. Mattis

Walk by that picture of the Predator drone, turn right at the MH-47, then turn left at the RQ-11 Raven B photo. Perhaps one could give directions in U.S. Special Operations Command's headquarters this way.

Through one windowless corridor after another, we make our way, passing rows of framed images that hang throughout the headquarters. The emphasis here on display: how SOCOM fights. To move through these corridors is to glimpse the capabilities that have formed a lethal nucleus for U.S. Special Operations since 9/11.

Just a few years earlier, the walls had been filled with Americana, decorated with pictures of Elvis, baseball, and Mount

Rushmore. General Doug Brown, who led the Command from 2003 to 2007, described the photographs as showing what they fight for, whom and what they protect: "Why are we here? . . . As everybody walks around, hopefully they'll stop for a second and think, 'That's what this force is all about: defense of this nation and the American way of life.'"[1]

Now, these walls exhibit the tangible instruments of the special operator's physical battlefield—from bullets to gunships to microdrones—and their objectives of lethality, mobility, stealth, and precision. The thematic focus is manhunting—and perfecting its art through technological advancement—not a sign yet here of the alternative approach that the commander has raised this morning.[2]

———

A hedge fund manager in our Council group, and a veteran of special warfare, points out a set of photographs that shows a quick evolution of U.S. military eyes and ears, of varied goggles, scopes, and lasers. He notes that most of these refinements weren't yet available to his unit in the 1990s—he left the force in the springtime before September 11, after a decade of "not much going on."[3]

He—along with Bones and our Command-designated guide—points out several differences in the images: night-vision goggles, here with four image-intensifying tubes, no longer just the monocular or binocular version. Headsets—light frames that skip over the eardrum to rest on facial bones—are now better at amplifying softer sounds, such as rustling leaves, while still muffling the noise of combat as earlier clunky over-the-ear models had done. Some of the newer scopes cut through atmospheric obstacles, from water to tall reeds, and when combined with suppressors of thermal and flash signatures, increase visibility and reduce detection. Handheld trackers, our guides explain, are now more reliable and offer a sort of mobile intranet of overlays to spot themselves, friendlies, and targets.

Turning the corner, we shuffle along to the next hallway until we reach an immense close-up photo of a Reaper in flight—an MQ-9 aerial drone. A sort of mechanical pterodactyl, one of the SOCOM staffers calls it, with its sensor attachments that create the Gorgon stare, its name conjuring the legendary creatures known for hairstyles formed from venomous snakes. The sky watch of multiple targets simultaneously, a many-eyed giant without the so-called blink of earlier models, is a system of over two billion pixels that can now detect a man's limp or a woman's hair color from over 20,000 feet. The Argus, a similar drone peripheral with a nod to Greek myths, is a sensor so advanced that 600 gigabits are processed in a second, or about 6,000 terabytes in a day.

One picture of a Predator MQ-1 from the nineties offers a close-up of its whale-shaped head and inverted V-turned tail, a small fiberglass airframe, propeller-driven and single-rudder, with a four-cylinder engine initially designed for about eighty horsepower. Later, the extensive telemetry of Predators transformed this basic spy in the sky with wide-area sensor pods providing near real-time imagery, increasing thermal and infrared sophistication from ultra-distances and at ever higher altitudes, intensifying SOCOM's sights a continent or two away. Prowling the skies with steady hovers and continuous data-streaming, the Predator ultimately fulfilled a core technical objective, the much-heralded unblinking eye. Weatherproof avionics, more-over, kept Predators more reliably overhead and less dependent on platform altitudes for azimuth resolutions. A split operation provided separate streams of full-motion video and designated information to ground units as well as command-and-control crews, thereby generating data that could be fused or integrated. With its further refinements, even a feeble glint of an object, in a grey murky dawn watch, could be detected, tracked, and targeted with precision.

A few of us lag behind, reading the captions of the pictures of airpower and armed overwatch, learning more from the SOCOM staffers about the general evolution of these machines.

On one wall here are the Reaper's most recent antecedents, drawings of drone prototypes from the fifties through the nineties including the early reconnaissance Firebees and Lightning Bugs, best known for their use during the Vietnam War. Next to those, the pictures of twin-tailed maritime Pioneers stand out as boxy machines. Launched with solid-propellant rocket boosters or by catapults, powered by two-stroke piston engines, they were sent out in the hundreds over the Persian Gulf and Balkans, offering image capabilities speedier than those available from extant satellite sensors. The subsequent addition of synthetic-aperture radars, signal-processing by magnitude, successive pulses, and backscattered echoes further expanded their use. Recovery remained a problem, though, whether missing a net or an arresting wire on a runway. On some ships, electromagnetic interference proved their undoing.[4]

Adding Hellfire missiles to these reconnaissance Predators, we are told, led to their ubiquitous presence in U.S. Special Operations, with many plans now not only built around, but wholly dependent upon, the coalesced use of remotely piloted vehicles—or at least as much as satellite bandwidth and airframe assets could offer. The mechanics of the shift are not inventive, but the policy decision to do so is new—to attach the fighting functions of killing and destruction onto the find-and-film systems. It is a tactical option of strategic significance, one that grew with the iterative actions of the unmanned fleets, such as the addition of targeted lasers for bomb strikes as well as the bundling of sensors and beams. Such innovations can permit tactical patience. As one commander explains, this capability gives an operator or an analyst both the visibility and the time to determine if an individual on the ground is a young boy carrying a shovel, or a man carrying a rifle. With the full Predator system in place, operators could complete their tasked loop of find, fix, and finish in an unbroken cycle on a single platform. Once approved to do so, Predators over Afghanistan could then locate, target, and, as needed, strike in one rotation, a capability quickly expanded to Yemen, Iraq, Somalia, and elsewhere in the twenty-first century.[5]

A series of images here show a CV-22, or Osprey as it is also named, taking off. One shows the craft pointing its rotors straight up and rising, then a moment later in the air, after the bird has tilted these rotors to a ninety-degree angle, converted into a turboprop airplane. A last picture shows where the pilot has stopped the rotor covers midway so the mechanical fish hawk flies like neither helicopter nor airplane. Designed to combine the best of both—a helicopter's lift and an airplane's speed and range—its electronic interface performs the switches required for each configuration without pilot input, changes including pitch, roll, and yaw axes, allowing among other things, a quick departure from a hot landing zone. All the more remarkable, the aircraft flies 2,000 miles on a single tank of gas and can land on a rooftop—no staging bases, refuelings, or runways required.

Farther down that same wall is a series of framed posters of gunships—flying arsenals with overwhelming firepower from their cannons, howitzers, and missiles. On display here are the variants of the AC-130. The aircraft's outer shells have changed little since the Vietnam War; propeller-driven, they continue to be the workhorses of austere conditions, flying at low levels, landing on short or narrow airstrips. Assigned to combat zones for close-air support and short-field assault operations, the AC-130s lurk, hunt, and unload sheer volume—a single side-mounted gun can spray 2,000 rounds in a minute.

Across from the gunships are silhouettes of a variety of heli-copters in recognizable forms—Black Hawk MH-60s, Chinook MH-47s, Little Bird MH-6s—for assault, supply, and troop trans-port. Standard rotary-wing designs and system components, in some cases, are modified to U.S. Special Operations specifica-tions, such as Black Hawks with their 2,550-shaft horsepower engines or Chinooks changed into heavy assault helicopters able to carry 20,000 pounds while maintaining sufficient speed at about 150 knots. Some rotorcraft refinements are more recog-nizable than others: a front probe for long aerial refueling. Less visible are electro-optical sensors, as well as more stealthy enhancements for clandestine infiltration and exfiltration. Active protection against infrared homing missiles, such as jammers, and adjacent negating technologies allow for some masking of flights in hostile territories or denied environments. State-of-the-art systems allow them to follow the terrain, to prevent detection even at low levels, and to land in brown-outs, among other capabilities.

At the end of the corridor, the last image stands out for its sheer magnetism. A small color photo here shows a Chinook hovering over a desert landscape and creating a dusty brownout. At the edges of the swirling dingy cloud, though, is a line that appears golden. The stunning burning glow, it turns out, is created by sand hitting the craft's spinning blades, shaving off metal particles which then ignite into thousands of sparks. This picture catches the bits flaring into concentric rings above—a spectacular halo effect—and then falling like a miniature meteor shower.[6]

———

Frequently hailed—or envied—as the best-equipped forces in the world, U.S. special operators are now routinely described as carrying the technological edge in the fight. In the decade after 9/11, it grew to be the most technologically advanced part of the force structure in the United States.[7]

SOCOM's seventh commander, General Doug Brown, noted that in the 9/11 wars, the "bottom line is that Special Operations Forces today are far more capable than ever in history."[8]

Special stuff for special operators—members of Congress have underscored their commitment to invest in U.S. Special Operations with a promise to go beyond the needs of combat and to create tools unrivaled on the battlefield at their congressional hearing for SOCOM, a formal two-day affair held in both chambers every year.

"The U.S. Special Operations Command, the lead command in the ongoing and, in all likelihood, perpetual war against terror . . . I cannot think of a higher priority for funding anywhere in the Federal Government than the SOCOM budget. It represents a direct investment in keeping America and Americans safe here at home," Representative Jim Saxton, chairman of the House Armed Services Committee, opened one hearing.[9]

That is a matter not simply of rhetoric but of federal law, a dedicated and visible budget for U.S. Special Operations. That's a rare type of congressional commitment, to provide direct funding to a combatant command, to ensure that the moneys will remain with these units, and to restrict their use to unique capabilities. The disbursement—known as Major Force Program 11, or MFP-11 for shorthand—is the primary mechanism for investment and innovation in special operations, and is dedicated to needs above and beyond baseline costs. General operating costs, such as personnel and benefits, are provided from the budgets of the four services. In both size and type, the MFP-11 budget is consequential, allocated at more than $2.3 billion in 2002, $10 billion by 2010, growing to $13 billion by 2020.[10]

To the extent that such an item perfects an extant capability, or significantly upgrades a combat requirement, the investment of U.S. Special Operations Command is sizable.

To take one example—bullets—the Command searches continuously for better ammo. Purchases already run a full and wide range, with orders of more than fifty different types of munitions—a combination of caliber, weight, and design needed for everything from single convertible rifles to belt-fed machine guns to aircraft cannons—and more than seventy million rounds per year. As a clear and obvious military item, open-ended requests to industry call for adaptations and refinements. These are not limited to combat differentiators, but rather are ongoing searches for modest or incremental alterations.

Any .50 caliber round, for example, already takes down a helicopter, but improvements to the explosive charge remain on the wish list. A sniper's location can already be partially masked with a smart bullet—programmed to arrive at an unexpected angle—but boosting the miniprocessors in the bullet's core would enable real-time data refinement from its sensors, increasing the likelihood of a moving target being followed until impact. Even a program evaluated as falling short of its goal, such as happened with one acquisition of combat assault rifles, didn't collapse from lack of policymaker interest or national investment. The desire to make a perfect rifle continues.

Challenges to SOCOM's capabilities, however, come in other forms.

While the Command is tasked to work outside the traditional system, it is bound by—not exempt from—its conventional process. It requires adherence to the basic Federal Acquisition Regulation, which runs over 2,000 pages—more than 200,000 Pentagon employees have graduated from the Defense Acquisition University to understand it—and that tome is not geared toward novelty or invention. That process further assumes the general desirability of defense work—advertising a list of requirements and expecting national talent to show up for an "awarded contract." Significant groups of technologists, however, have not sought or engaged military applications of their capabilities. Notable leaders have outright rejected entreaties from U.S. military developers, pointing out that their commercial legitimacy requires detachment and neutrality. In a range of subfields, from cryptographic algorithms to biometric authentications, their positions in the global marketplaces require clear separation from U.S. national security interests.

For a number of SOCOM's military objectives—cyber, robotic, cloud, and nano, among other fields—this presents meaningful obstacles to their missions.

Putting the problem in institutional terms, the days of the U.S. military-industrial complex, which President Eisenhower famously cited in his farewell speech, have passed. That term once referred to the most advanced and largest U.S.-based companies, from General Electric to General Motors, directly engaging in the U.S. defense arena in long-term partnerships with the Pentagon, with big businesses offering their domestic infrastructure and production lines to keep the nation safe. In their work during the second half of the twentieth century, in a concerted effort of mobilization across the nation, the United States achieved armed dominance against nearly all of its adversaries. Since the dénouement of the early nineties, however, the term has ceased to resonate, or even apply. International entities have grown increasingly sophisticated and by default, American capabilities have tapered in revised comparisons.[11]

Today only a handful of large national defense corporations express a shared vested interest to achieve breakthroughs in—and exclusively for—U.S. national security. Some new specialized firms—often led by those with a U.S. intelligence or military background—seek to infuse the defense sector with creative solutions and augment the industry with their entrance. They often excel in one or two products in instant and sharp relief, but struggle with scale and longevity.

If a problem set from SOCOM then does not have crossover appeal or relevance to other sectors, it typically remains in the domain of this small set of national commercial actors. That provides the advantages of creative containment and proprietary rights, but also a hurdle to overcome, requiring the Command to court the global private sector and woo its individual talent to ensure a wider range of expertise. At a minimum, that process has proven laborious and unpredictable.

With a timespan shortening between American invention and global duplication or imitation, a lapse of time further incurs a compounded cost in the discounted rates of return. Even in its most advanced areas, the near-copycats can erode American capabilities not simply by rapidly changing the new into the commonplace. Going beyond just the lost expenditure of resources, a quick replica elsewhere means a near-capability will now ricochet back to, and rival, U.S. forces. A speedy reversal of such a mechanism then spirals the need for the United States to defend against its own new technologies immediately. Such an application by an enemy, adversary, or rival puts the United States on the losing end of the money curve, generating an unsustainable cycle of expenditures, from both the initial output for the advance and the ongoing costs of sustainable U.S. defenses against its own adapted inventions.[12]

To tilt the economic imbalances of defensive measures would then be a further SOCOM objective. For instance, makeshift bombs—also known as improvised explosive devices (IEDs)—are cheap and easy to wire, but U.S. countermeasures—robots, sensors, and jammers—are not, and the stakes are life and limb.

Further mismatches in economic warfare are ever-present in aerial combat. An unusual but relevant example is the occasional use of a missile to destroy aerial remote-controlled vehicles. When an antiballistic missile is launched to take down a drone—traveling at five times the speed of sound—the exchange ratio in favor of the drone operator reaches a financial advantage in the extreme, a difference of a few million dollars per shot.

That is simply not sustainable—even for a U.S. defense budget that remains larger than the military budgets of the next seven countries combined.

———

Walking by a barred turnstile, down an enclosed hallway, through yet another card-credential entry, and into a newer building, our group at long last has an analog moment after all of the digital circuits. Each of us is stopped and told to sign a paper log so that we can proceed.

From there, we enter the Joint Operations Center (JOC), a single coordination point for SOCOM's global operations. With the swipe of a badge, the metal doors of the JOC open automatically to reveal one person standing alone in an immense space. The JOC director, a former Army soldier and Vietnam veteran, introduces himself and welcomes us into a room of theater-sized screens—blank and fuzzy at the moment, with the exception of one tuned to CNN—and rows of empty desks and chairs.

"You're not supposed to be here," he begins, with some flourish, "but that's okay, we have had other tourists in the building for a couple of years, and they're more of a problem."

At least we know where we stand with him.

"You are not indoctrinated," the JOC director says casually, without a hint of the word's Orwellian connotation. "So, I had to empty the room." If this space was in active use, he notes, then "I wouldn't let you in . . . but if I had to open the door to you, then there would be light strobes like an airport runway until you left." Even if we were individuals "fully adjudicated and indoctrinated . . . [with] a valid need to know," he continues, SOCOM would still require a local sponsor for initial confirmation, before any access authorization would be granted, as well as a guarantor to monitor the ongoing use of SOCOM's enterprise networks.

"You are in a SCIF within a SCIF within a SCIF," he elaborates, referring to the computer room as a Sensitive Compartmented Information Facility where nationally protected data is used, within a wing that is another SCIF, and a building that is another.[13]

That it is a SCIF introduces a laundry list of requirements which he goes on to detail. From beginning to end, the physical security protections are exhaustive, designed to prevent intrusions and other threats. The multiple defenses block a range of incursions, from visual to acoustic to electronic, but above all physical. In the unclassified explanatory documents and open accreditation requirements—a few thousand pages in length— the most intricate rules are designed to prevent mass casualties in the event of a large-scale assault.

A member of our group then poses a question, one that seems to be plain and innocuous: "Why are there so many trash bins?" referring to a corner crammed with them. The response is elaborate, as recycling and trash also take on a different meaning here. Magnetic media with classified information is degaussed, he explains, and any secure communications cannot be sanitized at all but have to be destroyed before release.

Above the basic category of classified waste, or the classified versus nonclassified distinction, is whether Alternate Compensatory Control Measures (ACCMs) are required. The latter may go beyond measures normally required to access top-secret information, rising to the level of Special Access Program (SAP)—"to apply extraordinary security measures to protect extremely sensitive information," as it is formally defined in open-source documents.

Publicly available, nonclassified materials describe such programs as generally falling into three umbrella categories—acquisitions, intelligence, or operations and support—and varying based on their institutional lead. SOCOM's criteria differ from the Army's, for example, but all such programs would be physically stored in a facility for SAPs.[14] That not all programs are created equal is consequential. Across that range, the degree to which information is closely held is affected by such determinations: 1) *acknowledged*, meaning that the existence of the program is acknowledged but its specific details, such as a particular technology or technique, are classified; 2) *unacknowledged,* meaning that protective controls ensure that the existence of the program is neither acknowledged nor affirmed; and 3) *waived*, meaning that the program is funded without marking, as when the secretary of defense or another designee determines that regular congressional reporting requirements would have an adverse effect on national security. At the highest level of security, even the existence of the program is off-limits to most.

Turning to the front of the room, our guide points to the large screens, saying, "When in use, that's where it all comes together." He describes a process of synchronization in which SOCOM teams synthesize information derived from a network of seven Theater Special Operations Commands, U.S. Special Operations Joint Task Forces, and affiliated organizations and units, including allies and partners, as well as open multimedia sources, all tracking U.S. military campaigns and contingencies around the world.[15]

The director describes a continuous effort that seems Sisyphean, a system in permanent overload as a result of its collection protocols, a sort of vacuum approach to information. Piles and haystacks are assumed here—that materials can and must be gathered and interrogated in bulk.

We then follow our guide up to a small windowed gallery overlooking the floor of the ops center. Motioning in the direction of a wargame center on one side, he remarks that synthesized data is migrated to that space, becoming the empirical basis for SOCOM's planning exercises and decision-making. With the screens turned on, one could imagine an elevated degree of verisimilitude would be achieved with high-resolution visuals and narration, a sort of sound-and-light show. Difficult to assess, though, is how these representations could become verifiable knowledge. A later look into the parallel room shows a massive map on the floor with projections of scenarios, or what appears to be a cross between the old games of Twister and Risk in a new electronic format.[16]

———

In this gallery, behind where we are standing are some tiny images, a collage of fighter pictures. Most of the individuals are shown in the distance or with their faces partially covered, sometimes in the green glow of some night-vision photos. Others are backlit by sunshine as silhouettes of individuals, generally not displaying any specific physical features. Occasionally, a personal preference shows up—a type of knife carried, a scarf or sunglasses worn—but otherwise the individuals remain unrecognizable. That is in keeping with the U.S. Special Operations ethos—and operational security and proficiency—of unnamed personnel who possess some measure of tactical autonomy.

In a few unit photos, the pose is different. The fighters are lined up in rows by height, standing a couple of rows deep, as if assenting to the conventions of a class school arrangement. In these frames, no features of individuals are blurred or hidden. Their appearances run the gamut from serene to jaunty, clean-shaven to shaggy-bearded. In these team pictures, what is most distinguishable are the badges, tabs, pins, and patches. Each points to a different squadron, team, regiment, or other unit.

Here is a visual display of distinction and identity, of service and group, within the broader community of U.S. Special Operations Forces. Those differences are meaningful. Indeed, the generic term "special operator" elides two important categories: service and group. SOCOM, and the special operations community as a whole, is charged with blending the various forms and types as needed—while also keeping sufficiently disaggregated to ensure that variance or difference is maintained. To "be SOF," as some say, carries a meaning that applies to a collection of varied personnel that is neither a solitary affiliation nor a singular organization.

U.S. Special Operations Command is not comprised of its own home-grown workforce but rather draws from, and is comprised of, service operators, each with a distinct culture and separate heritage. Part of the Command's responsibility is to interweave these service cultures and ensure an overall equilibrium among the forces.[17]

The four armed services each maintains its own form of special operations: U.S. Army Special Operations Command (USASOC); U.S. Naval Special Warfare Command (WARCOM); U.S. Air Force Special Operations Command (AFSOC); and U.S. Marine Corps Forces Special Operations Command (MARSOC).[18] These institutional branches provide the core personnel of U.S. Special Operations Forces.[19] This joins the operator with SOCOM but institutionally locates the service member in the Army, Navy, Air Force, or Marines. In basic terms, Special Operations is not a separate service—and that masks some fundamental institutional realities.[20]

That U.S. Special Operations Forces is not a service—and is heavily dependent on the four services—is strategically significant, even existentially so. Decision-making processes—including major resourcing and planning decisions—are carried out in a service structure of which U.S. Special Operations is not on the same echelon. While SOCOM refers to aspects of these four branches as its components and subcommands, and U.S. Special Operations leaders contribute, cajole, nudge, and otherwise seek to alter arrangements, they cannot control institutional outcomes. Because the Command does not have its own separate personnel system, and the institutional branches actually predate the existence of SOCOM, with the exception of MARSOC, it has a shared role in recruitment and promotion. The four services largely determine the pool from which the Command can draw individuals. With the services, SOCOM shares the responsibility of preparing and developing, of training and equipping fighters.

In general terms, the Army, Navy, Air Force, and Marines, in each of their component commands, have their own criteria for choosing and developing their part of U.S. Special Operations Forces. Most recruits undergo an elaborate selection process, one that focuses on differing aspects of conditioning and resilience, tailored to the service-selected specializations. Acceptance rates to such programs are their determinations. SOCOM states its preferences and levies requirements for both operator capabilities and numbers. Its leadership has publicly expressed concerns about dilution if the four branches accept too many candidates or reduce standards to grow the pool.[21]

Formally, service centrality is ever-present. Throughout, the operator's professional longevity, and ability to rise to higher ranks, depend on heeding that underlying expertise, culture, and mindset. Each branch has its own career-management processes that incorporates its special operations personnel, from assignment to retirement and from compensation to promotion. Meticulous attention to institutional proclivities is essential to the continuation of the personnel's careers.

Informally, each service functions as a group, with distinctive tribes, clans, kinships, and totems. Each retains a separate identity, with differing strengths of ties. At times, U.S. operators have an uneasy relationship with the broader culture of the general purpose forces—at times as a minority group or odd men out—but leaders of the general purpose forces have also fought to hold on to their special operators and to retain their distinctive branch inside U.S. Special Operations Forces.

At SOCOM, the overall personnel system has approximately 70,000 individuals. Of that number, about half are deployable forces, including logistics and headquarters staffs, and fewer than a quarter are specially selected, assessed, and trained to conduct special operations. The number of special operators—formally defined as those who engage in close-quarters combat with the enemy or, more commonly, those selected to be a tip of some sort of spear—is significantly smaller than that of the overall force structure.

Within SOCOM, components and units have separate facilities and places located across the United States. To oversimplify, more than a dozen major categories exist inside the four major groupings, and far more if the personnel codes of U.S. Special Operations Forces are taken into account. When placed in the policy context within U.S. national security matters, though, the general term "special operator" is more typically applied. That term glosses over these distinctions, but it also provides a unifying frame and commonality.

Collectively, then, by formal definition and military doctrine, U.S. special operators, with advanced combat training, are expected to carry out a range of activities including foreign military training and information warfare and nonconventional operations in remote, austere, or politically sensitive environments. They are typically equipped for short-term operations, maintaining limited logistics support inside their units. Special operations is further defined by limitations to its force structure—not easy to replace, reconstitute, or expand, thus not designed for attrition warfare.

Whether organized into small units or teams, some of these forces are further trained to work as clandestine fighters, alone or in pairs, to be an independent and unilateral option as well as to work closely with the full range of practitioners of U.S.

national security strategy and international partners. For those concentrating on manhunting and thing-hunting, or its close inverse of hostage rescue, a high degree of readiness is prerequisite, from a no-notice deployment to contingencies. These skill sets are designed to be adjustable so that special operations can rapidly start up, adapt, redirect, or close down in response to any forthcoming national need.

As a whole, then, the work of U.S. special operators is incomplete in perpetuity.

In the broadest sense, special operations have existed in one form or another for as long as there has been war. In military terms, such operations constitute a category of practices deemed outside the traditional or conventional operations of a particular time and place. A special operation is, in part, defined in the negative: by what it is not.

Integration of the various official descriptions provides a broad way of thinking about U.S. Special Operations that could be synthesized to five major concepts: 1) risk, including political sensitivities and hostile environments; 2) visibility, such as clandestine networks and other activities otherwise not on display in denied or constrained areas; 3) scale, to include small deployment numbers, an economy of force, and moving with a light footprint; 4) all-encompassing, from humanitarian activities to capture/kill operations; and 5) exceptionalism, to provide force where general U.S. military forces would be ill suited, including factors such as technique and reach, or in which the primary objective of force is not strictly military.[22]

Put a different way, U.S. Special Operations Forces manage "everything else," or the nontraditional and nonconventional—

those military objectives that are not already assigned as the responsibility of another branch of the U.S. armed forces. Frequently, such objectives are also expressed in the form of a negative: counterterror, counterinsurgency, counterproliferation, among other activities.

Given that the meaning of conventional warfare changes over time, what is deemed a special operation is by definition not fixed. The particular characteristics of such force vary with wartime conditions and operational environments. In World War II, for example, sabotage and subversion behind enemy lines commonly characterized operators from the United States. In the early years of the Cold War, psychological warfare and propaganda efforts were at the forefront. Throughout the Vietnam War, unconventional forms of warfare, including insurgent and counterinsurgent operations and the development and insertion of proxy forces, were central. Since then, combating, countering, and deterring terrorism has been the focus. A special operation may be a single engagement—for instance, to eliminate a particular target; episodic, including a series of activities such as the training of foreign forces; protracted—for example, supporting an insurgency against a government deemed hostile to the United States or its interests; or habitual, including the ongoing development of the self-defense of other nations.

In select cases, special operations include the direct engagement of the U.S. president and the secretary of defense, traditionally known as the National Command Authority.[23]

———

Soon after we arrive in the glass bay overlooking the Joint Operations Center, the SOCOM commander rejoins us, bringing all military members to their feet. Our visiting group tries to do the same, but is awkwardly unsure of the protocol for whether to stand at all.

The clumsy moment ends when the commander asks for observations drawn from the tour. One in our group notes an apparent emphasis on equipment and technology throughout, with few representations of those who comprise the force—the people—and asks the commander to share his guiding principles on the intersections of personnel and stuff, or forces and equipment.

That query elicits a philosophical response, a subject that seems to capture the commander's interest. He responds indirectly, asking if we noticed or recognized the full-length portrait hanging in the lobby that we passed at the start of the day. A few of us nod.

It is that picture of William Donovan, founder of the OSS. President Roosevelt referred to "Wild Bill"—as Donovan came to be known, a fighting Irishman turned swashbuckler spy—as his "secret legs" in sending him overseas to build an international clandestine network of intelligence operators and special forces to undertake sabotage, espionage, and, when called for, assassinations.[24]

Both SOCOM and the CIA claim the OSS as their forerunner—drawing a line from those units formed to infiltrate Hitler's Europe and Emperor Hirohito's Asia all the way up to the post-9/11 teams that combat terrorism. Today, Donovan's portrait also hangs prominently at the CIA's headquarters, and the OSS's golden spear remains in the insignia of both organizations. The room we spent the morning in is also named after him.

The commander tells us that the painting is a daily reminder for him of both the historic challenges that America has faced and the finesse now required for today's counterterrorism and counterinsurgency missions. He goes on to describe a new OSS cadre that he would welcome, one that would offer alternative paradigms for examining ideologically driven violence. He expresses concern about current shortfalls in expeditionary endeavors, about the limited numbers of U.S. experts prepared to work alongside local populations at the diverse and ever-changing locations to which SOCOM deploys. Languages, histories, economies, and beliefs, he continues, constitute only part of the information and knowledge that SOCOM requires to develop sustainable relationships.

"But we are having a hard time understanding . . . We don't know them, and they don't know us," he explains, referring to potential partners as well as adversaries.

As a conceptual frame for today's U.S. special operators—both as a personnel idea and as a preferred form of warfare—Olson suggests a model for U.S. citizens to "go native" up to a point, temporarily, when downrange, and fight with deep local specifics at the forefront.

To that end, the commander relates, we are making use of a pilot program of the U.S. Department of Defense—Military Accessions Vital to the National Interest, or MAVNI—"an initiative to recruit individuals living legally in the United States, who are not citizens, and through military service, would be offered that path." Olson describes the policy change as coming none too soon, as SOCOM faces a grave shortage of personnel with the requisite languages for places to which they routinely deploy. He conveys the depth of the problem inside SOCOM—the delayed recognition and still insufficient resolution—where not only are U.S. special operators unable to negotiate like a local, but in many instances lack the linguistic skills to carry out necessary exchanges. The commander explains, U.S. special operators are sent to quick courses and schoolhouse training—if there is time before a deployment, and when its duration would warrant the expense. U.S. Army Special Forces, or Green Berets, have extensive language training, but across other components, only a few standing efforts are in place.[25]

SOCOM's geographic scope—it works in about 100 countries in any given year—results in contacts with more than 500 languages that top a million speakers each, a count that sets aside the further complexity arising from dialects and variants in the field. Achieving a degree of functional literacy across all areas may be an ideal—to train local forces or to infiltrate organizations, among other activities—but such literacy seems barely attainable for any institution, even one for which it is the sole objective.

For SOCOM, specifically, a universal basic proficiency would necessitate decades of investments, and potentially a shift from mostly American-raised, national citizenship criteria in operator selection. Short of that transformation, SOCOM commonly relies on the temporary hiring of local translators and interpreters, a scramble or on-the-fly approach, or a vetting by honed instinct.

"This is a high priority for us, to increase our regional expertise through the recruitment of native and heritage speakers," Olson explains.

It is also in keeping with more than two centuries of U.S. law that authorizes citizenship opportunities for immigrants who serve—putting their lives on the line—in America's wars. Since the declaration of the Global War on Terror, and President Bush's retroactive Executive Order 13269 of 2002, immigrants in the U.S. military have been immediately eligible for naturalization. In the first decade of the 9/11 wars, 75,000 service members became American citizens. With the addition of MAVNI offering expedited review of applications, 10,000 noncitizens enlisted and completed the naturalization process.[26]

"This is operationally critical," Olson continues. With MAVNI, SOCOM has possessed a new recruiting tool to diversify the language skills of its forces—the entry point has been available to native speakers of Igbo, Urdu, and Dari, among others on the U.S. government's list of thirty-five high-priority languages. It has further meant assigning foreign-born individuals to its units while still maintaining formal exclusion from certain roles in U.S. Special Operations Forces.

If it were only that easy. The second word of MAVNI's name—Accessions—has an odd connotation of possession that is incongruous in this context of human aptitude. It is not only the program's name that appears to miscue, but also some of the policy delineations that sidestep the program's reality—recruiting noncitizens into the U.S. military—as if the pipeline might be perceived by others as a dangerous ingress inside America. MAVNI entrants, though, if successful in the adjudication of their citizenship application, join a large number of foreign-born individuals—over 100,000—who are already serving in the U.S. armed forces. More than 30,000 noncitizens are currently in uniform, and about 8,000 legal permanent residents, or green-card holders, enlist each year.

Even setting the caps and legal problems aside, "this won't be enough . . . our needs are greater," Olson continues.

For that reason, he relates, he is working on an idea, one "that I call Project Lawrence . . . We need our Lawrence of Pakistan, our Lawrence of Paraguay, our Lawrence of Indonesia, and our Lawrence of Mali," referring to T. E. Lawrence, the Oxford man who trained to be an archaeologist, enthralled by digs in Syria and Egypt, whom the British army sent to fight among the nomadic Bedouins, and who ultimately became a warrior respected by the locals.[27]

The commander presents this as a general ideal for a U.S. special operator to emulate. Lawrence, whose boyhood bedroom walls and university thesis were centered on the planning of crusader castles spanning West and East, placed himself astride a thin line in the British Empire, one that divided his role in a British intervention on the side of Arab tribes to defeat the Ottoman Empire. As a new soldier in 1914, he was Ned Lawrence of the Welsh countryside, apprentice-excavator to the British Museum, a cog in the mass mobilization of the world war. He returned to England in 1919 as an unlikely hero—Lawrence of Arabia—extolled for battlefield prowess and beneficent diplomacy. A mystical soldier, embedded in the tribes of the desert war, draped in creamy white robes with a gold dagger at his waist, steered camel cavalries into the desolate Wadi Rum, in today's Jordan. In the lore of the British Empire, Lawrence led local tribes to victory, developing a strategic force in the battle, a strength that culminated in Allied dominance—fleeting though it was—over long-standing Ottoman monarchical lands extending from Constantinople to Baghdad to Damascus.

Olson further cites Lawrence's essay "The Evolution of a Revolt" as an autobiography of this personal method. Lawrence proposed an irregular form of fighting and a regular type of war. An unconventional fight, he explained, uncorks in independence, blazed by volunteers who storm for freedom and justice. The other end, traditional and conventional, Lawrence depicted as bit parts in military machines, conscripts and cannon fodder rolling as a mass to serve the interests of empires and states. On the irregular-to-regular continuum in that personal account, the techniques of a U.S. special operator align with the guerrilla principles and simplicity that Lawrence favors.

The U.S. military's counterinsurgency manual has also been revised to incorporate aspects of Lawrence's instructions, both from the "Revolt" essay and from his weighty book *Seven Pillars of Wisdom,* of which it was published as a single chapter. Coedited by General David Petraeus, when he directed the U.S. Army Combined Arms Center, and General James N. Mattis, when he led the Marine Corps Combat Development Command, the manual called on readers to broaden how they conceived of combat skills and nonmilitary approaches, to be "culturally astute leaders," to be "ready each day to be greeted with a hand-shake or a hand grenade . . . to be nation builders as well as warriors, to help re-establish institutions and local security forces, to assist in the rebuilding of infrastructure and basic services, and to facilitate the establishment of local governance and the rule of law."[28]

Included in the book are Lawrence's specific directives—that persuasion of the populace comes via protection, the provisioning of essential services, and investment in local economies. In the manual's opening chapter, Petraeus, Mattis, and their cowriters pay specific tribute to Lawrence's practices of insurgency, praising him for bedeviling the Ottoman Empire, war experiences that "made him a hero and provide rich insights for today." They further adapt Lawrence's twenty-seven "commandments," as he described them in 1917, into a series of teachings for U.S. forces, one that emphasizes local culture as the necessary context for U.S. decision-making. That tome entreats lofty standards for special operations personnel on two- to twelve-month rotations: "Learn about the people, topography, economy, history, religion, and culture of the Area of Operations . . . Become the world expert on these topics"; understand that success depends on "agile, well-informed, culturally astute leaders" who know "every village . . . group . . . and ancient grievance."[29]

Although the manual was originally intended for Army and Marine service members, Petraeus and Mattis were encouraging its use more globally, attempting to apply microregional approaches across time and space.

The conjuring of Lawrence of Arabia here at MacDill also fits a thinly veiled zeitgeist of discontent over the 9/11 timelines and durations. Those special operators who predicted a year's fight in Afghanistan back in 2001 welcomed their rapid victory after just two months. That this would be the pinnacle for some of their combat operations, though, and the start of inexorable drift—a slow but steady erosion of their strength—proved puzzling to those who were not taking a generational view of the fight, as well as disillusioning to those who expected a series of easy wins against a less-advanced enemy. When the orders to invade and reconstruct Iraq were added to that calculation in 2002–2003—at a time when officers expressed grave concern about the U.S. operational plans, questioning both their viability and sustainability—and former and retired national security advisors, chairmen of the Joint Chiefs of Staff, and CENTCOM commanders publicly objected, "Don't attack Saddam"—the whole equation teetered on a strategic precipice. Fast forward through years of SOCOM's forces in and out of the region, still in Afghanistan and Iraq in ebbs and flows, drawdowns and surges, and the desire for an alternative way is palpable. Most visible of all is the longing to make sense of these longest wars.

While Lawrence's argot has come to the fore at both SOCOM and CENTCOM, Lawrence himself warned any future reader against such appropriation, asserting that such ideas are not applicable to alternative times and spaces. Lawrence preemptively admonished those who would seek to apply his personal notes to anything other than "the work in hand" of Bedu tribes in 1917, writing in his introduction: "They are, however, only my personal conclusions . . . townspeople or Syrians require totally different treatment. They are of course not suitable to any other person's need" and are only to be used "as stalking horses for beginners in the Arab armies."[30]

Setting aside the admonition from Lawrence, though, the ambiguous tale of combat over years, even decades—blurring the lines of how to fight, yet combined with a clear-cut statement of war, while focusing on common cause as requisite for victory—may present a useful model for some at SOCOM and CENTCOM. In certain respects, it offers an alternative to a U.S. doctrine of overwhelming force, which since the 1980s, has been called America's preferred way of war—dominate or vanquish.

Lawrence's is more of a wartime philosophy of inclusion. Embrace—rather than resolve, minimize, or eliminate—the differences and create a composite. That means, for example, scars on old maps—ancient and overlapping—are unlikely to be smoothed or disguised but can be incorporated. Today's fragile geopolitical constructions, and the theological struggles and territorial declarations that U.S. forces now confront across Iraq, Afghanistan, and the broader region, are found in parallel in Lawrence's chronicles of the same subjects in the Arab-British military campaigns a century ago.

Looking at the long ago provides a way to think about the future activities of U.S. Special Operations, the commander asserts.

Olson further offers a single graphic as the rendering of a future choice—a circle with colorful spokes. The concept has been crafted by SOCOM, the Command's work to synthesize the nation's plan for global counterterrorism activities. It provides their framework for two approaches to influence the behavior of U.S. adversaries in ambiguous conflict: the direct approach and the indirect approach.

In the U.S. Special Operations environment, the direct approach is well understood. It is present at the creation, listed first in its legislated activity. The direct approach—or direct action, terms often used interchangeably in U.S. Department of Defense documentation—is largely violent in nature: urgent, necessary, and chaotic. In the parlance of special operations, it has further meaning as a strike capability—manhunting and thing-hunting—and is a euphemism for both capture/kill and interdict/disrupt. Its further twenty-first-century connotation of prevention and preemption—to attack before they attack us—has resulted in a high-tempo mission, often with lethal force, over the past decade. The direct approach can be described as warfare relying solely on physical force.[31]

The indirect approach is less defined in U.S. Special Operations, but in a general sense stands for the opposite—a method that does not primarily rely on brute action from U.S. forces. It takes an eternal idea in warfare—exploiting the cognitive, moral, and psychological dimensions of conflict—and formally labels it the indirect approach. It is a philosophy that calls for attacking the mindset of adversaries, to render them hopeless, paralyzed, incoherent, and bewildered, explaining the method as focusing on root causes. The indirect approach incorporates information operations as well, such as electronic warfare, activities to interrupt or influence the opponent's systems and networks.

Such efforts may be indirect, but these approaches are not always bloodless. Fomenting instability to undermine governments deemed illegitimate and hostile is one example.

To some in the U.S. Special Operations community, the term indirect approach also has a narrower and somewhat different meaning—conducting activities through surrogate or proxy forces. In this sense, U.S. forces are achieving their objectives indirectly—"by, with, and through" is one shorthand phrase—as locals are trained and equipped to apply. This approach includes enabling foreign forces with training, advising, and mentoring, and often equipping through transfer of technology and operational support. That is to say, it is a kind of foreign internal defense: building the capacity of another nation, supporting and assisting them as they strengthen their own security. These methods aim to help nations fight their own fights and govern their own territories, and thereby to reduce the need for major incursions by U.S. troops on foreign soil. At its broadest, such a U.S. action is as much civilian as military in nature, applying resources drawn from across the federal government, from diplomacy to development, from justice to defense.

It is clear that such balanced warfare will by no means mark the end of SOCOM's capture/kill programs or herald the start of a social constructivist model—the dig-and-build or wells-and-schools tactics advocated as one part of a counterinsurgency strategy. Rather, this is a change in emphasis, one that signals the potency but inadequacy of decapitation as a primary means to degrade or erode violent jihadist organizations, while perhaps envisaging a dual modus operandi to generate more enduring effects. At a minimum, balanced warfare acknowledges that the decapitation strategy may be militarily necessary, but is insufficient—or worse, that the strategy could result in an enemy that grows back even larger than before, akin to a metaphorical starfish.[32]

Here is a presentation of one ideal, or one preferred roadmap. In addition to its review inside the Pentagon, it continues to circulate throughout the U.S. armed services, the intelligence community, the White House, the U.S. Congress, and further elements of the U.S. national security structure. Whether this would have the desired effects remains wholly uncertain.

SOCOM can recommend strategic changes—including budgeting and personnel decisions—but requires a range of executive and legislative approvals to implement them. While SOCOM may wish to increase its support of the indirect approach, it is not fully enabled to act for that strategy by its civilian leadership, and even if authorized, would have limited resources to contribute. Above all, SOCOM is expected to maintain its lethal skills, and while it may receive increased support for nonlethal activities, that acceptance has been shown most likely when still tied to lethal force or planning.[33]

Our visit ends in the glass bay with a lively discussion of global shifts in perceptions of American presence: the extent of its tarnishing abroad and the decreasing number of countries that advertise an American military presence as defense insurance or that display U.S. military support as a badge of honor.

"Most of those countries that do request assistance prefer American efforts that don't make the news," the commander adds. With that overarching meaning of America's grand strategy left in doubt—a substantial geostrategic shift—our visit to SOCOM draws to a close. Olson concludes our time at SOCOM with a bracing observation in a humble tone: "We've never been in war this long . . . There is a lot we don't know."

4

MORE BOOTS YET TO COME

Far more important are . . . those big ideas outside the
wire under Kevlar, under body armor.
—General David Petraeus

GET AGGRESSIVE, the bumble-bee colored sign orders—our van driver is taking a different way back to MacDill. Just a five-minute drive from yesterday's leafy waterfront arrival, this route prefigures a day of sharp and blaring contrasts. Amid a sprawl of pawn shops and check-cashing kiosks, billboards offer help for gambling addiction and cheap policies of life insurance. Contact the accident attorneys of Winters & Yonker. CASH is Queen, calls out the next sign, Welcome to She Money Pawn. $$ We Pay the MOST $$. Vasectomy. No Needle. No Scalpel. (727) 462-MALE.

"Stay classy, Tampa," one officer later says with a grin, about this main artery into base.

The Dale Mabry Highway ends at a massive concrete gate block, adjacent to greenery cut to read "MacDill." Well before we reach the perimeter, we come to a standstill as security guards inspect each car, opening trunks and gas tank covers, running mirrors along the underside of cars.

"Do you see the pink-windowed building . . . the massive one, on the other side of the gate?" a Council staff member asks.

"Do you mean the Death Star?" the guy next to me replies.

"I guess you could call it that—it's CENTCOM's Joint Intelligence Center."

The very place we are headed, where we'll soon learn about the "comprehensive approach" to the wars of Afghanistan and Iraq, from livestock management to parliamentary procedures, a method only made real when we meet young soldiers just back home.[1]

————

Driving up to the center, we pass rows of manicured shrubs and reach an immense stone fountain set in its circular driveway. CENTCOM's glitz provides a sharp contrast to the understated aesthetic of SOCOM. The welcome—even more so. At first, we see no one. It feels oddly deserted, or as though the building has only just been constructed and its occupants have yet to move in. No one is coming out, or going in, the large glass wall of doors, and I later learn that staff use a small door in the back. After a few minutes, though, a group of sharply dressed civilians come outside and call out a friendly "Welcome, welcome . . . welcome to U.S. Central Command."

We follow the greeters into a lobby that is massive—in length, width, and height—and luxurious, set off with walls covered with a tropical mural. We walk around a bold circular rug that fills the space. CENTCOM's insignia sits at its center and below it lies a partial map of Africa and Asia, covered in part by America's soaring bald eagle, with its claws holding a shield in red, white, and blue. It is a colossal overlay of American political imagery atop the outlines of the region.

Passing into a cavernous conference room, we are approached by more amiable staffers who take turns introducing themselves—public affairs officers, strategic communications staffers, or engagement team members. I cannot distinguish between the three occupational categories—they all seem to fit the stereotype of boosterism that others had cautioned us about. It feels unsettling given the deadly nature of the business at hand.

Our group initially sticks to safe topics and small talk: "When was this center built? . . . What did it replace? . . . What other new construction is expected?"

The staffers are polite and knowledgeable, responding to each query in turn, offering a steady stream of facts and figures. They describe nearly $1 billion in construction at MacDill since 9/11, including more than $200 million for lodging and $100 million for healthcare facilities. Referring to the ground we are standing on, "The old CENTCOM buildings had been built in the 1980s and 1990s, but most have now been demolished to make way for these new structures," a public affairs officer tells us. Keeping pace with the accelerating technology demands and avoiding overprovisions, though, has spawned many requirements.

"The building we are in here has literally thousands of miles of encased cables and steel pipe piles running more than 200 feet down." We learn that when the twin building now under construction is complete, it will add a half-million square feet to the U.S. Central Command facility.

A few others join the conversation, then more, until one of the staffers makes an off-script comment: "General [David] Petraeus, Representative [Kathy] Castor, and Representative [Bill] Young used golden shovels to symbolically break ground . . . At the dedication, Young apparently said, [this] 'building is proof that MacDill is no longer in danger of being closed down.'" That touch of bravado, with its allusion to pork-barrel politics, abruptly ends the conversation. The statement is perhaps too candid in this setting.

Interposed into that awkward silence is a gravelly voice from across the room, calling all to take their seats. Formal name placards mark the places, so we crisscross each other until we find our assigned leather swivel chairs. Around this immense horseshoe-shaped table, the ramrod-straight bearing of our hosts is in stark contrast to our slouchy posture.

A rear admiral speaks first, with a genteel welcome, and then sets out the Command's operations in a PowerPoint presentation. The slides start with broad objectives: Defeat extremist networks. Enable partners. Deter aggression. Build multilateral relationships. That is followed by the "pillars" of counterinsurgency operations—a slide with three verbs tucked inside drawings of columns: Establish. Consolidate. Transfer. The next lays out the Command's priorities in three countries—Iraq, Afghanistan, and Pakistan—as the major areas of challenge.

He goes on to describe CENTCOM's mission as protecting the population. The method is to "win" the war by swaying groups to one side through appeal rather than superior force, a type of nation-building from the ground up. It harkens back to the earliest days of the American republic, when President John Adams described the country's democracy project: "The Revolution was in the minds and hearts of the people." Or, picking up the expression from when President Lyndon Johnson advocated its inverse parallel in Vietnam: Victory depends on the "hearts and minds" of the people who "live out there."[2]

Over the next few hours, several military officers file in. The speakers are careful with their appraisals, varnished in their analysis. The diction is taut and clipped. They take turns describing how to eliminate underlying causes of violent extremism and how to build the capabilities of their local partners. One officer gives an example of provincial reconstruction teams bringing medical and educational assistance to remote mountain communities in Afghanistan; another offers details of building a new children's hospital in Iraq. One emphasizes security force assistance in both Iraq and Afghanistan, including establishing new law and order standards, building prisons, and training army and policing units. Another presents slides of U.S. soldiers training Afghan recruits, culminating in an enlistment ceremony at an Afghanistan base on July 4, complete with American flag and regalia.

The speakers' overarching theme is how to achieve America's objective—greater stability in the entire CENTCOM area of responsibility—through wide-ranging socioeconomic operations in Afghanistan and Iraq. Barely a mention is made of the twenty-plus other countries in CENTCOM's area of responsibility—Iran, Syria, and several other nations of geopolitical import. The omission, in part, could be chalked up to classification sensitivities—not wishing to give official word on unacknowledged programs, for example, or not wanting to draw attention to certain activities in Pakistan and Yemen. Even discounting for that, though, the presentation still does not explain the dispositions and buildups the officers describe—the facts and figures show an actual overwhelming emphasis on just two countries—and does not provide an explanation of the underlying assumption that U.S. security is well served by a concentration on Afghanistan and Iraq, above all others.[3]

While the examples and assessments are generalized—similar to what would be found in a Congressional Research Service report—the briefing as a whole does provide a timeline of the major shifts in CENTCOM's 9/11 campaigns, a trendline from precise to nebulous to abundant. A few times, the briefers use the same phrase to end their remarks: More needs to be done. This approach is inclusive—extraordinarily so—and here they link their objectives to broad counterinsurgency principles of community, legitimacy, and development. It looks like a method once derided inside CENTCOM—and publicly scoffed at—in the early days of the 9/11 wars, dismissed as "armed social work," a form of "do-goodery." Now, CENTCOM is promoting a dig-and-build strategy for the deployment of U.S. armed forces.[4]

That strategy has not satisfied skeptics who have dismissed these proponents of counterinsurgency as true believers who go to unreasonable, even reckless, lengths to achieve their military, defense, or security objectives. To many, the counterinsurgency method is unaffordable and unsustainable. Approaching Iraq as America's fifty-first state, and attempting to bring that state out of its multiple forms of bankruptcy, they argue, is an ill-conceived, extraordinarily expensive, all-consuming occupation unlikely to strengthen America's national security—and more apt to weaken it. No amount of money, they contend, can achieve a sustainable prosperity, and current levels of funding are not simply counterproductive but also corrupting.

One U.S. Marine officer assesses the past dexterity of U.S. armed forces to carry out such work and advises circumspection: "Unprofessional failure. These words best describe the eleven counterinsurgency actions that the United States has been involved in during this century."[5] A British Army officer, from its intelligence corps, points to counterinsurgency moves as the start of a new enterprise, not the end. He explains: "Building indigenous armed forces is not an exit strategy. It is the entrance strategy." Furthermore, he continues: "An obsession with meeting targets and gross numbers is self-deluding." Killing those judged to be "irreconcilables"— a decapitation strategy—is not much better, he adds.[6]

Just one briefer describes the combat zones differently— dramatically so. He presents examples of recent U.S. operations and intelligence, nearly all on the subject of violent Islamist networks, organizations, and individuals, and projects mugshots on the screen, a few of which have red X's over their faces. The following month, when Abu Ayyub al-Masri and Abu Omar al-Baghdadi, leaders of al-Qaeda in Iraq, are killed in a raid in Tikrit, I think of his slide deck: two more flipped to X.[7]

A decade ago, that first objective of the military campaign, as set on September 12, 2001 by President Bush, had been so specific and vivid. The Command's mission—and that of the U.S. forces as a whole—focused on a singular hunt. Both the president and Vice President Dick Cheney spoke in sledgehammer terms of bin Laden's demise: Bush referred to an "old poster out West ... Wanted: Dead or Alive" to convey the message of America's primary objective. Cheney, when asked if he would take bin Laden's head on a platter, responded without hesitation, "I would take it today." When that immediate objective—more significant than toppling the Taliban and eliminating a sanctuary for al-Qaeda—was not achieved by December 2001, CENTCOM's targeting widened. The invasion of Iraq was already in its third month of tightly held discussions at both the White House and MacDill's dual four-star commands of CENTCOM and SOCOM. Intermittent hunts in the high rocks and dry plains of northwest Pakistan proceeded with some regularity, but in two years, as one U.S. special operator describes it, there was a "flipping of a switch" to Iraq, and ultimately a leap then into ground wars and nation-building, first in Iraq and then in Afghanistan. "I can remember exactly when. It was not a slow slide. We were not dragged into it. Didn't stumble into it either. It was an off-on switch."[8]

As our group's first morning at CENTCOM comes to a close, there is an abrupt change in style—the showing of a video of smiling U.S. soldiers in Afghanistan and Iraq as the session's conclusion. It seems casual, like a group shot at summer camp, and not at all in keeping with the seriousness of the environment—massive weaponry slung over their shoulders and austere landscapes in the background. As the video continues, it has a back-and-forth quality; U.S. forces are undertaking a campaign that is simultaneously humanizing and destructive. On a single deployment, and even in as short a cycle as twenty-four hours, soldiers appear to be operating from two entirely different modes or mindsets. The film shows soldiers called to live among, support, and build relationships with local villagers on the ground. Then, within that continuous cycle, the same soldiers are called on to conduct capture/kill operations among the population, with the ever-present possibility of casualties among noncombatants—those they have worked alongside. The cycle is without a pause or reset, seemingly vulnerable to a dangerous short-circuit. Even the most rudimentary mechanism against cognitive rupture, if empathy and aggression unintentionally overlap—compartmentalization, suppression, or decompression —appears to have neither time nor space. The soldiers' rhythm is without break.[9]

After several minutes of this Hollywood-quality video, my eyes wander off-screen and around the room where we sit. Nothing about this meets the Spartan warrior ideal, the exemplar advanced by military leaders for more than two millennia. To the contrary, the tenor seems more comparable to the end of the Roman Empire. It feels as if we are sitting in Nero's palace, in an opulent setting in sharp contrast to—and literally a long way from—the downrange environment of the Command's soldiers on the screen.[10]

———

With a loud click, and then utter silence, the video ends. A staff member stands, informing us that the morning session has concluded, and that we are invited for lunch on the other side of base.

That meal with service members who signed up after 9/11—most of them cite that day as the primary factor in their decision—proves to be the highlight of the week. They delve swiftly into their personal experiences, forthrightly and earnestly, sharing observations of the security situation across CENTCOM's area of responsibility. Their collective report is largely one of volatility and deterioration.

Amid that uncertainty and turbulence, they describe one directive that remains fixed: zero defect. A Marine relates his understanding of that order, down to its most quotidian level, to entail the daily habits of every member of the U.S. force. "Interact respectively, drive responsibly, nothing bone-headed," all of which translates to behavior that must be well above reproach. That guidance is easy, he explains, but not all of us do it. The other meaning is to operate without a mistake, from "how we patrol a road to which project gets built up."

The corollary, the young Marine continues, is also hard. "Comprehensive . . . that's the word they give us. It means do everything and be everywhere . . . get all on board."

An Army captain joins the conversation and adds: "I am expected to finish the task of establishing security in my district in a half-year."

"Keep in mind" that some are "looking at seventh, eighth, ninth tours" if they stay in, interjected another.

Putting the CENTCOM presentations together with these personal accounts, it seems difficult to conceive of this version of counterinsurgency—a protracted campaign to ensure a durable peace—as viable. The service members describe naiveté and shame, a mixture of heroism and the mundane—and a laundry list of expectations imposed on them, including humanitarian assistance, reconstruction, stability operations, as well as raids, assaults, and force projection. Their stories mix protection and combat, rural water treatment and dense urban conflict, the rule of law and the elimination of the enemy. And somehow, all of this is to be accomplished in a six-to-eight-month rotation, or perhaps fourteen months for those who receive orders that their deployment is extended.[11]

This may be an appealing theory or strategy on paper, but it requires a force of people that is difficult to imagine. The type of personnel who could carry out a counterinsurgent-counterterrorist program seems akin to an amped-up Marvel figure. Not just a cartoonish image of a superhero but an over-the-top composite—a soldier with the body of Superman, the brain of Hannibal Lecter, and the heart of Mother Teresa. An exaggeration, but not far from the picture the service members paint, which they label the "three Ds": defense, diplomacy, development. They offer a tale of stark disproportion, one that seems to fit the trite but true expression "rainbows and unicorns."

From color arches to spiraled horns, the conversation turns to costs and consequences, and to personalities. That includes the second unvarnished comment of the day, although this time it continues uninterrupted: "King David [a nickname for General Petraeus] is running for U.S. President, and your group is part of his campaign fundraising plan." Another discusses Petraeus's entourage—a 100-person Commander's Action Group—and his traveling team on his C-40 aircraft, where no detail is overlooked, from the cabin temperature to the menu selection, managed by a meticulous staff.

They go on to explain that Petraeus has more than once been described as having the appearance of a bookworm, not that of a warrior, that he made the unusual choice as a young Army infantry officer to pursue a doctorate in international relations at Princeton University. Petraeus is said to have credited the move to the advice of an Army superior: Raise your intellectual sights beyond the maximum effective range of an M60 machine gun. His cerebral stance became a professional differentiator in a get-things-done, muddy-boots organization, one that he expanded as he moved into the Army's senior ranks. A motley group of American scholars—anthropologists, sociologists, historians—now forms his inner circle, they explain, individuals that he has recruited to join the fight.[12]

"Okay . . . but what is it like for you? And how does it feel to be home, Stateside?" one in our group asks.

"Well . . . ," one begins.

Looking among themselves, no one seems eager to answer that one.

Then, after the awkward pause, "Well . . . you see . . . look . . . we spend our days here as PowerPoint Rangers, endlessly tinkering with bullet points on slides."[13]

The negative impact is far-reaching. As one brigadier general in the U.S. Army has explained it, there is a danger of reducing the complexities of war to bullet points [that] "create the illusion of understanding and the illusion of control."[14]

One soldier describes his own past participation in block-by-block fighting in Sadr City, Iraq, with its elaborate layers of airpower, as contrasted with his current assignment—making pictures of the fighting. Yet another points to the irrelevant brushfires that eat up their day, lurching from one email crisis to the next, last-minute visitors and schedule changes, crashing computers, misplaced presentations, and the like. They relate returning from deployments where they had significant responsibilities to a sprawling, sclerotic bureaucracy at HQ, to attend endless and redundant briefings, a mind-numbing battle rhythm, by turns irrelevant and occasionally worthwhile.

Defense Secretary Robert Gates will encapsulate the problem with potency in a farewell speech from government service a year later: "Men and women in the prime of their professional lives, who may have been responsible for the lives of scores or hundreds of troops, or millions of dollars in assistance, or engaging or reconciling warring tribes, may find themselves in a cube all day reformatting PowerPoint slides, preparing quarterly training briefs, or assigned an ever-expanding array of clerical duties . . . the consequences of this terrify me."[15]

A senior officer at the table then shares that General Stanley A. McChrystal had been shown a slide the previous year on how to ensure stability in Afghanistan, with a line for each factor in a village operation—fraction of workforce; illegitimate agricultural production; trade and employment; overall government reach, execution, capacity and investment; and literally hundreds more.

"They call it a spaghetti map," the officer says, referring to its countless lines in an endless loop on the page. To some, he explained, the image is vague, amorphous, incomprehensible, rendering more confusion than clarification—and an exemplar of an unwinnable effort built on faulty assumptions of threat-based logic.

Upon being shown the noodling, to sum up, McChrystal observed: "When we understand that slide, we'll have won the war."

"General McChrystal expressed how we feel," he explains.

At first glance, the map is difficult to absorb. It is a single visualization of a large amount of data. But it is not simply that. The slide attempts to depict the vast range of factors at work.

As General McChrystal has put it, you can win if you're willing to account for the complex and truly understand the interdependencies in the operating environment. If not, if these interdependencies are disregarded, then it's like "tuning a high-performance engine by just twisting bolts and valves with no idea how they are interrelated."[16]

———

After lunch, turning down a narrow path, we walk over to the office of General Petraeus, a low-lying building separate from the main Command area. It almost looks like a utility shed for the new twin buildings, and later it's not altogether surprising to learn it has been torn down.

The inside is similarly modest, a small lobby that can't hold all of us, so we head directly to the general's conference room, walking single-file through a hallway of crumbling yellow plaster. The CENTCOM designers have not made it into this corridor, but when we reach the end, through a set of glass doors, we see that they have focused on the inner sanctum. These rooms, while on a smaller scale, are similar in configuration and appearance to the Joint Intelligence Center—high-polish mahogany tables, deep leather chairs, altogether stately. We again take our seats around a conference table, and the opening remarks focus on the strategy known as "the surge."

We listen courteously as various charts are clicked through by CENTCOM officers, showing evidence of their comprehensive efforts in Iraq. Graphs display an array of development and stability efforts—health, education, infrastructure, communications—in a spectrum of primary colors. Team members start many of their sentences with "You have to get . . ." and various phrases fill in that blank, including good governance, population protection, willing partners. Even marketing and advertising become part of this method, underwritten by the U.S. military—they detail a large public affairs campaign, including providing content for television, radio, and newspapers, and hiring contractors to distribute the material widely. The approach incorporates information operations as well, such as electronic warfare, activities to interrupt or influence adversary systems and networks.

In a different setting, Petraeus has given an account of his explicitly whole-of-government approach, explaining that the United States "has focused enormous attention and resources over the past two years on building the organizations needed." He included major spheres of civil society in the U.S. military's counterinsurgency strategy: "You have to do politics. You gotta get laws and legislation and promote reconciliation . . . you have to help the host nation deal with the basic reasons why individuals might be prone to extremism in the first place: lack of adequate education, basic services, health, opportunity, and so forth, and then work on the source countries." And even then, while security progress will be achieved, he states that "it is also fragile and reversible . . . much difficult work lies ahead."[17]

This is not the traditional American way of war—to win by overwhelming force and destroy or defeat the enemy. Rather, the method is military actions that are socially constructive, designed to sway local populations. The logic is to focus on root causes, to fill in what the local government cannot or will not provide, to make a population less susceptible to others' ideologies.

Toward the presentation's end, the subject shifts—a bit abruptly and only briefly—to the metrics of conventional U.S. military operations in Iraq. Neither the counterinsurgency nor the counterterrorism link is immediately apparent in the recitation of numbers and counts, which appears to offer a glimpse of major operations that are seldom on display to outsiders. One chart tallies security incidents across five columns headed "mortar," "surface to air," "sniper," "grenade," and "bomb." Another lists the dates and casualty numbers of high-profile explosions. An outline of Sadr City is overlain with drawings of U.S. aerial assets, a representation, we are told, of the firefight against Muqtada al-Sadr and his militias in their Baghdad Shia stronghold—the U.S. response to their short-range rockets and mortars then being lobbed into the Green (or International) Zone.

A sudden switchback to Afghanistan brings us back to a now-familiar sequence: first, an emphasis on the all-encompassing approach, the necessity of an integrated civil-military effort; second, the opinion that the entire region remains volatile; and third, the assertion that the momentum is favorable but not yet solidified, and that success will be achieved by creating a so-named friendly network to isolate and eliminate the threat: "It is [our] assessment that the momentum achieved by the Taliban has been reversed . . . [and] with our Afghan partners we will solidify and expand these gains."

The CENTCOM talk is expansive—what a few here call a self-licking ice cream cone. Here they advocate long-term undertakings to strengthen global security; they promote the creation of large-scale systems for enduring engagement. But success in counterinsurgency, as defined here, seems illusory. It requires near-perpetual, or at least long-term, substantive attention and resourcing from the United States, preferably with some allies, to maintain these conditions. The geographic framing, though, is noticeably narrow. Even when discussing global strategies, the lens is predominantly on Afghanistan and Iraq.

Viability and outlay, though, seem absent from the officers' repetition of "We must do all that we can." Equally unclear—and arguably more important—was the lack of endpoint. What does "done" look like? What is "good enough"? These questions replay in my mind while we express gratitude to our hosts and leave CENTCOM.

As we depart MacDill, I am struck by how the spotlight on Usama bin Laden has grown dim. In this week's presentations of the priorities at SOCOM and CENTCOM in 2010, bin Laden's continuing survival did not make the list in any discussion—his name was not mentioned once. A small group of intelligence officers, though, were about to pursue a lead on the whereabouts of the wandering mujahideen. It brought them to a small town in northern Pakistan and an intense focus on identifying one man then taking daily laps in his yard. To some, the Pacer—as they dubbed him—was surely the 9/11 sponsor. By January 2011, this walker was the priority sui generis of Command leadership.

5

AMERICA'S SUPERHEROES

Wandering Mujahidin. Armed and Dangerous.

—Gina Bennett, Central Intelligence Agency

In 405 days, the environs of MacDill Air Force Base will demonstrably change. The U.S. Special Operations way of life will be illuminated, briefly, after the death of Usama bin Laden in the Pakistani military town of Abbottabad. Public attention to U.S. Special Operations Forces will reach its apex.[1]

From the East Room of the White House late on the night of May 1, 2011, President Barack Obama will announce, "Justice has been done . . . For over two decades, bin Laden has been al-Qaeda's leader and symbol, and has continued to plot attacks against our country and our friends and allies . . . his demise should be welcomed by all who believe in peace and human dignity."

Public recognition of bin Laden's death will be immediate. Across the street in Lafayette Square, hundreds will sing the "Star Spangled Banner" in a spontaneous gathering under the American elms. On Eighth Avenue in Manhattan, firefighters from Engine Company 54 and Ladder Company 4 will open their red steel doors to the community and share a collective sense of relief—they had lost fifteen firefighters on 9/11—and they will hear an impromptu rendition of "God Bless America" at midnight by their neighbors streaming into Times Square.

America's media outlets will reach near-unanimous agreement on their characterization of the operation: a "tectonic victory" and an "astounding military and intelligence triumph." The *New York Post* will blare "Got Him!" Headlines of high-circulation newspapers will read: "Rot in Hell" . . . "Vengeance at Last!" . . . "U.S. Nails the Bastard." A few front pages and magazine covers will display the same image, a headshot with a single-word overlay: DEAD. Several accounts will emphasize a feel-good sentiment—high-fives and raw celebrations—punctuating a long, drawn-out war on terror that has otherwise gone astray. Here at last is a heroic deed interceding in a fight of otherwise questionable merit, they will relate.

Some sources will go even further in that first news cycle, offering impassioned accounts of how the "world's most wanted man was vanquished," dying from a single shot to the face, a bullet fired in response to his "last act of desperation" when he picked up his automatic weapon and sprayed bullets at American forces, at which point a "full-scale firefight broke out." All four claims will later be reported to be inaccurate—an exuberant rush to print a graphic tale—but the overarching declaration will remain consistent in ongoing news coverage, that the May Day raid is a clear win in America's fight against terrorism.

"Finally, a military action we can feel completely and utterly good about," another newspaper will declare.

Selective releases by government insiders will provide a glimpse, even if skewed, of U.S. Special Operations Forces. Members of Congress, White House officials, and Cabinet secretaries will share enough tidbits—in attributed quotes and background interviews—about the intelligence collection and raid preparations to form an outline of the manhunt for bin Laden.

One witness on the ground, though, will provide a remarkable timeline for the ages:

Bin Laden is dead. I didn't kill him. Please let me sleep now.

Sohaib Athar tweets these lines to his more than 100,000 followers in early May 2011 after unintentionally being the first to alert the world of the raid in Abbottabad. As a result of unknowingly documenting the arrival of a U.S. helicopter in his adopted hometown, Athar became Pakistan's most popular tweeter in a matter of hours—known as @ReallyVirtual.[2]

There goes the neighborhood :-/

Athar, a computer programmer born and raised in Lahore, moved to the resort area the previous year. Triggered by the trauma of nearly losing his family—a police van hit the car carrying his wife and six-year-old son, critically injuring both and leaving a permanent scar on his son's face—he described the change to his friends as a family escape to the serenity of the mountain views, a safe distance away from the bombs and turbulence of

Lahore. In the green velvet valley of Abbottabad, an old cantonment of the British Empire at the start of the ancient Silk Road, and a bucolic spot on the way to the snow-clad peaks of the Himalayas, the Athar family sought their new lifestyle.

An Athar tweet captures the slower pace:

drinking (my son's) chilled chocolate milk—growing old has its benefits.

Athar's one-line bio on the blog and Twitter account he updated for family and friends in 2011 noted that he had spent "seven years in parenting and twenty years in computing, the latter passion first sparked by an Atari XL computer in 1991." His posts gave a steady stream of self-deprecating observations about his quest for a reliable wi-fi connection, better batteries, generators, and a decent cup of coffee. Coming up empty in their search for daily roast, Athar and his wife had just opened a gourmet coffee shop with beans imported from Yemen and Italy. They invested in a generator and modems for a future community of kindred spirits they sought to create and develop in the neighborhood. Athar continued to write of their discoveries and setbacks and chronicle their efforts to build a simple—and secure—life.

Serious earthquake in Abbottabad a few minutes ago :-/

I have every intention of staying safe, if only the planet will let me.

Athar remarked with characteristic dry wit, in his second year living in Abbottabad, that he may not have escaped calamity after all, but only traded one disaster for another. His karma was further open to debate a month later when his new hometown became known as the long-time hideout of Usama bin Laden.

If Athar had followed Google Maps to walk the few kilometers from his house to bin Laden's, he actually would have arrived at the wrong place: An inaccuracy in these directions to the Garga segment of Thando Choa, in the province of Khyber Pakhtunkhwa, was soon corrected after the search trended high on May 2, 2011.

But Athar had never tried to find bin Laden's house. There was no reason to, as he hadn't been invited and had only one notable thing in common with his suburban neighbor: children. At the bin Ladens', nineteen children were at home, seven of whom were close in age to Athar's one son.

Usama lived with three wives, Amal, Siham, and Khairiah; their eight children, ages twenty-three, twenty-two, nineteen, ten, eight, seven, five, and two; and four grandchildren, of ages ten, eight, seven, and five. Also residing in the compound were four Pakistani employees, Abrar, Bushra, Ibrahim, and Maryam Ahmed, and seven of their children, ages eight, seven, six, five, five, eighteen months, and four months.[3]

In one sense, bin Laden had been the kind of neighbor that Athar and others in Abbottabad would like to have: a family man, living quietly and comfortably amid the rolling hills and apple orchards. One farmer in town described planting some vegetables for them, tucked into the side courtyard, but that was a rare example of an outsider noticed to be passing through their massive emerald-green gates. Even the milkman was directed to drop their bottles at a different spot. Neighbors remembered the occupants—whom they knew only as the Ahmed brothers and their children, an extended family of eleven people and not the total number of twenty-seven residents—as quiet, reclusive, not particularly charitable or supportive of local causes, but also not a source of trouble or problems. From afar, they appeared similar to others who sought the placid locale.

In the late hours of Sunday, May 1, 2011, in a tweet for the history books, Athar wrote with his usual understated clarity of the dramatic disruption to these quiet environs:

Helicopter hovering above Abbottabad at 1AM (is a rare event).

A moment later, unfazed, even nonchalant, Athar continued his literary improvisation.

Go away helicopter—before I take out my giant swatter :-/

That noise—the chuff-chuff, thump-thump—cropped up as a U.S. special operation neared its end. It was the third and last helicopter to reach Abbottabad that night from Jalalabad Air Field, or J-bad, a distance of about 160 miles when flown directly. The U.S. Army pilots, though, also known as Night Stalkers, had taken a roundabout route with their Black Hawks and Chinooks, in an effort to lessen the likelihood of identification, or worse, interception by Pakistan's Air Forces. Traversing the Afghanistan-Pakistan border near the Torkham Crossing and the Khyber Pass, their blades then slipped through the north of the Federally Administered Tribal Area and followed alongside the silty Indus River. On its embankment near the village of Kandar, pilots of the two Chinooks set down first, idling their engines, on standby to provide refueling, fire support, and exfiltration as needed. The two Black Hawks then continued on the remaining sixty miles south, carrying an assault squadron to its target location at lat-long coordinates 34°10'9.50"N 73°14'32.94"E. If things were to go sideways, more aircraft waited near the Afghanistan border, including HH-60G Pave Hawk rescue helos and AH-64 Apache attack helos. If the operation went truly awry, the catapults of the U.S.S. *Carl Vinson* in the Arabian Sea were ready to fling F/A-18 Hornets into the air.

At half-past midnight, Amal bin Laden heard a different sound, one she later described as thunder, perhaps a storm. In the third-floor bedroom of their home just off Safia Masjid Road, she lay awake while her husband, Usama, and their two-year-old son, Hussein, slept soundly beside her. For a few minutes, as gusts of wind blew past, Amal watched their yellow-flowered curtains flap up. As the din grew louder, she got up to peer out their balcony, but Amal could not see what was about to be the near-simultaneous arrival of the two Black Hawks, and the bellowing plunge of one that immediately followed.

A "noise of a magnitude I had never heard before" is how Maryam, an employee living in an outbuilding inside the compound's walls, and the one surviving Pakistani, described the next moment. The whole family—all twenty-seven residents were at home that night—was jolted awake by the screech. One of the Black Hawks had hit its tail rotor on a perimeter wall and careened into the compound's vegetable garden, its nose falling to the ground in a hard landing. One of the Chinooks on standby got the order straightaway: Come in overhead. Ten minutes later, over a crest reaching an elevation of 10,000 feet, the Chinook reached the cantonment.

What followed was quick, the details released by the Pakistani government a year after the raid. In the first eight minutes, three of the four Pakistani employees—the two Ahmed brothers, and their wives, Ibrahim and Maryam, Abrar and Bushra—were shot. Only Maryam survived. In the two-room annex Ibrahim shared with his wife and their four children—cots lined up in one room, the kitchen as the other, separated from the main house by locked gate—he was the first to be killed. Maryam watched as her husband fired his AK-47 from the front window, then fell backward, hitting the floor. Maryam was shot twice, once in the shoulder, the second bullet grazing her cheek. Next to be killed were Abrar and Bushra, who were hiding in a single room they shared with their three children on the ground floor of the house, adjacent to the bolted door leading to its second and third stories.

Khalid bin Laden, the twenty-three-year-old son of Usama and Siham, was the fourth to be killed, while holding a rifle and crouched at the top of the second-floor staircase.

Usama and Amal were shot in their third-floor bedroom. As she explained in a later interview with Pakistan's judicial commission, she saw "a red beam of light but I heard no sound." One of the U.S. operators later recounted that the bullets tore into Usama bin Laden, slamming his body into the floor until he was motionless," the fifth and last to die that night.

Sumayya, Usama's nineteen-year-old daughter, described hiding on their outside balcony as her father was killed, and then how, a moment later, she was grabbed by a U.S. operator and ordered to identify him. She later recalled standing over him, looking at the hole above his left eye while "blood flowed backwards over his head," and then watching as they lifted his body.

As one observer later put it succinctly: "Their safe house [had become] a death trap."

About twenty minutes after the raid began, the operation had eliminated the target. That information, conveyed through the chain of command to President Obama, brought a formal end to the long chase.

For the operators on the ground, exfiltration remained.

A huge window shaking bang here,

Athar next tweeted at 1:09 a.m. The blowing up of the downed Black Hawk, an attempt to destroy the modified helicopter before the squadron's return trip to J-bad, was heard by all awake in the area.

all silent after the blast . . . seems like my giant swatter worked!

Funny, moving to Abbottabad was part of the 'being safe' strategy

Amal remained in their bedroom, finding it too painful to walk on her wounded leg. She later described to the Pakistani investigators that she also felt frozen in anger, mostly directed at the two returning family members who had recently arrived in Abbottabad. She told the investigators that Khairiah bin Laden, third wife of Usama, who had been absent from the clan for nine years, had moved into the Abbottabad compound three months earlier, after corresponding with Usama for several months and receiving his all-clear to travel from Waziristan. Khairiah's one child, Hamza, who had not seen his father since he was thirteen years old, visited with his wife and two children at the start of that weekend, for just one night, before departing for a safe house in Peshawar. Amal recounted Hamza's visit in detail, including the iPods and jewelry that he brought, and how he left with his father's promise that they would all soon move to a larger home, one that would add not only the four members of his family but also more than ten additional relatives then being released by Iran.[4]

Both Khairiah and Hamza had been held in detention in Iran for most of the decade, arrested by Iranian authorities in 2002. On September 9, 2001, with Usama making final preparations for the planes-into-bombs operation, he had told his family—which then consisted of three wives, ten children, and three grandchildren—to pack one suitcase each and be ready to flee their Kandahar home of four years. As one caravan, they first traveled back to a camp near Jalalabad for two months, one they dubbed "Star Wars." Then some of the caravan crossed the peaks into Pakistan, dividing into smaller groups so as to move into a series of temporary safe houses in Swat, Quetta, and elsewhere. Khairiah, Hamza, and a few others traveling with them went first to Karachi before briefly returning to the southern desert of Afghanistan. They traveled through its barren rock fields on their way to an isolated farmhouse in Zabol, Iran, where they were soon found and detained by Iranian authorities. The conditions they experienced in the ensuing years ranged widely, from a four-star hotel with pool and gym in the nation's capital, serving as a temporary residence for war widows and orphans from Afghanistan, to windowless concrete cells with motion sensors and surveillance cameras. They were ultimately placed in the Block 300 of Tehran's Imam Ali University for Army Officers.[5]

In August 2010, Iran ended its custody of most members of the bin Laden family on condition that they immediately leave the country. When one in their coterie questioned why Iran did not let them live freely as invited guests, why family members could no longer take refuge in Iran except under direct custody, the responses ranged from heedful—"The Islamic Republic is going out of its way to be hospitable to al-Qaeda despite its appalling track record"—to blunt: "You destroyed Afghanistan and you came here to destroy the Islamic Republic of Iran," a Revolutionary Guard seethed. "We will not risk the future of more than seventy million Iranians for ants like you."

Amal believed that his returning wife, Khairiah, had exposed their location in her travels from Iran, and Hamza, she thought, also coming from Iran, had unknowingly confirmed it. It turns out that her assumption was correct. In late April 2011, just a couple of days before the raid, Hamza's travels were tracked by the U.S. intelligence community as he passed the cricket grounds and golf courses of the maple-lined avenues of Abbottabad.[6]

Nazar Mohammad, a constable from the local police station, was the first official on the scene in Abbottabad on the night of the raid. He found several neighbors already standing inside the compound's breached metal gates. A few were filming the fiery helicopter with their cellphones. The second official, a local civilian who later reported details anonymously, entered the compound alone. He spoke with Maryam in the annex and then with Amal on the third floor, but later cited his lack of Arabic as a limiting factor in his reporting of the events that had transpired. Next to arrive were Pakistan Army officials, a battalion commander from the Frontier Force Regiment, and the commandant of the Pakistan Military Academy, both based in the cantonment.

When a colonel from the Inter-Services Intelligence (ISI) ulti-mately reached the compound, he ordered all local officials outside, directed them to cordon off the area, and turned to over-seeing evidence collection and removal, from blood and hair samples to electronics and documents. Photographs of the dead bodies where they fell—of Ibrahim, Abrar, and Khalid—were soon circulated by Reuters.

From the bin Laden house, these first officials placed calls to their superiors, alerts that reached the heads of both the ISI and the Pakistan Army within minutes. At 2:07 a.m., the chief of the army called the head of Pakistan's Air Force, and a terse exchange ensued about an apparent raid by U.S. forces near the military academy, likely infiltration and exfiltration by helicopters, and the still-burning wreckage of a Black Hawk. It was that phone call—rather than any radar or electronic detection—that precipi-tated the scrambling of two Pakistani F-16 fighter jets and a mod-ified C-130 aircraft used for surveillance and reconnaissance. That process took about an hour—forty-three minutes preparing the jets to be launched, followed by fourteen minutes of flight time from nearby Mushaf Air Base to the south. A Pakistani F-16 electronically engaged a Chinook, but the U.S. pilot was able to evade electronically, and no missile ever left the rail.[7]

Before sunrise, the twenty-two surviving residents were moved out in three groups. Amal and two of her children—Safiyah and Hussein—were taken to a nearby base hospital of the Pakistan Army; Maryam and eight children—four of her own, and the four of Ibrahim and Bushra—were taken to a regional clinic; wives Siham and Khairiah, and Amal's three other chil-dren, were driven to Islamabad. By month's end, Maryam remained in detention. The Pakistan Army moved the surviving fourteen members of the bin Laden family to a new and undisclosed location in Islamabad, where they remained under house arrest for a year. They were flown to Saudi Arabia in April 2012, three days before the first anniversary of the raid.

Athar, reacting to a news report two hours after the explosion that a helicopter had crashed in a training accident near the military academy, interjected:

and now I feel I must apologize to the pilot about the swatter tweets :-/

At 5:41 a.m., Athar shared a sinking feeling after the correction came on air:

Uh oh, now I'm the guy who liveblogged the Osama raid without knowing it.

But his observations—and the details later provided by the surviving family members—did provide a fuller context for the actions in the air, and on the ground. Moreover, Athar's Twitter timeline later provided a reality check, piercing the rumors that quickly swirled in Pakistan, in the United States, and around the world, as Athar anticipated when he observed:

I think I should take out my big blower to blow the fog of war away and see the clearer picture. @ReallyVirtual

———

One year earlier, in May 2010, the public remarks of U.S. Secretary of State Hillary Clinton put the manhunt's delay squarely inside Pakistan: "I believe that somewhere in this government are people who know where Usama bin Laden and al-Qaeda is . . . and we expect more cooperation to help us bring to justice, capture or kill those who attacked us on 9/11."[8]

Bin Laden responded to America's clarion call for his capture/kill with a "visual statement to the American people" emphasizing the upcoming tenth anniversary of 9/11 and the indefinite state of peril for all Americans. Donning his usual white keffiyeh and military cargo pants, he sat inside the media room of the Abbottabad house and auto-recorded a home video to show "our just cause to the world." Prominently displayed behind him was his beloved snub-nosed Kalashnikov from the Jaji battle of 1987, a talisman from the jihadists' victory over Soviet attackers, a three-week fight that ended with the retreat of the large and more amply equipped Soviet force. Bin Laden had the tape delivered to al-Jazeera, with copies made for the *Independent* in the United Kingdom, a paper that had carried interviews with him from Sudan and Afghanistan over the years, and for a major U.S. television network yet to be determined, but "before the American Congressional election" to ensure maximum impact.[9]

According to U.S. surveillance reports of this time period, following a suspected courier provided a path to bin Laden. After a string of near misses, they locked on a Suzuki jeep on the road from Peshawar to Abbottabad, one that ended up confirming the connection of Ibrahim Ahmed, a bin Laden family employee, to the compound. The property had several odd features that further attracted their attention, including two feet of barbed wire on top of the eighteen-foot perimeter walls; tiny windows mirrored or covered in privacy film; a seven-foot partition blocking views in and out of the third floor; low levels of electronic and digital connectivity; and four separate gas and electricity meters, each registered in one name, but not matching the homeowner or its known residents. Some occupants appeared not to leave the place at all. Even their method of trash disposal was unusual—burning refuse inside, dumping ashes outside.[10]

From that time forward, the mobile phones of bin Laden's four household employees, the Ahmeds, were monitored. Others were aware of the widening surveillance: a cleric near the Margalla Hills, Islamabad, remarked on a shipping container outside his madrasa in August 2010, which he presumed was actually intended for reconnaissance.[11]

Abbottabad was already a known site for many in the U.S. military. Less than a mile away from the bin Laden compound was the Pakistan Military Academy, a prestigious institution comparable to Sandhurst in the United Kingdom and a one-time camp of the British Indian Army. In the year prior to the raid, the then-head of U.S. Central Command, David Petraeus, had visited the academy as part of his routine travels through the region. U.S. Special Operations Forces also occasionally traveled to the academy, to train their counterparts and to conduct joint exercises nearby with Pakistan's Frontier Corps and Special Services Group.[12]

In 2010, U.S. intelligence officials turned to an old hand for the local assignment, Saeed Iqbal, a retired Pakistan Army officer turned private security operator whose teams the United States had employed as spotters, drivers, and bodyguards for many years. Iqbal set out to Abbottabad on the pretext of buying property, reaching out to homeowners in the neighborhood of the bin Ladens. He rented an office downtown and hired locals to handle surveillance from a nearby building and to photograph the comings and goings along the clay paths just off the half-loop of Safia Masjid Road. They became friendly with the bin Ladens' neighbors, one of whom, Shamraiz Khan, who lived across from the compound's entrance gates, told them about selling a cow to a young man who lived there and tilling an adjacent field at their request. The family received few visitors, Khan said, and he had been inside the compound walls just once, only in the courtyard and not in the home, as the ladies observed pardah.

Iqbal's team created a pattern-of-life profile that included the children being home-schooled and rarely playing outside, and noted that when the female residents took an occasional outing, they were fully covered and driven in either a red van or the white jeep. The watchers counted the laundry hung in the yard to verify the number of inhabitants and to confirm if any were wholly reclusive—they noted ten children, three women, and two men who had not gone beyond the walls during the weeks they watched. One of the men walked in the courtyard most days for an hour or so—he was quite tall, wore a hat, and kept to a path under a cloth sheet. Iqbal confirmed that the extended family had been living an isolated Abbottabad lifestyle—but in plain sight—and he further tracked the telling details of a new arrival, Khairiah. Her travel took place in the same period as the arrest of Umar Patek in an Abbottabad apartment building. A fugitive from Indonesia charged with the Bali terrorist attack of 2002, Patek had only recently arrived from a hideout in the Philippines by way of Saudi Arabia. Security checkpoints and bomb sweeps had been set up in the area as a result.[13]

Iqbal's team and others monitored these moves, and ultimately such reconnaissance details from Abbottabad informed the tabletop model of the house and grounds—from the design of its emerald metal gates to the angle of its satellite dish—for a scenario planner at CIA headquarters and a presidential review at the White House in late winter.[14]

A variety of military options were then under consideration. One option forwarded to the White House included an airstrike by a B-2 bomber, so as to "avoid the risk of having American boots on the ground in Pakistan," but it came with no mechanism for verifying mission completion. It would also have created significant collateral damage from 50,000 pounds of ordnance, as it would have put a massive crater in what had long been a pastoral hub of education and tourism. For these and other reasons, an airstrike was eliminated as nonviable.

It was not until after the raid that U.S. and Pakistan intelligence work, among other efforts, confirmed that the bin Ladens had been in the same location for six years and had made the decision to move to the cantonment soon after the planes-into-bombs operation. In the mid-1990s, bin Laden had rented a place in Abbottabad, but he was already well acquainted with the region, having lived there on and off for a quarter-century. In his first extended visit, in 1980, he answered the call of global Muslim leaders to support Afghans fighting the Soviet occupation. He came alone, one of fifty-seven children by twelve wives of the bin Laden patriarch—seventeenth in the line of succession—but brought weapons, money, and medicine and then stayed to develop supply routes across the Pakistani border. As a scion of the billionaire Saudi real estate clan, most celebrated for its development of Mecca and Medina, bin Laden's backing had been welcomed. Some described his support in heroic terms as a moral offering by a "prince who left everything for jihad." Others underscored his continued links to the royal kingdom, asserting that his move portended greater contributions from wealthy Arabs in Saudi Arabia and elsewhere—that he was not just a single donor but a conduit for Islamic charitable dollars.[15]

In 2003, bin Laden had sent one of his employees, Abrar Ahmed, to Abbottabad with cash to make the arrangements for a new residence. Abrar, in turn, received assistance from Abu Faraj al-Libi, then functioning as al-Qaeda's in-country chief of operations, to secure the location. Abrar, using forged identification, hired a local broker and told a tale of developing a homesite on behalf of an uncle relocating from Waziristan. Abrar and the broker selected a small agricultural tract available from the Abbottabad cantonment and purchased adjacent pieces of land from private owners, creating a plot of a bit less than an acre at the end of a dirt road. Abrar conveyed the family's criteria to a local architect: a two-story house with four bedrooms on each floor, seven bathrooms, a separate entrance to the second floor through the backyard, and a courtyard large enough for a garden. In the construction phase, they added a third level, just a single room with a balcony.

From blueprints to completion took two years. One complication, even derailment, came midway through the project when Faraj was arrested. General Pervez Musharraf, then Pakistan's head of state, identified Faraj as the man responsible for two attempted bomb assassinations against him. Abrar and others discussed jettisoning the family's move to Abbottabad given that

Faraj could now point officials straight to bin Laden if he chose. Abandoning the location may well have been the most prudent decision after the public announcement. However, with options limited, cash committed, and the property already well along, Abrar continued to implement their building plan.

In completed form, the bin Laden house seemed to fit in with its surroundings. Its exterior was unremarkable, a square white concrete block with a flat roof. From the perspective of Amal and Siham, the two wives who stayed—bin Laden left two others in Sudan, a third in Afghanistan, and a fourth was in Iranian custody—moving into the house in August 2005 was a relief. Their decade-long string of temporary sites since their exile from Sudan had included at least seven locations in Pakistan, safe houses that ranged from a luxurious residence near Swat to the humble home of Abrar's parents west of Kohat. In Abbottabad, they set up a ground-floor space as a classroom with whiteboards and bookshelves and equipped a second-floor media room with their husband's audio and video recordings for distribution.

Two months after they moved in, on October 8, 2005, a catastrophic earthquake hit the region, the tectonic result of two regions literally colliding, one plate under India and Pakistan split by the Eurasian plate underlying much of China, Russia, Europe, and the Middle East. The rupture of fifty miles on the earth's surface was singular in scale in the recorded history of the seemingly timeless Himalayan peaks and caused catastrophic loss: 100,000 people killed and four million left homeless. Landslides engulfed entire communities. More than 1,000 aftershocks were recorded in the next month. Nearly 800,000 buildings collapsed or crumbled, including more than 17,000 schools and 800 medical facilities. In Abbottabad, more than half of the houses and two-thirds of the schools were damaged or destroyed.

At the bin Laden compound, twenty miles from the epicenter of the earthquake, only the outer walls caved. The concrete enclosure had initially been built to the maximum zoned height of twelve feet per the town-approved constructions plans. Now, in a quick rebuild, the walls were increased to eighteen feet, which the family members later said was to provide more privacy and seclusion.

It had the opposite effect, as now it was the only house in the district to have such a perimeter, a change that increased the bin Ladens' visibility to their neighbors.[16]

Their everyday living fell into a set pattern. For needs outside the house, such as purchases in town—they were within a short walk of Sajid's General Store for the basics and Rasheed's Store for candy and pop—the two Ahmed couples managed the errands. These four live-in employees provided a blend of caretaking and concealment. In addition to filling the kitchen cupboards with staples such as nuts, dates, and olive oil, they used a side yard to house cows for fresh milk and nearly 100 chickens for eggs.

Such self-sufficiency measures and the protection offered by the Ahmeds proved effective—a U.S. government review in 2005 indicated no current intelligence on bin Laden's location. A U.S. intelligence unit dedicated to the manhunt since the mid-nineties was subsequently eliminated, to the frustration of its founding officer, a downgrading of the effort he considered both bewildering and imprudent. America's focus turned elsewhere.

A few in the district had their suspicions of a criminal element—perhaps a drug smuggler—but no incidents or concerns had been noted in district records of the property or its inhabitants. Most of the community would learn only after the killing of bin Laden that they had lived alongside a global liability for six years.

According to interviews with surviving family members after his death, Usama had rarely ventured beyond the compound walls. They remarked that he had made some travels through the territories of northwest Pakistan in the first years in Abbottabad, and that he had made efforts to change his appearance, initially by shaving his beard and cutting his hair short, and later by dressing as a Pashtun elder, wearing a traditional long linen top over loose trousers.

––––

Family members later filled in some of the details of the earlier years. Najwa, his first cousin and first wife—she was fifteen and he was seventeen when they married in her family's seaside home in Syria—described the first few years of their marriage as peaceful. They lived in Jeddah while her husband finished high school, then college, and worked in the family construction business.[17]

But, she recounted, the Islamic revolutions of 1979 transformed his political outlook, first inspiring him with Iran's turn to theocracy, and then horrifying him during the two-week siege of Mecca at year's end. By the time he graduated from college that spring, the gilded days of extended family holidays—one to Denmark and Sweden included an additional jet in their private fleet to carry their Rolls-Royce for countryside touring—were gone. Gone as well was their low-key travel as immediate family—Usama, Najwa, and their boys had spent two weeks in the United States, in Indiana and California, in 1979.

In the place of such pleasure travel was jihad. Bin Laden increased the frequency and durations of his trips to Pakistan in the eighties. For a decade, religious resistance in Afghanistan consumed him. Fighting the infidel Soviet occupation drew both his assets and energy; he was one of many, with China, Egypt, Iran, Pakistan, the United Kingdom, and the United States among the countries dedicating assets to the expulsion of the Soviets. U.S. forces initially supplied materiel such as plastic explosives and heavy weapons—some bought from China, most delivered to Pakistan—and then expanded its support for the mujahideen to include shared intelligence—intercepted communications, satellite imagery—and more targeted weaponry such as wire-guided missiles. After the Soviet Union's special operators (Spetsnaz) increased their helo assaults and night raids in the mid-eighties, the United States countered by deploying special operators and intelligence officers to train mujahideen near the Afghanistan-Pakistan border. And so the Cold War proxy fights continued. Upon the mujahideen's victory in 1989, Pakistan, Saudi Arabia, the United States and other past supporters foresaw diminishing returns on their militant investment, as well as vulnerabilities arising from such surreptitious support. The United States, in particular, anticipated fewer threats after 1991 and decreased its reliance on this type of proxy war. If its quick Coalition victory in the Persian Gulf War augured the future—"more like a one-sided clay pigeon shoot than armored battle"—then its fights would be swift and precise.[18]

That strategic shift in Afghanistan and Pakistan suited a number of Saudi Arabia's national interests, and the kingdom adopted the broader narrative of the region's new peaceful era. Bin

Laden, in stark contrast, emphatically rejected it. This was a contributing factor to his failed resettlement to Jeddah, and soon thereafter he was banished by the kingdom and stripped of his citizenship.

In 1991, as an expatriate new to Khartoum, bin Laden contemplated, at least publicly, the end of his so-named lesser jihad against the West. Upon arriving in Sudan, immediately after his banishment by Saudi Arabia, bin Laden seemed at first to accede to President Omar al-Bashir's condition of public depoliticization—Egypt, Saudi Arabia, and the United States, among others, monitored his activities in-country but noted little of concern or significance. In those early days in Sudan, bin Laden presented himself as a gentleman warrior turned industrious business leader. In one media interview, dressed in white robes with gold edging, he spoke of transferring the construction skills he learned in Allah's Ancient House of Mecca, first to the faithful fighters in the peaks of Afghanistan, and then to major civil works in his adopted Sudan. Laying down arms, bin Laden explained that he was now simply "an agriculturalist" and "a construction engineer." The family settled into a pastel stucco home in the capital and purchased a retreat in Soba on the Blue Nile. Near the home in the countryside, he oversaw a number of farming projects, including salt extraction and growing sunflowers. Given the contract with the Sudanese government to build a coastal airport, in a joint venture funded by Saudi leadership, bin Laden's company commenced a 500-mile highway from Khartoum to the Red Sea.[19]

Bin Laden remained in Sudan for five years, until his hosts' calculation of their political hospitality shifted, brought about by new U.N. Security Council sanctions: regional embargoes as well as explicit demands from Saudi Arabia, among others, to stop "facilitating terrorist activities" and "giving shelter and sanctuary to terrorist elements." The Sudanese government, as part of its reversal in the face of declining economic fortunes, offered its thick folders of surveillance on bin Laden, among others, to the United States in 1996.

When Sudan further proposed shifting custody of bin Laden to either Saudi Arabia or the United States, both nations declined, and Afghanistan became the lead site of his potential exile, with Yemen a distant alternative. To accelerate that move, the Sudanese government leased Afghan planes to transport the bin Laden family from Khartoum to Jalalabad in 1996—bin Laden's old 747, rusted and inoperable, was left behind. On arrival in Afghanistan, bin Laden applied a similar method of ingratiation, promising to undertake construction projects—from mosques to military facilities—from the eastern Hindu Kush mountains to the southern flats of Kandahar. Most of his personal funds, though, were no longer on offer, having been left behind in Sudan—mostly seized, stolen, or spent.

Omar, his fourth-oldest son, later recalled the contentment, even attachment, that his father felt for the mountains bordering Afghanistan and Pakistan, and his acceptance of their second exile. His father, he said, felt affection for the range of fractal canyons and fault scarps, describing it as his most comfortable home, a sort of earthy plenum, wholesome and refreshing, where he could "breathe a pure, free air." Figuratively, it was a sort of aerie with hollows, monsoon clouds and the dark crowns of conifers on its steep slope.[20]

Omar shared none of his father's affection for the area. "Sheer misery" is how he recounted their new, confined life in the mud shells they constructed on the plateaus of northeastern Afghanistan. Later descriptions by those who never visited the austere nest hyped a sort of cosmopolitan village—a bakery, a hospital, a hotel, and hydroelectric power generation figured in that mythology. The natural landforms were decidedly uncultivated. Overnight guests described no fresh bread or cakes, but a culinary aroma of rancid eggs mixed with the scent of diesel fuel. Medical facilities consisted of jars of honey, and when a visitor asked about a washroom, a denizen laughed, "Where do you think you are, at the Sheraton? . . . There you may fulfill your need and make ablution," and pointed toward some ground.[21]

While luxury had become anathema to bin Laden, artifice still remained; he grandly named their first borrowed housing in Afghanistan—a mud fort with guard towers—the Star of the Holy War, which his third son, Sa'ad, renamed Star Wars. Bin Laden's indulgence was a different kind of materialism, one that can afford a feather bed but chooses wooden slats. To those who followed him, he touted eternal purity; to those who only visited, he lobbed ad hominem critiques of others. He spoke of leading a bleak and burdensome existence, but in front of a camera he donned starched white clothing, leather-bound volumes at arm's reach, and all the while surrounded by a large retinue eager to serve. "A cave is the last pure place on this earth," Usama told his followers.[22]

Bin Laden's holier-than-thou outlook would be risible, bordering on parody as camping deluxe, if he had not been so violent. Omar explained it as a sort of "jihad vacation" for those who made the pilgrimage, "nothing more than a suicide camp for wayward Muslims." Omar viewed their dirt-and-rubble bunker as a site of crude survival skills, of handling Kalashnikovs and memorizing holes in the limestone. His father's vision of living simply included skipping blankets in the mountains and covering his body with dirt and twigs.[23]

The Islamic Emirate of Afghanistan extracted a promise of loyalty and nonviolence from bin Laden but received neither. As in Sudan, bin Laden exceeded the Taliban's tolerance and patience, overstaying his welcome. This time, however, he rejected the entreaties for his departure. Labeling even the Taliban's appeal as contrary to the religious teachings of jihad, he stayed put, keeping his family in Kandahar and using a stretch of land at the Afghanistan-Pakistan border as his own, an area that one journalist called the Arab Afghan Emirate.

It was in those Spīn Ghar mountains that bin Laden first listened—amazed and delighted—to the pitch for an astonishing planes-into-bombs operation, and five years later learned of results greater than even he had hoped. "An epoch begins today," bin Laden grandly asserted to the small group of men with him. At long last, he exclaimed, they had fulfilled their promise to bring their proclaimed righteous cause to America's shores, moving from a first faint glow to the finest glory.[24]

It was also in these mountains that U.S. special operations and multinational teams tracked bin Laden in December 2001, in the twelfth week of the manhunt after September 11. Bin Laden, however, escaped from Pachir Aw Agam district, fleeing from the Milawa Valley toward Parachinar, Pakistan.

In the months that followed, one U.S. special operator offered these mountains as emblematic of the growing distance between wartime rhetoric and on-the-ground reality as the 9/11 mission shifted. The Safēd Kōh range, he explained, showed what a small operation this had actually been. The resources of bin Laden and his so-called Base (the literal translation of al-Qaeda) were meager. In fact, the jihadists functioned barely at a subsistence level. "[T]hey weren't these crazy mazes or labyrinths of caves that they described. Most of them were natural . . . They weren't real big. I know they made a spectacle out of that . . . we see all these reports. Then it turns out, when you actually go up there, there's really just small bunkers, and a lot of different ammo storage."[25]

Al-Qaeda's resources were scant, but the take-away was immense: a small number of individuals, intensely determined with meager resources, could still create a cataclysmic event with immense global impact. By simply playing not to lose, they could wreak havoc.[26]

———

Two staffers at the White House worked on Saturday, April 30, 2011, to finalize remarks for the president ahead of that evening's White House Correspondents' Dinner, an annual tradition of spoofs held in a beige basement ballroom at the Washington Hilton, complete with an actual red carpet and Hollywood celebrities who join as arm candy.

The writers received a request they found puzzling. "I love all these jokes, I think everything is great, I'm ready to go tonight," President Obama told them. "I have one edit . . . I would just get rid of bin Laden and go with another bad guy."[27]

Then a serious request that augured against the usual end to the annual media dinner: "Could you also make sure—I'm probably going to remember this on my own, but just in case—at the very end of the speech I want to say, God Bless America and May God Bless our troops and keep them safe."

The next morning, Sunday, May 1, started quietly at the White House, recapping the long-gown-and-tuxedo night before—the punchlines about President Obama's birth certificate and the real versus fake billions of two men interested in the office of the presidency—the genuine fortune of Michael Bloomberg and the self-proclaimed riches of Donald Trump. For many, the evening's most memorable lines were the skewering of the reality television character, turned into a punchline as rhetorical payback for his birther conspiracy campaign. "So ultimately, you didn't blame Lil' Jon or Meat Loaf. You fired Gary Busey . . . these are the kind of decisions that would keep me up at night," Obama jabbed from the podium.

Of course, what the speechwriters for the Correspondents' Dinner did not yet know was that the raid into Abbottabad had been initiated, that the two comments from the president, which they had thought a bit off-tenor to the event, were far from lighthearted. "We realized after that we were these three idiot comedy writers in the middle of the most serious, serious thing."

At about 2 p.m. that Sunday in the United States, nine hours behind Pakistan, small groups gathered around video and audio feeds in the White House, the CIA, the National Security Agency, the National Geospatial-Intelligence Agency, and other sites of U.S. national security along the eastern seaboard to observe a strike taking place over 7,000 miles away. It was a soda-straw view of Abbottabad, made possible by the aerial stack of U.S. reconnaissance assets thousands of feet over the city, including Sentinels, Reapers, Predators, and Global Hawks. In under an hour, the forces completed their objective. "We got him," the president stated calmly.[28]

Two days after Abbottabad, a black-tie dinner was held at the Ritz-Carlton Hotel in Washington by members of the Atlantic Council to mark the think tank's fiftieth anniversary. The conversation that Tuesday evening became an impromptu toast to the May Day raid.

As the keynote speaker, Vice President Joe Biden focused on the celebration, admiration, and outpouring of emotion that had overtaken the nation since the raid in Abbottabad, while singling out the trigger-pullers. Biden described the astonishment he had felt while watching this "staggering undertaking . . . the incredible events, extraordinary events this past Sunday . . . I was in absolute awe . . . it was actually breathtaking." He then characterized the significance of the operation: "I think one clear message has gone out to the world: There's no place to hide . . . the world is a safer place today, not only for the American people, but for all people." He expressed his appreciation of the nation's military, asserting that there was "no one else, I believe, other than an American group of military warriors who could do it," and his gratitude to "those brave professionals who tracked and killed Usama bin Laden." He called out one unit, "the phenomenal, the just almost unbelievable capacity of Navy SEALS and what they did—last Sunday." The reference to the Navy unit, the ones who undertook the raid, was an identity detail that had not yet been officially released. Biden paused after the naming, interrupted by spontaneous clapping from the attendees at that remark.[29]

That same night, in an interview on PBS NewsHour, anchor Jim Lehrer asked Leon Panetta, then CIA director: "Now, where were you . . . during this operation?"[30]

Panetta initially replied with a description of the leadership structure of a covert operation: ". . . And then, I am, you know, the person who then commands the mission." After a second's hesitation, though, Panetta added: "But having said that, I have to tell you that the real commander was Admiral McRaven because he was on site, and he was actually in charge of the military operation that went in and got bin Laden." Shifting the credit for the raid's success, Panetta observed that "it's the base commander that you should be thanking."[31]

Lehrer concluded the interview by explaining that "the commander Panetta referred to is Vice Admiral William McRaven. He is in charge of the Joint Special Operations Command, known as JSOC"—knowing this to be an organization unfamiliar to many in the PBS audience.[32]

———

By month's end, the director of the Central Intelligence Agency offered his support of an Abbottabad movie script—already predicted by the *Hollywood Reporter* to become a studio blockbuster—and members of Panetta's staff invited the screenwriter of the to-be-written *Zero Dark Thirty* to its internal celebration at its Langley headquarters.[33]

At the celebration, the screenwriter learned the identities of key analysts and operators who were recognized for their contributions at the white-tent event. A commander from SOCOM was visibly shocked when he learned of the security breach at the end of the event, which had been described to the participants as a closed gathering and was known by all to be a classified setting.

That same month, the chair of the House Armed Services Committee, with responsibility for legislative and financial oversight of SOCOM, opened his first meeting with U.S. special operators after the raid by addressing the entire room with: "You look like movie stars!"[34]

6

FOURTEEN MINUTES OF FAME

These days, the sun never sets on America's special-operations forces.

—Wall Street Journal

The steep drop into the Aspen airport, onto its single unforgiving runway, gives a quick glimpse of the glitzy Colorado resort. Even from the air, the stone-and-timber houses seem oversized, jutting out from the Elk mountainside, set high above the old silver mining town that is cut through by tributaries of the Roaring Fork River. A short drive from the airport, on the west end of town, near the formidable Ajax Mountain and downtown's Old West–style brick buildings, is perhaps the most bucolic spot for an American think tank.

Set up in the 1950s, in part to raise the cachet of a then-fledgling ski resort, the Aspen Institute is a forty-acre campus of spruce groves, fir trees, and stark modernist architecture. Its unofficial motto could be "Pinnacle air focuses the mind." Today it coexists easily with—and draws from—a well-heeled, built-in audience for its wide-ranging public events, all in a setting that appeals to even the most jaded. While the town is most associated with winter frolics, the institute is more akin to an esoteric summer camp—but where your espresso will still be properly tamped and the spa massage will offer bamboo sticks with ginger oil. The institute's signature event, which they name an ideas festival, is lofty in its purpose: to be an inspirational sanctuary for world leaders to discuss and reflect on ideas that define a good society—at a minimum, hundreds of bold-faced names, from heads of state to social activists, arrive for the week in this pastoral setting.

Its target audience includes the area public—many of whose upmarket homes are within walking distance of the grounds. One mid-summer Wednesday evening, a year after the Abbottabad raid, the institute has invited the Aspen community to a ticketed event under a big tent lined with twinkle lights. They have filled the 500-plus white wooden folding chairs planted in the grass. CNN's Wolf Blitzer will be interviewing the ninth commander of SOCOM, William H. McRaven. Despite the time that has passed, the raid remains very much in the public eye, a military operation of continuing intense interest. A few national security professionals are also in attendance, those who have arrived early for a three-day security forum that begins the following day. Dressed a bit more formally—and staidly—than the rest of the crowd, they sit in a row of reserved seats in front of a raised platform, a nearly empty stage save for two bar-height chairs separated by a small table with a pitcher of iced water.

After a brief welcome by the institute's leadership, Blitzer and McRaven walk the two steps up to the platform and take their seats on the stage's front center, their clear acrylic bucket seats marked by stickers with their last names. The event has been billed as an insider's look into U.S. Special Operations Command—and the Usama bin Laden raid one year earlier—by the man who oversaw the raid then, and now leads the Command. Blitzer, who became a household name during the 1991 Gulf War as a foreign correspondent on the nation's then only twenty-four-hour news network, is now a longtime CNN news anchor and serves as the evening's moderator.[1]

———

"When you ordered the raid . . . you didn't even know for sure that bin Laden was in Abbottabad at that compound?" Blitzer opens with a question to McRaven that addresses the public's interest in the bin Laden raid head-on.[2]

McRaven is quick to set the record straight: "Well, let me make one thing clear. I didn't order the raid."

Blitzer tries two other approaches, saying that McRaven "had the guts to tell the Commander-in-Chief we should do it, let's do it," and again, McRaven has to correct the record: "This is not a small point. The fact of the matter is it was the President of the United States that ordered the raid. My role was to execute the order to conduct the raid," he explains. And he did, from selecting the team's leadership to go forward to Afghanistan to launching the squadron's raid into Pakistan.

And so this back-and-forth goes. Blitzer first presses a lone-warrior trope, and when that fails to break through, he turns to a celebrity SEAL caricature: "You were runner-up for *TIME*

Magazine's Person of the Year. How disappointed were you? . . . What did it feel like . . . when you [sat] next to the First Lady . . . before a joint session of the United States Congress . . . and the whole world was watching?" McRaven bursts the bubbles with matter-of-fact reality and a pointed pause: ". . . I'm not even sure how to answer that, Wolf."

As one special operator noted in the year of the bin Laden raid, the conventional fifteen minutes of fame is fourteen minutes too long. That observation captures the essence of this Colorado evening, a contrast between one who spends a career learning and conditioning to operate unseen, unnoticed, anonymous, and the other whose professional expertise is the probing interview, who repeatedly though politely prods for specifics. At either ends of this range, of transparency and confidentiality, the rules of engagement remain starkly clear to McRaven, and Blitzer states that those ground rules are a given at the outset: Identities must be protected, intelligence sources and methods are classified, tactical details remain off-limits. McRaven is open to speaking in generalities: "We did [go] on helicopters, we [do] go to objectives, we secure the objectives, [then] we get back on helicopters and we come home."

But McRaven is asked so many adaptations of the off-limit questions that in a space of thirty minutes, he scrambles to find more than a dozen different ways to say basically the same thing: "No, I'm not going to answer that question." Variations include reminding Blitzer of what they both said at the beginning, that tactical details of recent operations are too sensitive to disclose.

"As I said, I have made a point in not talking about the tactical piece," McRaven reiterates, and when Blitzer pursues an awkward line of questioning—"You don't want to discuss that? You don't want to talk about other places?"—McRaven again unavoidably states the obvious and now repetitive response about the clear, bright lines at the spectrum's closed end: "Yeah, well obviously I'm not going into specifics on what we do and do not know," and "Not my place to discuss that . . . Not in my lane." And finally, to the great amusement of the audience, which breaks into laughter after McRaven finally responds in feigned exasperation, "Do they teach you this?" McRaven, who once studied to be a journalist himself at the University of Texas, Austin, asks rhetorically but knowingly, "To do the end run when the first question doesn't work?"[3]

Somewhat abruptly in the exchange, Blitzer tries a different way to engage:

"You don't do a lot of these interviews, do you?"

"No, no."

"Is this the first interview like this you've ever done?"

"It is the first interview."

"How does it feel so far?"

"Ask me again in an hour."

And so it continues, with one brief but significant exchange. When Blitzer asks, in general terms, about the impact of multiple deployments on the forces, of the enormous stress, of suicide rates rising among special operators, McRaven responds with specificity. "Our suicide rate. It is as high as it has been." Without further prompting, McRaven describes acute problems inside the force, referring to Command data on substance abuse, pain, and the unraveling of relationships. While noting that "[it's] worse than we thought," he stops short of discussing the levels of family violence, the extent of drug addiction, and a personal behavior standard that one operator describes as "a culture of 'anything goes.'"[4]

Much of the remaining time centers on audience questions, and the openers turn indirectly to the fraying of forces and ways to bolster and broaden the existing all-volunteer force, from the potential of mandatory national service to the growth of women's roles in U.S. combat and special operations. Other questioners emphasize drones—ethics of use, law of armed conflict, transparency, and foreign manufacturing—and McRaven gives full responses about rules of engagement, legal protocols, and technology transfer agreements. Three questions do turn the conversation back to the Abbottabad raid—one from a *Newsweek* reporter about the political courage of the president's decision to launch the raid, and one from a Los Angeles film producer asking when to expect the release of further details about the raid. The last question comes from an aerospace executive, who notes that on those occasions when leaders of U.S. special operations publicly discuss a success, they do not name a single branch or unit.

"Right, right," McRaven replies. So, the audience member asks, how was the decision reached in the case of Abbottabad to identify one of the units in the overall operation? Can McRaven share some pros and cons of that decision from a risk standpoint? The response is intriguing, both in terms of McRaven's pivoting from his initial agreement that the singling out of Naval Special Warfare diverged from the military's usual practices, and in terms of where he draws the line.

"I think it's a little misleading to think that we don't talk about specifics . . . if you say it was . . . SEAL Team One or the 75th Rangers that conduct the operation . . . we're generally okay with that . . . [but] we don't generally get into the names of the individuals."

The naming of individuals is a line that many recognize as bright—and SOCOM discourages the release of identities, among other categories of sensitive information.

Blitzer points out, though, that U.S. Special Operations Command—and military leaders in general—routinely request journalists such as himself to hold back information other than the names of specific individuals downrange. "This is a sensitive subject . . . but just to press you on this . . . when somebody in a position of high authority, the military or the civilian rank, comes to us and says, if you report this, lives will be endangered, we listen. And very often, we don't report it." But, Blitzer continues, the authorities can't abuse such requests; "it's really got to be the real thing."

In response to this comment, McRaven goes in a different direction, pushing those who work at U.S.-based media outlets "to protect this country" by holding back information. "You're going to see things that you think the public needs to know. And I will tell you, I'm not sure the public needs to know all that . . . Are people affected by the information that comes out? You bet they are."

Blitzer follows up, pressing for specifics, an example or two of how McRaven would calculate this risk scenario and balance democracy's requirements of public transparency and account-ability with a military's wish to limit the circulation of informa-tion. Blitzer points out that he and his professional colleagues are open to adjusting their practices, but it is also clear that a "trust me" argument is insufficient to them. Guarding information, and keeping it away from the American public, requires a compelling reason. Put a different way, a take-my-word-for-it, on a practical level, doesn't supply journalists with the information they need to make such judgment calls.[5]

McRaven himself has just lived through a public identification, feeling the effects first-hand of the rare naming of the identities of those involved in a U.S. special operation. Such a public profile brings forth a number of changes, including navigating a wide range of specific questions about raids and tactics.[6]

This break in norms will also become apparent in the Aspen Security Forum over the next few days, where U.S. special operations become a central part of the agenda, a novelty in the institute's half-century analysis of national security policy and strategy. McRaven expresses confidence that the newfound attention is for a job well done; he believes that it will serve the community well to have such positive feedback on the good-news story. He downplays the complexity of the raid itself—from "a military viewpoint, it was a standard raid and not really very sexy." The phrases "rock star" and "celebrity quality" are applied by others—this is unfamiliar for U.S. Special Operations Command as a whole, and exerts a different kind of unsettling and disconcerting pressure.

Despite the bright spotlight, McRaven expresses confidence in the discretion of the operators. Public attention, he says, will not materially impact the special operations culture, since the operators recognize that such work is collaborative and never implemented by one person. "And what's important is that not one name of any of the Navy SEALs who went into Abbottabad has been disclosed." McRaven states that the secrecy of sources and methods will be retained, and appropriately so, and concludes that the morale of U.S. Special Operations Forces is boosted by the public appreciation.

The visibility does, however, ripple the surface of U.S. Special Operations Command. The small team of Americans who took part in the raid in Pakistan experience the glare of the national spotlight in unexpected and diverse ways, ranging from humble pride to self-aggrandizement to utter indifference. In the weeks and months after the operation, SOCOM's institutional practices also vary, from refinement of clandestine norms to lapses in accountability to personal profiteering.

Nearly all uphold the ideal of quiet professionalism as advocated by the Command. A couple of operators, though, do not, and their stories soon garner intense interest.

———

Make origami with Post-It notes. Stack erasers into grand pyramids. There's only so much you can do as a book publicist without a title to talk up. At Penguin's Dutton—an imprint with a storied history—this is a common problem. That's not because of trouble in their acquisitions department: half of the books Dutton has published are on the bestseller lists of the *New York Times* and Amazon in this decade, a tradition of wide appeal that dates back to the house's first literary hit in 1874. A so-called boutique house, Dutton limits its annual list to some fifty books, in a marketplace that generates more than 200,000 new titles a year.[7]

In September 2012, Dutton leads its list with *No Easy Day* (also known as *NED*), the first account of the bin Laden raid told by an operator (a second book appears five years later). *NED* is published just sixteen months after the operation, and one month after the Aspen Security Forum where discussion centered on the anonymity guarded by raid participants.[8]

Inside SOCOM, senior leaders express embarrassment and concern. One charges the book's author with self-promotion and self-dealing. Another calls the author out, in a letter broadly circulated to the special operations community, for "hawking details about a mission against Enemy Number 1 . . . I am disappointed . . . Most of us have always thought that the privilege of working with some of our nation's toughest warriors on challenging missions would be enough to be proud of, with no further compensation or celebrity required."[9]

Untitled by Anonymous is how it's first known. Because of the nature of the book, details are a closely held secret inside Penguin.

The sales team knew for one month that they would have a major add-on to the autumn schedule, possibly even the biggest book of the year. They worked on a campaign—generating whispers and shouts—to create a mystique around a product about which they knew almost nothing. They sent notifications of the book by Anonymous to their digital outlets and a network of more than 15,000 bricks-and-mortar stores. They promised a massive media rollout, including embargo arrangements—a highly orchestrated release more usual for a splashy new book from tent-pole authors like J. K. Rowling or Dan Brown. As with Oprah's Book Club selections, they pushed major booksellers to place blind orders, giving them little more than the $26.95 price and the 316-page count.

Dutton typically has the more usual and easier task of selling fiction from celebrated authors with track records of large sales.

This will soon be announced as a military story, a memoir, a coauthored work of nonfiction, titled *No Easy Day: The Firsthand Account of the Mission That Killed Osama bin Laden.*[10]

Dutton promotes the book as "an essential piece of modern history," the inside story of one of America's most important events in the twenty-first century and a surefire hit. Names throughout the book, including the author's, have been changed for security reasons. There will be no photographs or images of the author, and no identifying information that would unmask the author. The sales calendar is also unusual: the tight publication timeline—two weeks from announcement to embargo—mirrors the highly compressed writing process, a matter of months. Bookstore buyers are told that they must sign a contract with an embargo agreement, to coincide with remembrance activities on September 11.[11]

On the dust jacket is a man in silhouette, with a thick neck and broad shoulders. In a press release, Dutton describes the author as a hero to America, a tough man of action who has earned five Bronze Stars and a Purple Heart on his many deployments, including being on the team for the hostage rescue of Captain Richard Phillips off the coast of Somalia in 2009, then in production as a movie starring Tom Hanks. In the text, the author further describes a previous manhunt near Jalalabad in 2007 in search of bin Laden, "a tall man in flowing white robes in Tora Bora . . . For all the time and effort, we essentially bombed some empty mountains and my teammates went on a week-long camping trip."[12]

Dutton presents the author as selfless: most of his book earnings will be donated to support the families of fallen SEALs. The publisher describes his motivation in writing the book as a desire to set the record straight, and explains that the work was coauthored with a professional writer, a reporter from North Carolina who spent many years covering Fort Bragg for the *Fayetteville Observer*. The reporter embedded with U.S. Army Special Forces in Afghanistan and published some of those accounts in *Gentlemen Bastards*.[13]

Bright gold lettering runs along the book's spine. At a quick glance, the packaging is straightforward in its artwork, schematics, and graphic elements. The compressed timeframe for printing—from first set of galleys, to the proofs with maps and photos, to the copyediting of widows and orphans—seems to show up in small ways, as might be expected given the truncated three or four rounds needed by the editorial, design, and production teams. What's here is sufficient for piles of advance readers' copies to send to reviewers.

Given the author's cloaked identity, it will be an unconventional media tour, replete with physical disguise and voice-masking. No book tours, parties, public launches, or festivals are anticipated—just specific interviews in select news outlets, and embargo strategies designed to compress purchases into the first week of sales and push the book to the number-one slot. The publicity relies on a special one-hour episode of CBS's *60 Minutes*: "Newsmakers like Mark Owen . . . [that] warranted the entire hourlong broadcast, are the exception . . . Mark Owen's book was newsworthy on a number of fronts, including the fact that he was even talking about [the mission] and writing a book about it."[14]

Speed to market will be essential to its sales. This is not the only account of the raid that is expected to appear. Celebrated author Mark Bowden, the apparent inspiration for the pen name of *NED's* Mark Owen, is clearly the rival to beat. Bowden's book, *The Finish*, which ultimately hits the shelves one year later, is a different sort of project: though written by an outsider, it benefits from extensive information from the White House on the decision-making processes leading up to the Abbottabad raid. Moreover, it is built on Bowden's deep knowledge of U.S. special operations, as conveyed in such books as *Killing Pablo* and *Black Hawk Down*.[15]

Of course, *NED* is bound to sell well no matter what. To flip through the manuscript is to know this immediately—the hook is so simple and compelling. Here is a historic work. Above all, it's the patriotic story that the country has been waiting for and wanting to hear, a litany of feel-good descriptions, a Stars and Stripes narrative, pure in purpose and cathartic in its outcome. "This is unabashedly about the best of America," one reviewer declares. Others hail the book as a "God Bless America patriotic page-turner" and a "flag-waving tale of righteous retribution and payback" against the 9/11 terrorists who killed thousands of people on American soil—a tale of glory wrapped in the flag of American courage and ingenuity.

And second, it is unique and gripping—no other account exists, the first-hand experience by one of the shooters on the last night of the terrorist leader's life. It's a cinematic story, aimed at the audience that wants to go along for the ride in an edge-of-the-seat way. Even though the end is universally known, vivid details enable the reader to picture the shooter boarding the helicopter for the ninety-minute ride from Jalalabad: a helmet with attached night-vision; a Heckler & Koch 416 rifle; radios to communicate with both the ground team and the commander; pictures of people living in the compound; bolt cutters and an explosive charge; some cash and a camera.

The book begins with the helicopter crash that made global headlines—a suspenseful and visceral start to the narrative. Owen takes the reader on Chalk One and describes how the MH-60 helicopter lost its hover when over the compound, pitching out of control. "Suddenly the helicopter kicked to the right 90 degrees . . . The rotors above me screamed as the Black Hawk tried to claw its way back into the air." Instead of fast-roping onto the roof, he and the other assaulters climbed out of the crash in the compound's courtyard and made their way from the ground up.

The author also shares details of his upbringing. He is an American boy, the son of missionaries, who grew up on Wrangell Island, where logging and fishing have been the economic mainstays, part of Alaska's archipelago of a thousand islands ringed by fjords and accessible by boat and plane. In this austere environment, Owen describes thriving on, and learning from, any physical challenge. As a kid, he was inspired by stories of SEALs in Vietnam, as related in the book *Men in Green Faces*. After graduating from a small liberal arts college in southern California, he enlisted in the Navy. Owen writes of discovering his calling when he was introduced to U.S. special operations, driven by honor and duty, wanting to take the fight to the enemy. He describes enjoying the manhunting responsibility, the "creep" and the "pounce," that he first experienced extensively in the invasion of Iraq—being brought on target at night, eliminating occupants of a building—"the only way to permanently take them off the street was if they were dead"—and returning to base before day-break. "Nothing got our blood pumping more than creeping into an enemy compound, sometimes directly into the rooms of enemy fighters while they were sleeping." He shares how he thrived on the adrenaline rush of his intoxicating job—and further highlights the camaraderie of the teams.

Remarkably, no one knew anything about what would soon be the biggest book of its kind. The U.S. government officials expressed displeasure at being blind-sided. "Bin Laden death book rattles Pentagon," was a headline the day after its publisher's announcement. The lead spokespeople at the White House, the Department of Defense, and the CIA, as well as congressional leaders, all responded that it was also the first time they were learning of the book. A spokesman for the Department of Defense said that "the Pentagon and CIA were shocked" that Penguin Dutton had already printed "575,000 hardback copies." They had expected a tell-all one day—maybe several years away—but this was only a little over a year after the raid.[16]

The Pentagon had tried to stop distribution of the book and sent a warning letter of legal action to prevent publication from proceeding. A civil suit was filed by the U.S. Department of Justice. The general counsel of the Department of Defense, Jeh Johnson, notified Penguin Dutton of the department's prosecution of the publisher, author, and coauthor, for divulging information about sensitive national security matters. Shortly thereafter, the Pentagon's legal office identified sensitive information and again sought to halt its publication. They underscored that the author was in violation of two nondisclosure agreements that he had signed in 2007. They noted that he did not submit the book for prepublication review, as he was required to, based on documents he had previously signed. They argued that by signing the agreements, the operator acknowledged his awareness of the process. Therefore, the author was in "material breach and violation."

This Pentagon letter from counsel went on to state that "further public dissemination of your book will aggravate your breach and violation of your agreements," that the nondisclosure agreements obliged him to "never divulge" classified information . . . This commitment remains in force even after you left the active duty Navy . . . [that] disclosure of classified information constitutes a violation of federal criminal law." In conclusion, it stated, the Pentagon is "considering pursuing against you, and all those acting in concert with you, all remedies legally available to us in light of this situation."[17]

Penguin Dutton rejected the premise of this letter and proceeded to print and distribute the book as planned. Their response was simple: "Owen is proud of his service and respectful of his obligations. But he has earned the right to tell his story; his abiding interest is to ensure that he is permitted to tell it while recognizing the letter and spirit of the law and his contractual undertakings." In the book, the author also provided a preemptive explanation in both the introduction and the conclusion, stating that a personal attorney had provided oversight of the manuscript— but did not explain how a civilian attorney would be able to make such a determination of national security information.

Without waiting to see how the legal dispute unfolded, Penguin Dutton moved up the publication date by a week, from September 11 to September 4, 2012. The publisher expected controversy and decided that the legal risk was worth taking: in addition to the economic incentives, there was a cachet for landing the book, a sort of publisher's bragging rights. If they managed the campaign well, with its elaborate marketing and roll-out, it would further build their reputation to recruit other such authors, selling other books of intense national interest.

And so the selling began. *NED* found its audience, fast and wide, selling over a million copies rapidly. Even before it hit the shelves, on its preorders alone, it displaced an already record-setting *Fifty Shades of Grey*.[18]

Owen went forward with the rare hour-long interview on CBS's *60 Minutes*, his appearance and voice disguised, dressed simply in button-down shirt and khakis. In a dramatic voiceover, the network advertised that the interview would cover details of the raid that had never been made public before, with the author walking journalist Scott Pelley through a reconstruction of the compound.

The show attracted more than twelve million viewers that night. That surge of media interest sold even more books.[19]

On the day when the book actually reached bookstore shelves for sale, according to reports, a Department of Defense spokesman announced that the Pentagon had reviewed the publication and concluded it had revealed "sensitive and classified" material.[20]

Owen's new legal team, from the Washington law firm of Patton Boggs, had a strong reputation for representing others in similar situations, including Karl Rove when he was an aide in the White House and accused of leaking the name of Valerie Plame, a covert operative for the CIA, in the lead-up to the Iraq War. In response to the Pentagon's further claims, Patton Boggs asserted that the author "is not in breach of the nondisclosure agreement." They went on to write that Owen had "sought legal advice about his responsibilities before agreeing to publish his book and scrupulously reviewed the work to ensure that it did not disclose any material that would breach his agreement or put his comrades at risk. He remains confident that he has faithfully fulfilled his duty."[21]

Owen challenged the practices governing the U.S. government's hierarchy of disclosure, whereby the president, as commander in chief, can categorically declassify whereas a special operator cannot: "If my commander in chief is willing to talk, then I feel comfortable doing the same." In his book, Owen further criticized both the president and the Joint Special Operations commander for talking about the raid and for getting details wrong. He argued that if these leaders could—and did—declassify matters, then he should not be hushed or forced to remain in a cone of silence.

A federal court subsequently found, in keeping with an earlier decision by the U.S. Supreme Court in a similar matter, that these unauthorized disclosures about U.S. Special Operations Forces impaired the government's ability to perform its statutory duties. It ruled that the author owed the government a formal apology immediately for his noncompliance and breach of contract—and the book's royalties.[22]

Within the broader military community, the consensus seemed to be that Owen's narrative was deemed too specific in tactical detail and too fast in its disclosure. For some, operational details are to be brought to the grave, especially as they relate to the specific names of those who put their lives at risk. With regard to other narratives, some have argued for a statute of limitations, asserting that when the tactical risk to the operator is no more, then the strategic value of sharing the experience comes to the fore and circulation is expected. In both cases, though, a certain measure of time is expected to pass, often starting with the end of hostilities—and whether that point had been reached in Owen's case was far from certain. He would address some of these issues in his follow-on book, *No Hero: Evolution of a SEAL*.[23]

In conclusion, Owen offered his own perspective on the decade-long war on terrorism. In his opinion, it came to an end with the killing of Usama bin Laden. Owen framed the 9/11 wars as centered around a decapitation strategy, one so determinate that a singular factor served as both its origin and its ongoing rationale: "Lying in front of me was the reason we had been fighting for the last decade. It was surreal trying to clean the blood off the most wanted man in the world so that I could shoot his photo."[24]

That assessment was soon challenged by many in U.S. Special Operations.

————

Inside SOCOM's headquarters, at an annual gathering of the leadership of U.S. Special Operations a few days after the Abbottabad raid, the mood was subdued. Doubt, rather than satisfaction over a completed mission, pervaded the discussions. While some U.S. leaders were then describing the death of bin Laden in Pakistan as a strategic milestone—one significant enough to call for the end of the 9/11 wars—many in the U.S. Special Operations community challenged the idea of a singular enemy, and the notion that the death of any one person would have a transformative effect on the fight.[25]

While some assessed the Pakistan raid as an inflection point in their mission—a strategic turning point—others appraised Abbottabad as necessary but insufficient given the malignant character of al-Qaeda and the rising intensity of Islamist alternatives in Iraq, Syria, Yemen, and elsewhere. Several found common ground in the belief that this protracted fight faced a rocky transition, from known and understood enemies to more splintered adversaries and enemies dispersed among civilian populations across metropolitan centers and rural lands.

That position—aspects of which were publicly debated—attracted far less notice than the storyline the paparazzi sought about the operators and their specific personal details as well as the raid—its tactics, techniques, and procedures.

Just how the death of bin Laden would bolster the standing of other jihadists was as yet unknown—as were what forms the metastasis of al-Qaeda's principles would take in this void.

Several SOCOM leaders braced for Islamist up-and-comers to be more erratic and nihilistic, strengthening their more virulent strands of *takfir* (the Islamist practice of purifying apostasy) and finding adherents beyond the traditional center of the Middle East. Of more immediate concern, though, were the aftermaths on the field of battle—and the expected blowback from the Abbottabad raid.

7

FALLEN ANGEL

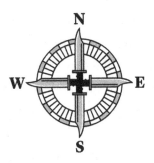

You want Pashtun boys to shoot their cousins—this is a strategy?

—Dr. Roshanak Wardak

In the Tangi Valley, Afghanistan, farmers plow with water buffalo and live in multigenerational clusters behind stout pine-plank doors and high clay walls. Hectares of wheat fields grow waist-high on land fed by thawing snowcaps. Canals souse the apple orchards, apricot trees, and pomegranate groves. Bare red mountains surround the green bowl, but in the windy season, the funnels move downward through the jagged cliffs, kicking up clouds of yellow silt.

In the summer of 2011, despite the U.S. news headlines announcing the end of the 9/11 wars, deployments of U.S. special operators are unchanged—and soon to increase. Raids continue apace. In the four months of operations after the Abbottabad raid, the Department of Defense reports 2,832 raids across the entire region. Locals describe ground operations in Tangi on a nightly basis.

One, in particular, goes disastrously wrong.

The failed raid is reported in U.S. media outlets but attracts little notice among the general public. Late in the night of Friday, August 6, a 40,000-pound loaded U.S. helicopter—call sign Extortion 17—is shot down in the Tangi Valley by a rocket-propelled grenade. That downing results in the greatest loss of life for U.S. Special Operations in its history, surpassing Operation Eagle Claw and Operation Gothic Serpent.

It is the deadliest day for the United States in its then decade-long war in Afghanistan.[1]

———

"Welcome to Tangi . . . it's like getting kissed by the devil." The lieutenant offers an apt simile of the valley's destructive allure, to no one in particular.

"To be honest, they didn't want us here," another young man explains, referring to the 1,500 U.S. personnel who arrived in Wardak province to take over outpost responsibilities.[2]

Each morning from Combat Outpost (COP) Tangi, they set out on foot patrol, up and down and up. The work is tedious—to find tiny wires beneath them—and ever on the verge of deadly, requiring their complete attention to conduct the bomb sweeps. Stray cords, fresh dirt mounds, awkward rock piles—any of these is a sufficient reason to stop. Fail in the hunt and any heavy vehicle that drives over buried pressure plates—but most likely a U.S. Humvee or an MRAP (Mine-Resistant Ambush Protected vehicle) in this area—is enough to connect the underground lines and set off its detonation. Miss an oddly placed object—a can of soda or a packet of cigarettes makes adequate casing—and the device's crude charge is left for a truck to trigger in passing.

The area of patrol for COP Tangi has been just south of a physical checkpoint recognized as the Bab al-Jihad, or the Gates of Jihad. To pass through that marker is to leave the grit of Kabul and enter a pastoral landscape of birches and wildflowers growing on a terrain with well-trained militias, fierce antiforeign defenses, and a heritage of liberation struggles.

Where a newcomer gazes up at the sandstone peaks and sees barren spaces, a local points to a crisscross of sunken dirt tracks leading to the Kabul-Kandahar corridor, the road linking the country's two largest cities, a part of the ring road forming Highway 1. Natives know that the remote appearance of black scree and headward gullies creates an illusion of a journey by crawl. Pile into a Hilux or hop on a Honda, speed along the upland passes, and you'll soon reach the capital. The older residents of Tangi speak with pride of the locally quarried white marble, framed by arches and pillars of Himalayan cedar, used to erect the city's dazzling buildings. They recommend a visit to Kabul's Bamyan caves in the neighboring Hazarajat, the site of the world's oldest oil paintings.

New arrivals who take the short trip to Kabul, though, describe a grim fortress, a city enclosed with concrete blast walls and razor wire, the air thick with mustard haze. City dwellers warn these outsiders against traveling any further north, even to Hazarajat. No painting is worth the peril, they remind the foreign traveler, and in any event, the Buddhas of Bamyan—the sixth-century golden, rock-cut statues of the central highlands, the largest of their kind—have been destroyed.[3]

"If you are an Afghan traveling by road, wear a ragged tunic, abandon all government ID, and say your prayer," explains Umaidullah Azad, a telecom official who recently made the trip. "If the Taliban flag you down, you have a good chance of surviving if you look like a country bumpkin. But no chance if you have government or foreign connections."

Better to stay put in Kabubble, as Azad and others prefer to call the cordoned capital of Kabul, inside the security ring of spruced-up civic buildings and posh foreign embassies. Steer clear of the outskirts, the narrow, crowded streets of Soviet-era apartment blocks, dotted with tires burning for cooking fuel throughout the day. Avoid the polluted sludge of the Kabul River and the black smoke of motor exhaust that will sting your eyes and clog your lungs. You won't like staying in the neighborhood of poppy palaces, among residents of questionable sources of income, but you're better off there than out in the countryside, they add. The narcotecture may not be to your liking—massive cement houses painted in a cacophony of colors, accented with chrome and mirrored tiles—but at least there you should be able to walk outside. Those houses have sandbagged bunkers out front with armed guards that keep watch over the sidewalks and SUVs with blacked-out windows idling in the driveways behind heavy steel gates to whisk you away if danger arrives. Be aware, though, that there is a lion—an actual lion—on the roof of one residence. The roar is just a creative security feature demonstrating the owner's eccentric need for attention, they are fairly certain—and don't worry, the lion is chained to the house.

Thirty miles to the south of all that, from the perspective of the young U.S. Army soldiers stationed in Tangi Valley, that poppy neighborhood is a vacation destination. Even the outer rings of Kabul are a luxury spot in comparison to where they live and work. A few years earlier, they may well have included the Tangi inside that perimeter. A generation prior, they may also have joined the flocks of Americans who meandered the celebrated hippie trail through this region.

Today, though, to be assigned to COP Tangi is to live in a single narrow corridor—the seductive beauty of Afghanistan is restricted to a view from afar.

"This daily grind is an exercise in absurdity," is how one soldier characterizes their routine. "It's a walk on Walter Reed Highway," a ticket to the Bethesda military medical center, he notes dryly, describing himself as a sitting target for an explosive sown into the rutted road or a bullet from a Talib dug into the mountain brink. He prays for a lucky break, to receive orders for chai missions—tea conversations with village elders. Pots of green tea, pails of apricots, or perhaps even a plate of spring onions and saffron rice—he would welcome the cross-legged circle with relief. But that change is not forthcoming.

The Tangi Valley is not the site of the three-cups-of-tea strategy being tried by American forces elsewhere in Afghanistan. These waves of U.S. operators are given the task of clearing out Taliban fighters in the valley who have been pushing toward Kabul. The placement of this personnel is an early step in what will be an upward spiral of U.S. Special Operations Forces across Wardak province, and part of a steep rise in U.S. and Coalition military deployments overall. The official numbers have now reached 100,000 U.S. troops in-country, doubling from the year prior, fighting alongside a further 40,000 Coalition forces from more than forty countries.[4]

Nearby to COP Tangi, but significantly larger, Forward Operating Base (FOB) Shank is given a shared objective: reverse the local Taliban revival. Their deadline is similar: eleven months. A member of a U.S. Army engineer company assigned to build watchtowers at FOB Shank expresses disbelief in the entire process—the mismatch among resources, objectives, and political realities. In an interview with his hometown newspaper, he wonders aloud whether there is any true local support for the buildup of a national government and describes regular attacks on FOB Shank and its outpost satellites, a string of sites with the appearance of ad hoc pinpricks.

That skepticism turns out to be well founded, and another service member, an Army doctor assigned to the expanded FOB Shank, soon describes a situation badly deteriorated. He reports no let-up in the hostile fire: "I was assigned to . . . FOB Shank . . . we were constantly under the threat of both direct [small arms] and indirect [artillery and rocket] fire . . . there was one particularly violent day . . . when a rocket barrage landed in our FST [Forward Surgical Team] area. I also had a surprise one morning when an enemy AK-47 round from a nearby firefight ripped through my tent and landed next to me."[5]

He and others expressed frustration that higher-ups had set unrealistic goals—goals unachievable in any timeframe and that, even if accomplished, would reverse after their departure. But they stayed dedicated to the orders, managing multiyear projects and passing extensions on to new arrivals. These major works of

FOB Shank went on without interruption from one unit's deployment to the next; cement was being poured for 80,000 square feet of taxiway and 452,000 square feet of paved space for large transport aircraft and more B huts, long plywood trailers without windows, to bring housing capacity up to 6,600 troops.

COP Tangi and others had been part of a growing number of U.S. outposts on this landscape. Their role had been not simply to contain the violent spike—Abdullah Wardak, the governor of Logar province, and ten French soldiers had just been killed—but to change political infrastructure and allegiances as well. The commander of COP Tangi had been given an explicit mission and a compressed timeline: Clear, hold, and build. In a year, the soldiers are told, eliminate local resistance fighters, at which point the national government will step back in, to govern the valley—suggesting, incorrectly, that a federal body had once administered the area.

For so many reasons, though, the entire concept seemed utterly unattainable. An Afghan soldier, of Tajik descent, points out that the flawed framing—the order to neutralize or eliminate the Taliban threat—had set them up for mission failure. "We're not fighting the Taliban in Wardak . . . We're fighting criminals who use the name Taliban." Gholam Mojatba, a twenty-year veteran who had been fighting alongside Coalition forces in the valley, asserted that attacking petty gangs and other lawless elements would require a different approach with the locals. Of greater significance, Mojatba pointed out, would be the centrifugal forces. He and other Afghan Army soldiers have ammunition and international support, but those resources are, at best, a temporary epoxy. The loose confederation that Kabul seeks to lead has not demonstrated sufficient unity in purpose or method to endure, he concludes.

Kabul politician and opposition leader Abdullah expressed a different sort of skepticism about the reach of Afghanistan's national government-in-progress, noting that several of President Hamid Karzai's ministers were still not able to travel to their own provinces—Wardak, Logar, and others: "We have not been able to reach out to the people and we have failed to provide them good governance."[6]

Many locals agreed with Abdullah's assessment, that Kabul had failed to protect their interests, much less provide even basic security. Village elder Ismatullah of Maidan Shahr, Wardak's capital twenty miles west of Kabul, was not opposed to alternatives to Taliban authority, but he was not new to the impasse: "What the governor said in our meeting was very good . . . He quoted the Koran very correctly. But . . . now I am going home—and the Taliban control my district, not him."[7]

A deputy governor in Wardak, Ali Ahmad Khashai, described the ground as frequently under assault. "Many attacks in Wardak are organized and planned in Tangi . . . the enemy is active and the military operations have not been effective, unfortunately."[8]

The duration of these fights presents another challenge. These contests are deeply entrenched. Competition for this land at the intersection of Kabul, Wardak, and Logar provinces is manifold, including among local village elders, Taliban religious leaders, and Afghan national politicians. Each is offering a different form of law with a range of inducements or coercion: in respective order, collective resources allocated through hierarchical governance; security guaranteed by virtue of religious adherence; or personal safety underwritten by taxes and payoffs.

Fighting for this land has been genocidal in living memory.

Hassan Kakar, a professor at Kabul University, provides witness. He returned to his homeland in the 1970s after years of study at Princeton and Harvard Universities, joining the civic resistance and chronicling the survival of his fellow Afghans during the Soviet occupation of the eighties. From its start on Thursday, December 27, 1979, watching from his rooftop on the western outskirts of Kabul, he recorded the attacks. He continued those writings through Friday, July 3, 1981, when mujahideen forces entered the city, bellowing, "Long Live Afghanistan." Then from a prison cell, after an arrest and trial on charges of subversion in 1982, Kakar documented the personal stories of fellow inmates. When released after five years, he expressed a mix of disbelief in—and gratitude for—his survival. Fellow prisoners had been executed on lesser charges.

In the countryside, such suppression devolved into genocide. "The actual number of the casualties is unknown . . . In many places dead bodies lay here and there. No one dared to bury them," Kakar wrote in his journal. Those who did not flee areas of mujahideen activity faced near-certain slaughter for their perceived support and harboring of the resistance. Rural doctors were killed for treating the wounded and trapped. Médecins sans Frontières, also known as Doctors Without Borders, briefly operated a hospital in Wardak province, but their personnel were soon arrested and worse, and in their first year of operations in-country, Soviet gunships leveled four of their clinics. Soldiers described their method as deliberate and systematic, to destroy:

We told them to "get up, go away . . . we are going to kill you [if you do not] go away." The forces moved in sequence: Mi-24 Hinds—a fleet of gunships—coordinated with T-62s and BMP-1s—ground forces and armored vehicles—to encircle a district, bombard its structures, and then set its villages ablaze.[9]

International monitors reported from the country's front-lines and borderlands that Afghanistan was being attacked as a single battlefield—Kakar said the Communists acted as if on orders to "clear the Afghan land of weeds." A photojournalist, on the ground in 1983, described the countryside's destruction as complete: "All the way from there . . . absolutely no one . . . they were just reduced to gray dust."[10]

By 1985, more than one-third of the country's population had fled. The neighboring nations of Pakistan and Iran hosted the majority of refugees, taking in more than five million Afghans. Of the population remaining in Afghanistan, more than two million were killed. Testimony given in Paris and Washington document-ed mass killings and the use of lethal chemicals on farming villages in Wardak and Logar provinces. Along the main artery to Peshawar, Pakistan, the preferred route for mujahideen to move their mate-riel, one survivor from a town near Tangi detailed a tragic day in hiding. Soviet tanks rolled into his village at dawn on September 13, 1982, he explained, scattering inhabitants to take cover, but families who sought shelter in an irrigation canal near the town square were quickly found. The soldiers "poured in a kind of yellowish-white liquid [from a vehicle] and I don't know what it is. And then you had men wearing suits and masks and goggles . . . [they] went down the steps leading to the canal entrance and . . . poured in a white powder" and set the tunnel on fire.

The U.S. Department of State confirmed that specific report through an independent inspector, and Secretary of State George Shultz reported to Congress, "Our suspicions that mycotoxins have been used [by Soviet and Afghan government forces] in Afghanistan have now been confirmed . . . reports during 1980 and 1981 described a yellow-brown mist being delivered in attacks which caused blistering, vomiting and other symptoms similar to those described by 'yellow rain' victims in Southeast Asia," a reference to the casualties of Soviet trichothecene toxin (T-2) attacks in Laos and Cambodia in the same years.

These foreign forces were driven out of the Tangi area in the early nineties when the Islamic Emirate of Afghanistan, or Taliban, took hold. The Taliban controlled the territory throughout the nineties, and while temporarily pushed out after September 11, 2001, they quickly regained their theological control of the area. With a mujahideen tradition well established here, a new generation of Talibs asserted their continuity, expelling outsiders, surviving massacres, and using all means necessary against forces hostile to local traditions, beliefs, and culture. Their new mullah provided a similar de facto government, including strict enforcement of behavioral practices, and they called on all holy warriors to join them in self-defense.

The Taliban's has been a ruthless justice but was long considered incorruptible, untainted by the usual forms of bribery and driven by ideological rectitude. In the capital's border provinces, they both initiated violent campaigns and interceded in the brutal strife. In the void of Karzai's Islamic Republic of Afghanistan, the Taliban's Islamic Emirate had revitalized. Local elders may not prefer this form of governance, but their leadership does provide a type of security they value.

Amanullah Ishaqzai, a government judge in Wardak, says, "I can't blame them . . . A court case in the government system takes five years and many bribes. The Taliban will settle it in an afternoon."

Habibullah Noori, who ran a bus service between Kabul and Wardak, says, "If you have a problem, the Taliban solves it. In the government offices there is only corruption and bribery. Last year, the Taliban did not have 80, 90, or 100 percent control . . . It was a mess. There were robbers, killers, everything. Now, you could walk around with 10 kilograms of gold on your head and no one would touch you."

That newfound sense of security may well resonate with Noori, but it is not simply thieves that threaten the new Talib sense of order, but also those local elites who appear to be insufficiently compliant. Dr. Ehssabullah Hakimi illustrates the problem with a personal story about receiving death threats from the Taliban for practicing medicine in Wardak. "Because I had a good job, they thought I was a spy." Fearing the nighttime letters were sufficiently credible and not an idle warning, Hakimi and twenty-two members of his extended family locked up their ancestral compound one night and fled to Kabul. The next month, a cousin who remained behind was hanged, roped to a tree a mile from a police station, with a sign that whoever took him down would meet the same end—he swung there for two days until international relief workers arrived.

Mohammad Rahim, a resident of the Tangi Valley, told a visiting reporter from Agence France-Presse, "This area is under full

Taliban control . . . They have patrols day and night here without any fear. They have walkie-talkies, cars, motorcycles. They have erected checkpoints on the Logar to Wardak road that crosses this valley . . . The Taliban have threatened people not to work in government offices or they will be killed."[11]

Roshanak Wardak, a physician whose rural practice is in Sheikhabad, a former member of Parliament, dismisses the new Talib as thieves, criminals, thugs. She explains, though, that the population is in straits. "They have no resources . . . I think you cannot understand what it is to have nothing." She is now the primary obstetrician in the area, in a country where one in six mothers dies during or as a result of childbirth and that also has the world's second-highest rate of infant mortality. After forty women died in childbirth in her district in the winter of 1996, Dr. Wardak opened the doors of a new clinic in the spring to address the local problem, one of her many civic and professional commitments. A journalist who stayed with her explained the extraordinary efforts of both the doctor and her patients, day and night, then in their tenth year with barely a pause: "Pregnant women walk all day to reach Dr. Roshanak's surgery, and then they walk back with their newborns."[12]

Dr. Wardak is known in her province for her courage, as one of the few government officials, present or past, who travel from Kabul to the Wardak province routinely, and is a strong opposition leader to oppression of any kind. She rejects outright the steady stream of men in both places who try to control her, her medical practice, or her movements. "If you can show me where the Qu'ran says I should wear the burqa, I will wear seven burqas.'"

She has been a target of the Taliban and local warlords. Her actions and words carry weight here. That an individual who would be a natural ally of the U.S. forces has been so alienated by their use of force against residents and neighbors—and even herself—underscores the problems the Coalition faces. Dr. Wardak notes that the raids, for example, are wholly unproductive, if not counterproductive, killing innocents and therefore fueling support for the Taliban. They occur "every night. We are very much miserable . . . These night raids have not brought security . . . The area . . . is completely under the control of the Taliban." She further explains, regarding area loyalties, that nearly all of the Taliban fighters are Afghans: "Every second or third house has a son or a brother in the Taliban," and even if they do not support the insurgency, they want to avoid any action that would provoke a Taliban reprisal or retaliation.

Dr. Wardak has experienced this first-hand—a bomb fell 200 meters from her house, waking up the village. "The curious went to see what happened. That's when the second drone struck." She flew to Washington, D.C., to describe the Farah airstrike that killed 143 people, of whom 96 were Afghan women and children. "Every time this bombardment happens by drone . . . [the] American country and their leadership, their soldiers, they are losing their popularity among the M.P.s and also among, especially, the people. Very much they are losing [it]," she testified at a congressional hearing.

Gul Agha, a resident of Tangi Valley, explains: "Frequent night raids in and around this district have angered local residents, who are offended by knocks on their doors in the middle of the night when families are sleeping." Agha explains, "The foreigners are guests, but what has changed in ten years?" Speaking to the Americans, he describes his summary of the period: "Yes, you are our guests, but you have done a lot of bad things."[13]

As the balance shifted, with the bad outweighing much of the good, the night raids were widely questioned across Afghanistan, even by those such as President Karzai working to keep U.S. forces engaged in Afghanistan. In April 2011, the mission of COP Tangi came to an abrupt end. After only a year in the field, the team was uprooting. The two young Army soldiers did not get the orders for chai missions as they hoped, but they got something they wanted much more—exit out of the valley altogether, a departure welcomed by both sides.

"As we lose U.S. personnel, we have to concentrate on the greater populations," said the commander of Task Force Warrior, explaining the reason for the transition of authority at the COP Tangi from U.S. troops to Afghan national forces. This was not a matter of mission accomplished.[14]

Such U.S. departure declarations at COP Tangi referred only to general purpose forces. Coming into the valley were U.S. special operators. They were not being formally labeled as combat forces or tracked in a conventional sense. Instead, their warfare was selectively declared, rarely identified in any detail.

The fight continued. Only the forces who would do the fighting would now change.

———

The special operations teams are getting on helos, the blades start, they lift off, they have some time en route, they stand ready to be inserted on target, get the job done, get back in helos, and go back to base, or what some of them refer to as "home." They do this every night and sometimes several times in a single night. On August 5, 2011, this Army CH-47D Chinook, Tail Number 84-24175, call sign Extortion 17, has already been in the valley once. At 10:58 p.m. they dropped a team on the ground for a capture/kill operation near Juy Zarin. Their target is Qari Tahir, then considered by the American commanders to be the leading Taliban strongman in the Tangi Valley.[15]

After Extortion 16 and Extortion 17 dropped a company element of the 75th Ranger Regiment, and a unit of Afghan commandos, they went back to base, refueled, and awaited the call to exfil. In addition to Extortion 16 and Extortion 17 that night were two AH-64 Apache helicopters, one AC-130 gunship, and UAVs as part of this operation. The element that landed near the compound, supported by aerial assault, killed six Talib fighters using 30mm cannon. Two escaped. At the compound now overtaken and secured by U.S. forces, they did not find Tahir.

Extortion 17 is called to join the hunt, to insert another team to block a northern escape. Planners sent a reinforcement team of thirty-eight, including thirty U.S. military personnel (Navy, Air Force, and Army) and eight Afghan personnel (seven Afghan National Army commandos and a translator). The new landing zone for the Immediate Reaction Force (IRF) was only large enough for one Chinook, so the full force flew in Extortion 17 while Extortion 16 flew empty, in from the northwest rather than the south. They took off again, this time at 2:22 a.m., from the nearby base, FOB Shank, about twenty miles west.

Three hours into the chase, the ground team is still hunting their high-value target, and an MQ-9 Predator visual feed shows a group fleeing to the north. Two AH-64 Apaches take aim, fire, and kill five fighters. The AC-130 gunship—Slasher 02—puts eyes on target. From overhead sensors, they picked up about nine or ten men and, thinking that Tahir could be in this group, call for an IRF.

Extortion 17 had requested the infrared spotlight, to illuminate the landing zone (LZ) as seen through the team's night-vision goggles. They requested sparkle—burn on, burn in sight, assault in sixty seconds, burn still out eleven seconds later, then twelve seconds later LZ is ice, indicating the landing zone was free of enemy activity. The infrared spotlight of the AC-130 circling above has lit up the site and Extortion 17 is clear to land.

"The crew of Slasher 02 . . . flipped the switch on their powerful light. 'Burn is on,' they radioed. Through the goggles, the landing zone shone brilliantly. The two helicopter pilots continued the descent. 'LZ is ice,' transmitted one of the Rangers on the ground." Extortion 17 was then about 100 feet above the ground and traveling at a speed of approximately 60 mph.

By 2:38 a.m., on short final, they are over the landing zone when hit by a rocket-propelled grenade, launched from a tower less than 250 yards away. Given an estimated velocity of the round at 120 yards per second, and then combined with the oncoming Chinook's airspeed, that translated into less than one second possible for the Extortion 17 pilot to identify, maneuver, and evade the threat.

Then a flash. Silence. A second flash, a hit. A Fallen Angel.

The rocket hits the aft rotor disk, severing ten feet of the lightweight fiberglass and honeycomb blade from its pylons, causing immediate and violent spin, the forward rotor system separating in air; and less than five seconds later, the forty-six-year-old Chinook crashes into the banks of the Logar River with its fuselage in flames.

It is a catastrophic loss.

All thirty-eight personnel aboard are gone in one blast.

The Apaches return with suppressive fires along the riverbanks and tree lines. A Pathfinder unit moves in to secure the ground. At daybreak, the three-day recovery operations begin. In full light, the wreckage is startling, flung across a vast area, along both sides of the Logar River, with some debris swept down into the river, inside the steep cliffs that run along it.

A local resident, Farhad, said that "Coalition forces worked several days to remove victims' remains. Then they blew up sections of the helicopter into smaller pieces, loaded them on trucks and took them from the site . . . Small, twisted pieces of the Chinook CH-47, though, remained scattered on both sides of a slow-flowing river in Wardak province." A full investigation commenced and witness accounts were recorded. They described the helicopter as being taken out "during ingress, at a time when it was flying low and slow . . . and then seeing the chopper burst into flames and break apart before falling from the sky."[16]

Extortion 16 and Extortion 17 operated with no lights, relying on night vision and helo instrumentation, and therefore were not easy to see—but they could be heard. "There are a lot of bullets out there that say 'To Whom it May Concern,'" explains a U.S. Marine F/A-18D weapons and sensors operator who was a senior watch officer for the Marine air operations center in southern Afghanistan.[17]

Agha, also a resident of Tangi Valley, described that "when the helicopter came at night, the Taliban were hiding in the bushes around the area." The second doctor said the helicopter was one of two Chinooks that approached Juy Zarin as an operation in Gulabkhil was under way. "The Taliban have their regular sentries to prevent American night raids," he said. "The two helicopters tried to land, but the Taliban fired two rockets at them. The helicopter was downed only about 100 meters from our house. Several small and big explosions were heard inside the helicopter."

Farhad told reporters: "After it started burning, it crashed. It came down in three pieces," he added. "We could see it burning from our homes."

A local newspaper reported that the Taliban took responsibility, and that its leadership had a general but not precise knowledge of the significance of their target. They hoped to boost local support with the news. According to Zabiullah Mujahid, "We didn't know exactly that it was that Navy SEAL unit, but we know whenever they have the night raids and they plan to attack mujahideen somewhere, they always use their special forces so we knew they were very important."[18]

Five days after the crash, in a bombing raid by an F-16 fighter jet at approximately midnight on August 8, 2011, the retaliation strike was complete. General John R. Allen, then the top commander of U.S. and NATO forces in Afghanistan, stated that "Coalition forces killed the Taliban insurgents responsible for this attack." The Coalition spokesman reported that at least thirteen militants, hiding in Siyab Dara, part of Chak District about twenty miles from the helicopter's crash, had been killed. The police chief of Wardak province, Abdul Kayum Baqizoi, also noted that the strike killed thirteen men and that two militants managed to escape.[19]

Less than one month later, though, the operation's overall objective had failed. In a stark territorial reversal, the Taliban overtook COP Tangi, selling off what remained of the outpost— bits of wire, pieces of aluminum—laying mines at its perimeter and then leaving it behind just one month later. They posted a video of their takedown on YouTube, including their arrival and departure on motorcycles, holding Kalashnikovs in the air, cele- brating the departure of the foreigners—and flying their group's banner high above the valley.[20]

Two years later, an Afghan soldier is killed trying to take down the black-and-white flag on the rocky outcropping when he stepped on, and detonated, one of those makeshift bombs.[21]

————

On the evening after the downing of Extortion 17, SOCOM held an informal dinner at MacDill, at the home of the com- manding officer of U.S. Special Operations. It is a long-planned event, intended to be celebratory, gathering senior leadership and some family members to join in the upcoming change of command. In the first couple of hours, there's no mention of Extortion 17, although the crash has just been publicly reported.

After dinner, casually relaxing in the kitchen, a guest asks, to no one in particular, "Will the change of command be post- poned?" It brings a long silence to the small group. No one replies to that specific question or interjects to move the conversation in a different direction. A quick scan of the faces shows the response is a marked blankness of expression. The Command's decision, though, had already been made: no change in the schedule. To do so would have been to shift because of the enemy's attack. To proceed equated to duty, to carrying the mission forward.

In the living room, a Vietnam veteran and Medal of Honor recipient considers the group's earlier reaction. "No one wants to talk about it," Tom says to another guest. He goes on to articulate a certain numbness when this happens, and not a discernible expression of grief or sadness. The deep human costs are a solemn responsibility, an oath taken at entry, and open grief or an emotive response would not be typical in this kind of setting. There's a quiet introspection when it comes to these deaths, even though the specifics of this crash cause distress since the loss of life seemed unexpected, avoidable.

The conversation briefly stops when a fellow Medal of Honor recipient, Mike, who also served in Vietnam, sits down. "Another helo, huh?"

"It's actually amazing it doesn't happen frequently," Tom replies.

When hit with a rocket-propelled grenade, at close range, there is little the pilot can do to avoid a crash of some kind, they discuss. Although in the case of Extortion 17, it has proven to be especially deadly given the large number of people that the helicopter carried that night.

The two go on to discuss newer munitions that present a potentially even more dangerous situation. A single MK211 shot can also destroy the craft.

"They got lucky a couple of months ago," Mike says, referring to the Night Stalker pilot who crashed a helicopter into the wall of the bin Laden compound in Pakistan, but managed to do so delicately enough that all on board went ahead with the infiltration.

"Lucky . . . and very, very, very good," Tom commends.

Three days later, after a full slate of events for the change of command, the leadership at the ceremony head to MacDill's hangar to depart for Dover AFB in Delaware. The remains of the service members are already en route from Bagram AFB, Afghanistan, to be met by family members, the commanders of CENTCOM and SOCOM, the civilian leadership of the U.S. Department of Defense, and President Obama. The service members will be honored in a private ceremony at Dover.

The crash of Extortion 17 is only briefly covered in U.S. media outlets. The summer after the Abbottabad raid, coverage of U.S. Special Operations is still almost entirely devoted to the events of that night. That includes a cover story in the *New Yorker* that appeared on newsstands this week, receiving widespread attention for recounting details of the ground operation, from the type of dog that flew in with the Naval Special Warfare team to the kind of pistols the special operators carried.[22]

After the downing of Extortion 17, there is no loss of confidence in the capabilities of U.S. special operators—but also loss has now become normalized, expected by SOCOM, the U.S. Department of Defense, and even the U.S. public at large. If anything, the lack of national—and military—reaction showed an inuring to combat loss in the 9/11 wars.

Unlike other catastrophic losses of its kind, the copter down in the Tangi Valley did not provoke a strategic shift by the United States. The history of U.S. Special Operations has been punctuated by crashes, some with extraordinary strategic effects, ending missions altogether. In the case of both Operation Eagle Claw (Iran, 1980) and Operation Gothic Serpent (Somalia, 1993), the impact on policymakers was so significant—undermining confidence in their use—that it transformed the utility and the development of U.S. Special Operations Forces.

This time, though, the fight continued without pause.

———

In late 2013, acts of terrorism spiked in both form and frequency, most notably with the rise of Da'esh—also known as the Islamic State and by the acronyms of ISIS and ISIL. Its offensive in Iraq in late 2013—taking control of Fallujah and parts of Ramadi, quickly followed by Raqqa in early 2014, and both Mosul and Tikrit in June 2014—posed a direct challenge to U.S. and Coalition forces throughout the Middle East. The announcement of their formation of a caliphate—the Islamic State—across the broader region of Iraq and Syria came with heightened attacks. The Kurdish towns of Sinjar and Zumar were quickly overrun; the Mosul Dam was seized; and then a series of public execution by beheadings—of journalists, aid workers, and tourists—attracted the world's attention to these territorial gains.

Da'esh's black banners came to dominate large swaths of Iraq and Syria, and its self-proclaimed leader, Abu Bakr al-Baghdadi, stated the organization's objective unequivocally: "We ask God, praised be He, to make this flag the sole flag for all Muslims."

Al-Baghdadi gave a detailed call to arms soon after the capture of Mosul. Speaking from the Nur al-Din Mosque, a landmark site built in the twelfth century in honor of an emir credited with defending the region from papal crusaders, al-Baghdadi preached: "I have been plagued with this great matter, plagued with this responsibility, and it is a heavy responsibility. I was placed as your caretaker," describing himself as a direct descendent of the Prophet. He spoke of the historical Caliphate—a swath of Islamic lands stretching from Spain to Iran to Morocco to the Arabian Peninsula—and of establishing a flourishing new Islamic country. In fulfillment of the Qu'ran's prophecy, he promised an Islamic paradise without corruption, fortified by virtue and prayer. Referring to blessings from Muhammad, and citing passages from the Qur'an, al-Baghdadi called listeners to the fight: "Arm the armies to fight the enemies of Allah to do jihad against the polytheists." To all those gathered, "Fight His enemies and do jihad in His cause to achieve this and establish the religion, to empower the Shariah of Allah."[23]

A range of offshoots of Da'esh—directly conducting operations or indirectly inspired by the message—have routinely carried out numerous attacks in international cities since the establishment of the Islamic State. After the capture of Mosul in 2014, that included attacks at a peace rally in Ankara; at an airport and a train station in Brussels; at a newspaper office in Paris; at two mosques in Sana'a; at a hotel in Tripoli; and at a museum in Tunis. In the following year, a shopping area in Baghdad, a shrine in Baluchistan, a Christmas market in Berlin, a church in Cairo, a restaurant in Dhaka, the Prophet's mosque in Medina, a train station in Moscow, a crowded street in Nice, and government buildings in Tehran were among the targets hit. Subsequent targets included London's Parliament building, a concert hall in Manchester, a crowded street in Manhattan, and a pedestrian zone in Barcelona.

Local fighters—more than 60,000 soldiers, particularly Kurdish and Arab militias, with support from U.S. and allied forces, growing to a Coalition of eighty countries—attacked the Islamic State. They fought in the Syrian towns of Kobane and Manbij, and in 2017 won back the Middle Euphrates River Valley and, most significant, Raqqa, which Da'esh had previously invaded and claimed as the caliphate's capital.

When al-Baghdadi's prophecy of creating a permanent Islamic State across Syria and Iraq failed, his followers left little standing. On June 21, 2017, Da'esh adherents blew up the twelfth-century mosque and minaret in Mosul—from where they had delivered the call to arms just three years prior—as they retreated.

In 2019, the White House declared the end of the fight against the Islamic State, the immediate draw-down of U.S. troops in Syria, and its intention to withdraw forces from Afghanistan. On March 23, 2019, the last town of the Islamic State—Baghouz—fell, ending the caliphate's claims to any territory. At least for that moment.[24]

General Tony Thomas, then leading U.S. Special Operations Command, observed, "While we resoundly defeated the Caliphate, the ideology is robust, resilient, and stronger than when we left in 2011."

Less than one month later, a simultaneous multicity assault in Sri Lanka, of suicide bombers at churches and hotels in the cities of Colombo, Negombo, and Batticaloa on Easter Sunday, killed scores. Just after the mass attacks in Sri Lanka, Da'esh claimed them as revenge for the taking of Baghouz, Syria: "Our battle today is a war of attrition to harm the enemy, and they should know that jihad will continue until doomsday." Da'esh further claimed ninety-two attacks in eight countries as evidence of their strength. In September 2019, al-Baghdadi, seemingly undeterred by the territorial losses, called on the carriers of the black banner to fight the "atheist Crusader campaign," declaring that "he who fights in the cause of Allah and is killed or achieves victory—we will bestow upon him a great reward." He went on to underscore that Da'esh remains a global force, one that will continue to conduct worldwide operations.[25]

By the end of October 2019, al-Baghdadi was dead, killed in a U.S. special operations raid of a compound in the Idlib province of Syria, near the Turkish border, among some sparse olive groves and nearby Byzantine ruins. The U.S. special operators, infiltrating on helicopters from the Al Asad airbase in Iraq's western Anbar province, secured the target area quickly. After engaging in small-arms fire, they followed al-Baghdadi into a tunnel, where he detonated his suicide vest.[26]

In one sense, this was another milestone in the global war on terror. The al-Baghdadi manhunt was many years in the making, and his targeted killing was a tactical marker. However, his death did not—and was not expected to—bring any changes to the operational or strategic activities of U.S. Special Operations Forces or CENTCOM.

"We're under no illusions that [Da'esh] is going to go away just because we killed Baghdadi . . . [we expect] some form of retribution attack, and we are postured and prepared for that," stated General Kenneth F. McKenzie, Jr., the CENTCOM commander, in a Pentagon press briefing.

Da'esh soon named their successor caliph. No one knows what form its fight will take next, but its ideology and their adherents have repeatedly demonstrated resilience.

Three months later, the targeted killing of Major General Qasem Soleimani marked both a strategic and tactical shift—and another U.S. operational marker whose reverberations it is too early to predict. The Iranian military leader, with considerable political influence across the Middle East, arrived at Iraq's International Airport en route from Damascus, on commercial Cham Wings Airlines Flight 6Q501. Landing just after midnight on January 3, 2020, he and his two escorts were greeted on the Baghdad tarmac by Abu Mahdi al-Muhandis, head of Kata'ib Hezbollah and a leader of Iraqi militias. Approximately ten minutes later, the two cars, carrying ten people, were destroyed by Hellfire missiles from a MQ-9 Reaper overhead.[27]

One U.S. official, in a meeting with reporters, called it a "target of opportunity."

Ryan Crocker, a career U.S. ambassador to Iraq, Syria, and Lebanon, among others, pointed to the aftermath: "But now what? . . . we've got some hard choices and vulnerabilities, but so do they." Successors to both leaders, in Iran and Iraq, were announced by month's end.[28]

8

USE OF THE GOLDEN SPEAR

Thus the long war, from everlasting waged.

—Lucretius

Peace and war now coincide in the Sun Belt boomtown of Tampa.

From the oval windows of the C-37A aircraft—the military version of a Gulfstream V—a few minutes before landing at MacDill Air Force Base, the downward view is that of both.

On the port side, shooting the approach from the east, are orange-and-white gantry cranes sited in the dredged silt of Tampa Bay, swinging metal containers from docked barges in continuous motion. Lined up are berthed freighters with phosphate and oil, the dominant commodities in bulk cargo here. Alongside its terminals are mega cruise ships, setting off for the Caribbean,

Mexico, and South America. In the distance, the Sunshine Skyway Bridge's bright yellow cables form a slender sail across the Gulf of Mexico horizon under which freighters, ships, and boats will pass.

Closer in, at starboard side, the city's Amalie Arena is easy to spot by its painted lightning bolt, the jagged symbol of its National Hockey League team. Its landmarked Ybor City cigar factories, built up between the Plant Rail Line and Port Tampa at the turn of the twentieth century, remain recognizable by their rows of red-brick stacked chimneys. A sage-green artery now connects the University of Tampa to a large residential neighborhood of white stucco buildings with Mediterranean-style clay roofs and stone-paved loggias. A mile-long stretch of waterfront houses forms a crescent leading to South Tampa's sprawling peninsula of MacDill.

Since the launch of the 9/11 wars, when the first C-37As were assigned to MacDill, these jets have ensured the smooth transport of the commanders of CENTCOM and SOCOM, military leaders of the fight. Throughout two decades of war, MacDill officers and staffers have made this aerial loop.

In its final approach, the C-37A's glide path is clear. On the flat terrain of what had once been swamplands, MacDill's two-mile-long runway is the dominant feature from above, cut in diagonal and flush with Hillsborough Bay. While its concrete-and-asphalt surface has been milled many times over, its contour remains the same as when first laid out in World War II. Then and now, vectoring that slot to Runway 04/22 is a routine landing. The aircraft's trailing-link landing gear drops, its flexible arm ahead of the wheel, to absorb landing impact and dampen vertical oscillation. At touchdown, the wing's large spoilers pop up to chop speed. The pilots nose up to the metal-clad vintage hangars, shutting down the Rolls-Royce turbofan engine at the usual, Spot No. 1.[1]

——

Since 2001, to fly into MacDill has been to look down on one perpetual and massive construction site. Not a year has gone by when the whole of MacDill hasn't been a place of cranes and concrete, of off-road haulers and excavators, of demolition and creation, of the jerry-rigged and purpose-built—all trying to keep up with the steep demands of the new global combat.

The ground conditions—here and now—demonstrate that policymakers and military leaders are readying SOCOM and CENTCOM for many fights to come. The unremitting and unending military activities at MacDill since 9/11 show a spectrum of war without end.

More than five million square feet has been in flux, including massive infrastructure projects. A large hospital was cleared for the construction of a new 280,000-square-foot comprehensive medical facility, finished in 2017, one that serves the approximately 5,000 people now living on base and a population of more than 200,000 people—both active duty and retired personnel, as well as their family members—in the surrounding community. An older U.S. Air Force officers club was bulldozed to make way for a 350-room hotel to accommodate base visitors, completed in 2016. A new 90,000-square-foot glass building, completed in 2016, provides a campus for the education and training of special operators. Underground water facilities, to sustain this expansion, have been linked to two 500,000-gallon reservoirs moving out over forty-three miles of piping. The installation's fuel system has expanded to a 16,000-foot pipeline and a 35,000-barrel operating tank with twelve hydrant pits.[2]

CENTCOM has added immense structures—two buildings of about 300,000 square feet each—visible from above by their red-tiled tops. SOCOM has sprawled across the interior of the base with interconnected low-lying structures. Alongside MacDill's main runway are also a cluster of buildings for a blended subordinate command, U.S. Special Operations Command–Central. SOCCENT, as it's called for short, had originally been stood up in the 1980s to prepare U.S. Special Operations capabilities in the geographic theater of U.S. Central Command—particularly in the Middle East, but also including parts of northeast Africa and Central Asia. With the launch of the twenty-first-century global war on terror, though, it has served a major campaign function, one with further links to forward operating components in Qatar, Kuwait, and elsewhere. Tasked with wartime planning and logistics immediately after 9/11, it then expanded into certain aspects of command and control, or warfighting. In 2011, SOCCENT moved into a dedicated headquarters. In 2018, the Command having outgrown its space, MacDill ordered a base impact analysis as a step toward SOCCENT's next round of expansion.

The work of CENTCOM and SOCOM further joins together at Coalition Village. More than fifty partner countries are based there, represented by their senior officers, sent from Albania to Djibouti, from Bangladesh to El Salvador, each there for some aspect of combined counterterrorist activities.[3]

The Village was established as a temporary operations unit in the weeks immediately after 9/11, initially as part of the mobilization effort then defined by President Bush in the following words: "Every nation, in every region, now has a decision to make. Either you're with us, or you're with the terrorists." In that first month, military personnel arrived from twelve countries: Australia, Belgium, Canada, France, Germany, Italy, Jordan, the Netherlands, New Zealand, Qatar, Turkey, and the United Kingdom. By the second month, that roster had expanded to twenty nations.[4]

For those partner militaries, CENTCOM's main parking area was converted into a high-low trailer park. At first, that meant satellite communications hookups but no running water. Each country was assigned an aluminum trailer, a lineup of tin cans that looked like they could be blown away in a single Florida hurricane. But they were soon built out—upgraded to prefab brown-and-tan structures, with water, communication, and electric lines trenched in. As one base employee put it, "a whole city is going up on a parking lot on the south side of the headquarters of the Central Command, or CENTCOM," complete with a couple of dozen national flags raised high.[5]

For many countries, joining a global fight against terrorism was not a difficult decision to make. The attacks on September 11, 2001, brought an outpouring of support. Allies, rivals, and even adversaries united. The prestigious Parisian newspaper *Le Monde*, frequently critical of America's role in the world, captured a widespread reversal of sentiment in its headline of the following day: "We Are All Americans." Political leadership from Nigeria to China, from Russia to Colombia described the attack in similar terms, as barbaric and evil, as not just an attack on one country but a brazen challenge to humankind. Presidents and prime ministers expressed a singular characterization of the war on terror as the world's fight, as civilization's fight, and as the global fight of all against a new virulent nihilism.

The United Nations, its headquarters four miles from the World Trade Center, smoke and ashes visible from its East River location, provided immediate agreement about the world's role, with the unanimous adoption on September 12 of Security Council Resolution 1368, a call to all nations to respond in a singular voice against the terrorist attack on U.S. soil and to work together to bring the perpetrators to justice.

On that same day, NATO's North Atlantic Council invoked its Article V collective defense responsibilities for the first time in its history: "The Parties agree that an armed attack against one or more of them in Europe or North America shall be considered an attack against them all and . . . [will take action,] including the use of armed force, to restore and maintain the security of the North Atlantic area." Signed by twelve nations in 1949, Article V had primarily been an invention of the Cold War, with the aim of solidarity against the Soviet Union's expansion into Europe, and a commitment by the United States to come to Europe's aid if the military requirement ever arose. For a half-century, this strategy was informally described as U.S. tanks lining the Fulda Gap, a hypothetical route that a surprise land invasion by the Soviet Union could have taken into Germany. Therefore, Article V, called an anachronism after the dissolution of the Soviet Union, was a remarkable basis for the first 9/11 counterterror operations when Operation Eagle Assist was launched to protect U.S. airspace, carried out by pilots from thirteen countries patrolling the U.S. skies in NATO aircraft.

As those initial countermeasures were underway, the Pew Poll on Global Attitudes undertook a survey of public views toward the international jihadists of the 9/11 attacks. It reported that "publics around the world support the objective of rooting out terrorism" and strongly approve of international coordination to fight this form of violence. It wasn't just Americans, of course, who lost their lives on 9/11—citizens of seventy-seven countries died that day. Several national leaders spoke about their own nations' grief. As one Australian leader put it, "We are in there in our own right as well—there were tens of Australians who disappeared on September 11."[6]

On October 11, 2001, President George W. Bush expressed gratitude to the global community and set out a unified approach: "And the world has come together to fight a new and different war, the first, and we hope the only one, of the 21st century."[7]

By November 10, 2001, when President Bush spoke at the United Nations, forty-five countries had joined the Global War on Terror as allied counterterror forces. This would be a global fight against a violent movement of radical Islamists, against organizations and individuals who carry out acts of terror and destruction in the name of jihad, Bush declared. That statement met with widespread agreement among members of the United Nations, and the Security Council adopted its third 9/11 resolution, again in unanimity, on November 14, 2001. It singled out Usama bin Laden by name and specifically "condemn[ed] the Taliban for allowing Afghanistan to be used as a base for the export of terrorism by the Al-Qaida network and other terrorist groups and for providing safe haven."[8]

At MacDill, allied military leaders gathered each morning at 9:00 to oversee the operations in Afghanistan. Overt combat formally began on October 7, 2001, when bombs were dropped on al-Qaeda's strongholds and training bases, with strike sorties from F-14s, F/A-18s, B-1s, B-2s, and B-52s, among others. Task forces also deployed in the Middle East, southeast Europe, Southeast Asia, the Mediterranean, sub-Saharan Africa, and elsewhere. On the third floor of CENTCOM headquarters, sitting around a horseshoe table, a multinational group of general officers reviewed the video and radar images beamed from J-STARS and other capabilities that tracked all aircraft, ships, units, and troops moving throughout the theaters. As one French officer put it, in past wars we would all forward-deploy. But this was a new way of fighting: "Now with the modern means of communication, where we have access instantly to information, it is not necessary to stand in a tent in the middle of the desert or on top of the mountains in the middle of Afghanistan in order to command and direct the war." At midday, a subset of the Coalition leaders would drive the few miles to downtown Tampa, for press briefings organized by the Pentagon. From the second floor of the Marriott Waterside Hotel, General Tommy Franks, then commander of CENTCOM, provided daily updates on the Afghanistan campaign, and allied military leaders responded to press queries.[9]

From the beginning, CENTCOM and SOCOM were both preparing for the "long war," as it was later dubbed, one that would depend on a global coalition. CENTCOM's deputy head of strategy and planning pointed out that the Coalition's counterterror fight would go on long after the initial 9/11 objective was met:

"We will not roll up our sleeping bags or untie our tents after we capture or kill bin Laden," he said.[10]

A U.S. spokesman from the Village summed it up: "Bush administration officials repeatedly have said that the war on terrorism will not end with Afghanistan. As a result, the Coalition Coordination Center [its official name at the start] apparently will be in operation indefinitely."[11]

By January 2002, more than thirty-five countries had offered to send forces and equipment to Afghanistan—and elsewhere as needed—for the global war on terror. Canada forwarded its navy ships and Hercules transport aircraft and ordered the deployment of 3,000 troops, more "than at any time since the Second World War," detailed the country's defense minister. Denmark, the Netherlands, and Norway sent fighter aircraft. When a Norwegian F-16 engaged a target in southern Kandahar, it was the first time that nation had dropped a bomb since the 1940s. The United Kingdom sent 4,000 forces forward, to patrol the skies over Afghanistan and the waters off Pakistan, including British special forces who joined ground activities with U.S. operators. British air marshal G. E. Stirrup, then his country's leading officer at Coalition Village, explained their outlook: "The United Kingdom has always made clear that the purpose of this campaign is to remove terrorism as a force in international affairs. Clearly that does not necessarily end in Afghanistan."[12]

Coalition Village expanded to include every NATO country and even countries that the United States had some notably difficult relations with—Russia and Yemen, among others—in unusual ad hoc arrangements to account for sensitivities in political matters and intelligence sharing. Visitors to the Village in

2002 and 2003 were told that the officers are part of the "the largest coalition ever assembled by the United States . . . [it] includes 54 countries." At another press briefing, in which the common enemy was described as "terrorism," a brigadier general from Kenya, a captain from Japan, and a rear admiral from Italy spoke of the shared purpose: "We're here, to fight together," explained the officer from Japan.[13]

When President Bush visited MacDill, to speak at a Coalition Village conference in 2004, sixty-five countries were flying their flags. Coalition forces were then deploying more than 40,000 troops. Bush expressed gratitude to the many nations "doing their part in the war on terror . . . for serving with America in the cause of freedom," as well as appreciation to the whole of CENTCOM and SOCOM. In describing CENTCOM, he compared their mission to that of their earliest days, when the combatant command had helped "protect our allies from aggression" during the Cold War. "Now, at the start of a new century, the men and women of CENTCOM have liberated two nations, and have rescued more than 50 million people from tyranny. Today your nation is counting on you to ensure the defeat of terrorists, to secure America, and to advance freedom throughout the Middle East. That's our mission." In expressing his appreciation to SOCOM, Bush stated, "MacDill is also the headquarters for our quiet warriors, the United States Special Operations Command. It is the nature of Special Ops that many of your victories are unseen and must remain secret—but I know about them. Our Special Operations Forces are the worst nightmare of America's worst enemies, and you're making us proud."[14]

When President Bush returned to MacDill three years later, he again expressed thanks to the nations represented at Coalition Village, underscoring the joint fight of liberation, of defending security. He underscored both the scope of the fight—"this enormous challenge in the 21st century"—and the shared mission of "defending the security of the civilized world." He also broadened the definition of the common enemy: "[In] the fight against radicals and extremists and murderers of the innocent, we stand as one."[15]

In September 2014, when President Obama spoke to the MacDill community, he continued the U.S. emphasis on fighting alongside Coalition forces: "We're going to keep on working with our allies and partners to take out the terrorists who threaten us wherever they hide. Because in stark contrast to those who only know how to kill and maim and tear down, we keep on building up and offering a future of progress and hope."[16]

By that time, thirteen years into the fight, the geographic focus had added Syria to Iraq and Afghanistan, while continuing to include smaller-scale efforts in Libya, Mali, Niger, Somalia, and Yemen, among other countries. Partners at Coalition Village still numbered over fifty countries, and in some fights in Central and South Asia, the Middle East, and Africa, Coalition forces were taking the ground lead while the United States provided airpower and equipment. For Coalition and U.S. forces, the fight increasingly emphasized the centrality of local partners, such as the Kurdistan Regional Government around Syria; Iraqi national security forces in Iraq; and the forces of Cameroon, Chad and Nigeria in West Africa.

By this time, a comprehensive and sustained counterterrorism strategy incorporated joint force in lethal operations. The president explained, "I met with representatives from more than 40 nations. It is a true team effort here at MacDill . . . We will lead a broad coalition of countries who have a stake in this fight. It is the world rejecting the brutality of ISIL [also known as Da'esh] in favor of a better future for our children, and our children's children—all of them. But we're not going to do this alone."

President Obama gave a further example of the Sinjar Mountains at the border of Iraq and Syria, where the previous summer refugees fleeing Da'esh had been stranded and surrounded. The United States conducted airstrikes on Da'esh while local forces, particularly the Kurdish Peshmerga, created a safe passage of escape and Coalition forces dropped supplies. The president described Coalition efforts to train and equip partners, to advise and assist, which helped "give space for Iraqi and Kurdish forces to reclaim key territory . . . [they] helped our partners on the ground break ISIL sieges, helped rescue civilians cornered on a mountain, helped save the lives of thousands of innocent men, women, and children."

The overall message of U.S. leadership stayed the same, to degrade and destroy: "Whether in Iraq or in Syria, these terrorists will learn the same thing that the leaders of al-Qaeda already know: We mean what we say; our reach is long; if you threaten America, you will find no safe haven. We will find you eventually."

When President Obama returned two years later, in 2016, to give a capstone speech on U.S. national security over his

Administration's eight years, he laid out to the MacDill community something that "you know all too well, your mission—and the course of history—was changed after the 9/11 attacks. For eight years that I've been in office, there has not been a day when a terrorist organization or some radicalized individual was not plotting to kill Americans . . . Now we did not choose this fight, but once it came to us, the world saw the measure of our resolve." Look ahead, he said to those at MacDill, we all know that "The terrorist threat is real and it is dangerous . . . But these terrorists want to cast themselves as the vanguard of a new world order. They are not. They are thugs and they are murderers, and they should be treated that way."[17]

In thinking about Coalition Village over the years, one MacDill airman described the different ways that the Coalition has come to be perceived on base, noting that the Village has an "emblem, [it's] the American bald eagle, wings spread with foreign flags visible underneath . . . If you're an American, it represents the U.S. covering and protecting the nations depicted under its wings. If you're a foreign ally, it represents all the nations supporting the U.S. and enabling the U.S. to continue to soar." A Danish brigadier general, a one-time chairman of Coalition Village, remarked, "Either way, it's a representation of what we do here at the Coalition, supporting one another to accomplish a common goal."[18]

By 2020, Coalition Village has now been promoted for nearly two decades as a site for the international community to unify for counterterrorism activities. The Village's completed structure, however, still remains apart—as well as dwarfed by America's massive CENTCOM complex. It is notable that the United States has continued to leave all nations, even its closest allies, outside the wire—while individuals are selectively allowed inside. Here, at the headquarters of the 9/11 wars, there continues to be an ambivalence about whether a tightly linked coalition to fight the scourge of terrorism is the Coalition Village's ground reality.

To some, the global war on terror—and its other, similar labels—has long been a demonstrably American endeavor, one that may seek assistance and symbolic support from other countries but which is not a joint enterprise on equal footing over collective ground. Even among the flags that fly in the Village, the highest is the American flag, some officers point out.[19]

Still others take a more aspirational approach, about the need for a global coalition, perhaps best summed up by former CENTCOM Commander James N. Mattis, at the end of his tenure as the nation's 26th Secretary of Defense:

> One core belief I have always held is that our strength as a nation is inextricably linked to the strength of our unique and comprehensive system of alliances and partnerships . . . we must use all tools of American power to provide for the common defense, including providing effective leadership to our alliances. NATO's 29 democracies demonstrated that strength in their commitment to fighting alongside us following the 9-11 attack on America. The Defeat-ISIS Coalition of 74 nations is further proof.[20]

To circle back to MacDill's physical markers is to see an index of the present facts and future trends. MacDill's third major war—its 9/11 wars, following World War II and the Cold War—is not yet on display here, and perhaps never will be. In the ongoing campaign referred to as the nation's longest war, a war without a typical battlefield or fronts, led by those inside CENTCOM and SOCOM, an outside form may not be apt.[21]

But these physical voids do not betoken a lack of military operations. That the 9/11 wars have not given rise to tangible objects at the wartime headquarters is a matter of significance. It attests to the war's overarching uncertainty: its nebulous objective, its hazy enemy, its amorphous battlespace. In this sense, the current blank spaces at MacDill may be exactly the correct fit. Perhaps in this conflict the traditional binary of victory/defeat is not fitting.

The 9/11 wars, centered on counterterrorism and counterinsurgency activities and practices, challenge those who define wars by the cessation of hostilities. Here, what constitutes the end of these wars, or even the boundaries of the mission, is intrinsically blurry, with few clear measures. Instead, for those who eschew win/lose formulations altogether, a different model may be offered at MacDill, one that does not lend itself to tangible form. The approach appears closer to perpetual vigilance, against roiling conflicts, with an acceptance that the results of U.S. forces will be neither finite nor conclusive. Their method suggests a sort of hedging by U.S. special operators, a strategic-risk-and-management approach to terrorism—a problem to be managed rather than a war to be won. That looks like reality, but it hardly sounds obviously heroic or made for celebration—or easy to form as touchstones to dot MacDill's landscape.

Without those readymade objects, to discover the tracks of activity, work that is both labor-intensive and frenetic, standing at MacDill's gates soon after sunrise provides a different and alternative starting point. Ford and Chevy pickup trucks stream in, filling up new parking garages. By early morning, the lots are already overflowing, with the last of the arrivals conspicuously marked by the location of their vehicles—parked on patchy grass, a sort of makeshift spot. Following those people into the buildings of SOCOM and CENTCOM, into their windowless rooms, to their desks and screens, is a more useful path. Theirs is an inside and compartmented war—away from exposed ridgelines or public celebrations. The inside work is not yet fully formed, even after two decades, but it continues to move fast and wide.

It was a fight that began in crisis—urgent and ad hoc—and is now routine.

At its start, a broad-brush and open-ended resolution, the Authorization for the Use of Military Force, was established for the global war against terror, and it remains in effect today as the basis for perpetual combat:

> The President has authority under the Constitution to take action to deter and prevent acts of international terrorism against the United States . . . That the President is authorized to use all necessary and appropriate force . . . in order to prevent any future acts of international terrorism against the United States by such nations, organizations or persons.[22]

Over the past two decades, the U.S. Department of Defense has invested trillions of dollars in these 9/11 wars.[23]

To date, CENTCOM has deployed more than two million service members to the wars in Afghanistan and Iraq—and by a conservative count, tens of thousands of raids have been conducted by U.S. special operators in counterterrorism and counterinsurgency fights ranging from Afghanistan to the Philippines, from Iraq to Libya. Combating terrorism became central to the U.S. military's mission, and these forces were charged to deter, disrupt, and defeat global terrorist organizations—a major shift in mission, scope, and pace. SOCOM's culture changed from a somewhat isolated command into a core part of U.S. national security. Its numbers tell part of that story: Over the past two decades, SOCOM doubled its personnel, tripled its direct budget, and quadrupled its deployments.[24]

Throughout these years, the global war against terrorism has continued nearly unabated. While the war is no longer fought under that moniker, and has broadened beyond counterterrorism, many of the same U.S. units have stayed in the fight against similar enemies and adversaries. There was a moment, briefly, after the Abbottabad raid in 2011, and again near the time of the Afghanistan withdrawal deadline of 2014, that some U.S. policymakers did call for a formal end to the 9/11 wars. A few declared a postwar era, stating that the war in Afghanistan would soon be over and that troop withdrawals would be completed from Iraq, marking the successful resolution of that country's violent instability. That has, though, largely gone by the wayside, either rendered unrealistic by events or overturned subsequently by decision-makers. Today's deployments continue apace and show a ground truth that this fight continues to be fiercely waged, not only in Syria and Iraq but around the world.

Today, rather than reduced commitments as some had predicted, U.S. special operators are now deployed not only in a global counterterrorism campaign, largely against nonstate actors, but also in support of another major pillar of U.S. national security policy: countering threats from state actors. Whether it be a revanchist Russia in eastern Ukraine or its commercial backing of the Libya National Army against Tripoli's central government, or the risk of military escalation by North Korea or Iran, U.S. forces are deployed to confront hostile actions short of full-scale and overt conflict.

That is the reality of U.S. Special Operations Forces by design. They are tasked with everything not meeting a conventional requirement, assigned as the nation's force to fill voids, niches, and contingencies—each new problem can rise to be an essential task, mission, or commitment, just by its very emergence. The new issue can remain its responsibility as long as its form is judged to lie outside the boundaries of traditional warfare. The list of tasks resulting from the infinite nature of that responsibility is therefore inexhaustible.[25]

Put a different way, by definition, SOCOM's work is unorthodox, ambiguous, and unending.[26]

At times, that has been characterized as a negative—that the role for U.S. Special Operations Forces is too wide and can be ever broadened. These forces have been called both the "easy button" and the "quick fix." At least two major hazards have been noted by critics. First, of scope: With few fixed boundaries on what may be relevant, nearly anything can be. Second, of agency: Created as an outlier in the U.S. national security establishment, and as an asymmetry inside the military at large, these forces are charged with anything too irregular or unconventional.[27]

To others, this unique structure provides an economy of force, one that has the potential for consequential interventions in U.S. national security. Those proponents call for sustaining an advanced U.S. special operations capability in the long fight, investing in a highly competitive selection process, long pipelines of training, and vanguard technology to ensure it remains unrivaled.

Where it will go next is unknown.

As former U.S. Secretary of Defense Robert M. Gates reminds us: "And I must tell you, when it comes to predicting the nature and location of our next military engagements, since Vietnam, our record has been perfect. We have never once gotten it right, from Mayaguez to Grenada, Panama, Somalia, the Balkans, Haiti, Kuwait, Iraq, and more—we had no idea a year before any of these missions that we would be so engaged."[28]

This is what war is.[29]

NOTES

1 FIRST DAY AT HEADQUARTERS

1. The opening quote, "The fire-breathers are almost always civilians," is offered by Robert M. Gates at the University Club in New York City in 2014, then on a book tour for his memoir, *Duty,* regarding his four decades of U.S. government service, including leadership of the U.S. Department of Defense and the Central Intelligence Agency. The remark was part of his broader assertion that U.S. policy leaders have been too quick to apply military force to international problems, citing the 2003 invasion of Iraq as one example, and the calls to bomb Iran's nuclear sites as another—and too slow to consider the phases, consequences, and aftermaths of warfare.

2. Both SOCOM and CENTCOM were established in the 1980s and are part of today's unified combatant command structure. For those elements, at the time of this visit, see the U.S. Department of Defense, *Directive 5100.01: Functions of the Department of Defense and Its Major Components* (Washington, DC: U.S. Department of Defense, December 21, 2010). For a discussion of aspects of the institutional history of SOCOM, see William G. Boykin, *The Origins of the United States Special Operations Command* (SOCOM Archives, 1991); Boykin, *Special Operations and Low-Intensity Conflict Legislation: Why Was It Passed and Have the Voids Been Filled?* (Carlisle, PA: U.S. Army War College, 1991); Lucien S. Vandenbroucke, *Perilous Options: Special Operations as an Instrument of U.S. Foreign Policy* (Oxford: Oxford University Press,

1993); Susan L. Marquis, *Unconventional Warfare: Rebuilding U.S. Special Operations Forces* (Washington, DC: Brookings Institution Press, 1997); and William C. Ohl, *Fixing U.S. Special Operations: Rational Actors Not Allowed* (Washington, DC: National War College, 1993). Regarding CENTCOM, see Anthony H. Cordesman, *USCENTCOM Mission and History* (Washington, DC: Center for Strategic and International Studies, 1998); Jay E. Hines, "From Desert One to Southern Watch: The Evolution of U.S. Central Command," *Joint Forces Quarterly* 24 (Spring 2000): 42–48. For an analysis of a predecessor organization, also at MacDill, see Henrik Bliddal, "Reforming Military Command Arrangements: The Case of the Rapid Deployment Joint Task Force," Letort Paper of Strategic Studies Institute, U.S. Army War College, 2011; Paul K. Davis, *Observations on the Rapid Deployment Joint Task Force: Origins, Direction* and *Mission* (Santa Monica: RAND Corporation, 1982); and United States Congress, *Rapid Deployment Forces: Policy and Budgetary Implications* (Washington, DC: Congressional Budget Office, 1983). For discussion of aspects of the legislative history, see James R. Locher III, "Congress to the Rescue: Statutory Creation of USSOCOM FY 1987," *Air Commando Journal* (Spring 2012): 33–39; Locher, "Has It Worked?: The Goldwater-Nichols Reorganization Act—Department of Defense Reorganization," *Naval War College Review* 54:4 (Autumn 2001): 95–115; Wade Ishimoto, *Reflections on Defense Reform: 25 Years since Goldwater-Nichols and Nunn-Cohen* (Quantico: Marine Corps University, 2012); Lynn R. Rylander, "ASD-SOLIC (Assistant Secretary of Defense for Special Operations and Low-Intensity Conflict): The Congressional Approach to SOF Reorganization," *Special Warfare* 2 (Spring 1989): 10–16; John D. Gresham, "SOCOM at 25—Part I: The Battle for Capitol Hill," *Defense Media Network* (July 13, 2012): 100–109; John W. Partin, "Interview with General E. C. Meyer," SOCOM Archives Collections (July 14, 1988); John W. Partin, "Telephone Interview with General James J. Lindsay," SOCOM Archives Collections (October 16, 2003); "Interview: H. Allen Holmes, Assistant Secretary of Defense for Special Operations and Low-Intensity Conflict," *Special Warfare* 7 (October 1994): 46–48; *U.S. Department of Defense Directive 5111.10: Assistant Secretary of Defense* (Washington, DC:

U.S. Department of Defense, March 22, 1995); and Steven F. Tomhave, *The Impact of Congressional Legislation on United States Special Operations Capability* (Carlisle, PA: U.S. Army War College, 1989).

3. See Michael S. Sherry, *The Rise of American Air Power: The Creation of Armageddon* (New Haven: Yale University Press, 1987) for analysis of aerial bombing and the rise of strategic air combat in U.S. military planning.

4. See Carl von Clausewitz, *On War,* trans. Col. J. J. Graham (London: N. Trübner & Co, 1873) for this classic military concept. Also see analysis by Antulio J. Echevarria II, "Clausewitz's Center of Gravity: It's Not What We Thought," *Naval War College Review* 56:1 (Winter 2003): 108–23.

5. See a three-part series by Dana Priest and William M. Arkin, "Top Secret America," *Washington Post* (July 2010), later published in a more comprehensive form as Dana Priest and William M. Arkin, *Top Secret America: The Rise of the New American Security State* (New York: Little, Brown, 2011). For earlier discussion, see Dana Priest, *The Mission: Waging War and Keeping Peace with America's Military* (New York: W. W. Norton, 2003).

6. See the series by Andrew Feickert, *The Unified Command Plan and Combatant Commands: Background and Issues for Congress* (Washington, DC: Congressional Research Service), which is updated regularly, as well as Dennis J. Quinn, *Goldwater-Nichols DoD Reorganization Act: A Ten-Year Retrospective* (Washington, DC: National Defense University Press, 1999); Clark Murdock, Michèle Flournoy, et al., *Beyond Goldwater-Nichols: U.S. Government and Defense Reform for a New Strategic Era* (Washington, DC: Center for Strategic and International Studies, 2004); Roger Z. George and Harvey Rishikof, eds., *The National Security Enterprise: Navigating the Labyrinth* (Washington, DC: Georgetown University Press, 2011); and James R. Locher III et al., *Forging a New Shield* (Washington, DC: Project on National Security Reform, 2008).

7. For the development of command arrangements, see Edward J. Drea and Ronald H. Cole, *History of the Unified Command Plan, 1946–2012* (Washington, DC: Office of the Chairman of the Joint Chiefs of Staff, 2013); Alice C. Cole, Alfred Goldberg, Samuel A. Tucker, and Rudolph

A. Winnacker, eds., *The Department of Defense: Documents on Establishment and Organization, 1944–1978* (Washington, DC: Office of the Secretary of Defense, 1978); and Alfred Goldberg, *The Pentagon: The First Fifty Years* (Washington, DC: Office of the Secretary of Defense, 1992). For its major reorganization in the 1980s, see James R. Locher III, *Victory on the Potomac: The Goldwater-Nichols Act Unifies the Pentagon* (College Station, TX: Texas A&M University Press, 2002); and U.S. Senate Armed Services Committee, *Defense Organization—The Need for Change: Staff Report to the Committee on Armed Services*, Senate Print Number 99-86 (Washington, DC: Government Printing Office, 1985). For the longer trajectory of U.S. military organization, see Stacie L. Pettyjohn, *U.S. Global Defense Posture, 1783–2011* (Santa Monica: RAND Corporation, 2012).

8. President Eisenhower's declaration—"Separate ground, sea, and air warfare is gone forever . . . we will fight it in all elements, with all services, as one single concentrated effort"—was part of his longer document sent to Congress on April 3, 1958, a contribution to their deliberations that resulted in major legislation later that year on the reorganization of the Department of Defense.

9. At this time, as part of the development of irregular warfare capabilities, President Kennedy authorized the establishment of SEALs as part of Naval Special Warfare and the expansion of Army Special Forces, or Green Berets. To the graduating class of West Point, on June 6, 1962, Kennedy drew attention to this type of warfare, "new in its intensity, ancient in its origin—war by guerrillas, subversives, insurgents, assassins; war by ambush instead of by combat, by infiltration instead of aggression, seeking victory by eroding and exhausting the enemy instead of engaging him. It preys on unrest."

10. President Johnson made the remarks on May 2, 1965, in a speech on the Dominican Republic intervention: "The American nations cannot, must not, and will not permit the establishment of another Communist government in the Western Hemisphere." And on May 3, 1965, to the AFL-CIO's National Legislative Conference: "We don't propose to sit here in our rocking chair with our hands folded and let the Communists set up any government in the Western Hemisphere."

For a deeper analysis of this era, see C. W. Borklund, *Men of the Pentagon: From Forrestal to McNamara* (New York: Frederick A. Praeger, 1966); Roger R. Trask and Alfred Goldberg, *The Department of Defense, 1947–1997: Organization and Leaders* (Washington, DC: Office of the Secretary of Defense, 1997); Edward N. Luttwak, *The Pentagon and the Art of War* (New York: Simon and Schuster, 1985); Allan R. Millett and Peter Maslowski, *For the Common Defense: A Military History of the United States of America* (New York: The Free Press, 1994); and Martin Van Creveld, *Command in War* (Cambridge, MA: Harvard University Press, 1985). Two books by Michael S. Sherry provide greater context: *In the Shadow of War: The United States since the 1930s* (New Haven: Yale University Press, 1995) and *Preparing for the Next War: American Plans for Postwar Defense, 1941–45* (New Haven: Yale University Press, 1977).

11. For the "difficult problem of terrorism," see Donald Rumsfeld's memorandum dated May 8, 1976, on his first tour as secretary of defense, in the chronological records of *The Rumsfeld Papers*, an e-archival repository, papers.rumsfeld.com, released with the publication of his book *Known and Unknown: A Memoir* (New York: Sentinel, 2011). For further commentary from Zbigniew Brzezinski, see the memoranda, reports, and correspondence in the Brzezinski materials of the Presidential Library of Jimmy Carter, including National Security Council, Weekly Report #81, as analyzed in Barbara Zanchetta, *The Transformation of American International Power in the 1970s* (Cambridge: Cambridge University Press, 2013) and as the basis for his memoir, *Power and Principle: Memoirs of the National Security Adviser 1977–1981* (New York: Farrar, Straus and Giroux, 1983).

12. President Jimmy Carter, State of the Union Address, January 21, 1980.

13. Christopher Ogden, "An Interview with Kissinger: Détente Should Not Become a Tranquilizer," *Time* (January 15, 1979).

14. In the seventies, several countries invested in counterterrorism expertise, including Germany, particularly after the killings of athletes, coaches, and a police officer at the Munich Olympics in 1972 and the Lufthansa airline hijacking in Somalia in 1977; Israel, already

well trained by the time of Operation Thunderbolt, its Entebbe airport raid in 1977; and the United Kingdom, particularly as it related to Northern Island. For some analysis, see Rolf Tophoven, *GSG 9: German Response to Terrorism* (Koblenz: Bernard and Graefe Verlag, 1984) and Konrad Kellen, *The Impact of Terrorism on the Federal Republic of Germany: 1968–1982* (Santa Monica: RAND Corporation, 1986); Daniel Byman, *A High Price: The Triumphs and Failures of Israeli Counterterrorism* (Oxford: Oxford University Press, 2010); and Steven Sobieck, "Democratic Responses to Revolutionary Terrorism: A Comparative Study of Great Britain, Italy and West Germany" (Ph.D. diss., Claremont Graduate School, 1990). For some overviews of this era, see Ian O. Lesser, Bruce Hoffman, John Arquilla, David Ronfeldt, Michele Zanini, and Brian Michael Jenkins, *Countering the New Terrorism* (Santa Monica: RAND Corporation, 1999) and Bruce Hoffman and Jennifer Morrison Taw, *A Strategic Framework for Countering Terrorism and Insurgency* (Santa Monica: RAND Corporation, 1992). For a conceptual framework, see Brian Michael Jenkins, *International Terrorism: A New Kind of Warfare* (Santa Monica: RAND Corporation, 1974) and Brian Michael Jenkins, *Combatting Terrorism Becomes a War* (Santa Monica: RAND Corporation, 1984).

15. The mandate for CENTCOM's establishment came from Secretary of Defense Caspar Weinberger in 1983, followed by legislation sponsored by U.S. Senators William Cohen and Samuel A. Nunn for SOCOM's creation in 1987.

16. For a practitioner's perspective on the events of this period, and U.S. policymaking with Iran at this time, see Gary Sick, *All Fall Down: America's Tragic Encounter with Iran* (New York: Random House, 1985). His subsequent book, *October Surprise: America's Hostages in Iran and the Election of Ronald Reagan* (New York: Random House, 1991), presents the aftermath in U.S. politics and the effects of the failed military operation on President Carter's reputation and legacy, as well as the decision-making by Ronald Reagan and his advisers in the final weeks of his presidential campaign and the opening weeks of his administration. The news coverage of these events was exhaustive and included a number of interviews with President Carter in which he reaffirmed his support of the shah throughout the street protests and uprisings. See, for example, the interview by Bill Moyers, PBS *Bill Moyers Journal,* on November 13, 1978, when Carter referred to the opposition as "villains" who were disrupting civic life.

17. See Janet Afary and Kevin B. Anderson, *Foucault and the Iranian Revolution: Gender and the Seductions of Islamism* (Chicago: University of Chicago Press, 2014).

18. The Foreign Affairs Oral History Project of the Association for Diplomatic Studies and Training has extensive interviews of embassy personnel based in Kabul in 1979. See, in particular, the interview of Bruce A. Flatin, the embassy's political counselor, who rushed immediately to the Hotel Kabul upon notification of the hostage situation: "We were told that terrorists had seized the Ambassador." Flatin was also given a copy of Walter Reed Hospital's autopsy report: "There were many bullets in the body, but the ones that caused death were .22 caliber bullets in the brain, about four of them. The official Afghan incident report to us, in the form of a diplomatic note, had listed weapons found in the room—and none of them were .22 calibre. And as you know, police and troops don't use .22 caliber."

19. See interview of Bruce A. Flatin by Charles Stuart Kennedy, The Foreign Affairs Oral History Project of the Association for Diplomatic Studies and Training (January 27, 1993).

20. The Foreign Affairs Oral History Project of the Association for Diplomatic Studies and Training has several interviews of embassy officials in Tehran during this period. See, in particular, the interview of Victor L. Tomseth, who noted, "Prescient political analyst that I am, I argued that if you close down the embassy every time there is a demonstration in Tehran, you might as well close it down permanently because hardly a day goes by when there isn't a demonstration in some part of the city about something." Chargé L. Bruce Laingen offered his perspective on the February 14 intrusions—"Thereafter the Embassy had revolutionary guards whom we referred to gently as thugs, on the compound . . . A squad of them, indeed at the beginning three squads of them from three separate revolutionary groups, were placed in the Embassy for our 'protection.'" Political officer

Elizabeth Ann Swift recalled: "The whole issue of having the Shah in the United States was an extremely emotional one for the Iranians. I don't think I really realized at the time exactly how emotional it was, but what it basically meant . . . they looked upon it as just one more sign that the United States government was really fully intent on restoring the Shah, or at least restoring a right-wing government to Iran. They were not about to believe that we were going to let the Shah in just for medical treatment."

21. See interview of Victor K. Tomseth by Charles Stuart Kennedy, The Foreign Affairs Oral History Project of the Association for Diplomatic Studies and Training (May 13, 1999).

22. See interviews by Charles Stuart Kennedy of Myles Greene (February 22, 2002); L. Bruce Laingen (January 9, 1993); Richard H. Morefield (April 18, 1990); and Elizabeth Ann Swift (December 16, 1992) for the Foreign Affairs Oral History Project of the Association for Diplomatic Studies and Training.

23. See Douglas Brinkley, *Cronkite* (New York: HarperCollins, 2012).

24. See Yaroslav Trofimov, *The Siege of Mecca: The Forgotten Uprising in Islam's Holiest Shrine and the Birth of al-Qaeda* (New York: Doubleday, 2007). On further context, see Tariq Ali, *The Clash of Fundamentalisms: Crusades, Jihads and Modernity* (New York: Verso, 2002); Ian Buruma and Avishai Margalit, *Occidentalism: The West in the Eyes of Its Enemies* (New York: Penguin, 2004); and Thomas Hegghammer, *Jihad in Saudi Arabia: Violence and Pan-Islamism since 1979* (Cambridge: Cambridge University Press, 2010).

25. See interview of Barrington King by Charles Stuart Kennedy, The Foreign Affairs Oral History Project of the Association for Diplomatic Studies and Training (April 18, 1990).

26. See Trofimov (2007), which includes a large number of cables released by the U.S. Department of State, as well as PBS *NewsHour*'s Jim Lehrer interview.

27. For analysis of Usama bin Laden in his earlier years, see Peter Bergen, *Holy War, Inc.: Inside the Secret World of Osama bin Laden* (New York: The Free Press, 2001); Steve Coll, *The Bin Ladens: An Arabian Family in the American Century* (New York: Penguin, 2008). Usama bin Laden is the

common spelling of this Arabic name in early U.S. national security documents, and "UBL" has been conventionally applied as shorthand. See, for example, Gina M. Bennett, "The Wandering Mujahidin: Armed and Dangerous," U.S. Department of State, Bureau of Intelligence and Research (August 21–22, 1993), declassified and released in full on November 23, 2007; and two Clinton administration documents, "Terrorism/Usama bin Laden: Who's Chasing Whom?" (July 18, 2006) and "Sudan: Bin Laden's Deal" (August 19, 1996), declassified and released in part on August 5, 2008. In bin Laden's correspondence in English, he signed with "Usamah," such as in the World Islamic Front's statement "Jihad Against Jews and Crusaders" (February 23, 1998). Western news outlets have used both "Usama" and "Osama." For example, the *New York Times* now uses "Osama" but used "Usama" in its earlier coverage, including its reporting on bombings and assassination plots in Jordan, "Jordan Dooms 11 Militants" (December 22, 1994), and a car bombing at a U.S.-Saudi Arabia training center in Riyadh, "Four Confess on Saudi TV to Bombing of U.S. Center" (April 23, 1996).

28. For broader context, see Mark Bowden, *Guests of the Ayatollah: The Iran Hostage Crisis: The First Battle in America's War with Militant Islam* (New York: Grove Press, 2006); Warren Christopher and Paul H. Kreisberg, eds., *American Hostages in Iran: The Conduct of a Crisis* (New Haven: Yale University Press, 1985); and Kermit Roosevelt, *Countercoup: The Struggle for the Control of Iran* (New York: McGraw-Hill, 1979).

29. On the mission, see James H. Kyle, *The Guts to Try: The Untold Story of the Iran Hostage Rescue Mission by the On-Scene Desert Commander*, with John Robert Eidson (New York: Orion Books, 1990); John T. Carney and Benjamin F. Schemmer, *No Room for Error: The Covert Operations of America's Special Tactics Units from Iran to Afghanistan* (New York: Ballantine Books, 2002); Alan Hoe, *The Quiet Professional: Major Richard J. Meadows of the U.S. Army Special Forces* (Lexington, KY: University Press of Kentucky, 2013); Paul B. Ryan, *The Iranian Rescue Mission: Why It Failed* (Annapolis: Naval Institute Press, 1985); Roland D. Guidry, "Eagle Claw Also Known as Desert One . . . A Successful Failed Mission," *Air Commando Journal* 1:3 (Spring 2012): 18–26;

Jim Greely, "Desert One," *Airman Online* (April 2001); Jim Greely, "A Night to Remember," *Airman Online* (May 2001); Gianni Koskinas, "Desert One and Air Force Special Operations Command: A 25-Year Retrospective," *Air & Space Power Journal* (Spring 2005): 113–14; Mark Bowden, "The Desert One Debacle," *The Atlantic* (May 2006): 62–77; Forrest K. Marion, "Air Force Combat Controllers at Desert One, April 24–25, 1980," *Air Power History* (Spring 2009): 47–55; David C. Martin, "Inside the Rescue Mission," *Newsweek* (July 12, 1982). An important new work, published in 2020 by a deputy operations officer and based on his journal, presents further details from conception to execution. See Keith Nightingale, *Phoenix Rising: From the Ashes of Desert One to the Rebirth of U.S. Special Operations* (Havertown, PA: Casemate, 2020). For available U.S. governmental reports, see Harold Brown, Melvin Price, and James L. Holloway, *Iran Hostage Crisis: United States Government Documents* (Washington, DC: U.S. Department of Defense, 1980) and United States Joint Chiefs of Staff, Special Operations Review Group, *Rescue Mission Report* (Washington, DC: U.S. Department of Defense, August 23, 1980), also known as the Holloway Report.

30. For broader analysis, see Abbas Milani, *The Myth of the Great Satan: A New Look at America's Relations with Iran* (Stanford: Hoover Institution Press, 2010). For details of the planning for the second attempt, see Michael Crowley, "The Incredible, Absurd Iranian Rescue Mission That Never Happened," *Time* (November 4, 2013), and Jerry L. Thigpen, *The Praetorian STARShip: The Untold Story of the Combat Talon* (Maxwell Air Force Base, AL: Air Force Press, 2001).

31. See Ronald Reagan, Message to U.S. Congress, *Regarding the President's Anti-Terrorism Legislation* (April 26, 1984); Ronald Reagan, *National Security Decision Directive Number 38: Staffing at Diplomatic Missions and Their Constituent Posts* (June 2, 1982); Mattia Toaldo, "The Reagan Administration and the Origins of the War on Terror: Lebanon and Libya as Case Studies," *New Middle Eastern Studies* 2 (2012): 1–17; George P. Shultz, *Turmoil and Triumph: Diplomacy, Power, and the Victory of the American Ideal* (New York: Charles Scribner's Sons, 1993); George P. Shultz, "Terrorism: The Challenge to the Democracies," Speech to Jonathan Institute Conference (June 24, 1984); Richard L.

Armitage, assistant secretary of defense, "To Combat Terrorism and Other Forms of Unconventional Warfare," Testimony to the Committee on Armed Services, U.S. Senate, 99th Congress (August 5, 1986); Caspar W. Weinberger, *Fighting for Peace: Seven Critical Years in the Pentagon* (New York: Warner Books, 1990); Caspar W. Weinberger, *In the Arena: A Memoir of the Twentieth Century,* with Gretchen Roberts (Washington, DC: Regency, 2001); and Alan Ned Sabrosky, *The Recourse to War: An Appraisal of the Weinberger Doctrine* (Carlisle, PA: Strategic Studies Institute of the U.S. Army War College, June 23, 1989). See also David C. Martin and John Walcott, *Best Laid Plans: The Inside Story of America's War Against Terrorism* (New York: Harper & Row, 1988); and Steven Emerson, *Secret Warriors: Inside the Covert Military Operations of the Reagan Era* (New York: Putnam, 1988). See the Holloway Report (1980) for a discussion of the national need for the counterterrorism—and hostage-rescue—capability in the context of Operation Eagle Claw and future scenarios: "the concept of a small clandestine operation was valid and consistent with national policy objectives. It offered the best chance of getting the hostages out alive and the least danger of a war with Iran."

32. At the time of this visit, the president, White House senior advisers, congressional leaders, and military officers were conducting extensive reviews of U.S. defense policy as it related to the global counterterrorism campaign, known for several years as the global war on terror. For examples of the types of appraisals then circulating, see Anthony H. Cordesman, *The Obama Administration: From Ending Two Wars to Engagement in Five—with the Risk of a Sixth* (Washington, DC: Center for Strategic and International Studies, 2014); Martha Crenshaw, *The Consequences of Counterterrorism* (New York: Russell Sage Foundation, 2010); Audrey Cronin, *How Terrorism Ends: Understanding the Demise and Decline of Terrorism Campaigns* (Princeton: Princeton University Press, 2010); Charles D. Allen, "The Impact of a Decade at War," *Armed Forces Journal* (May 2011): 14–36; and Bob Woodward, *Obama's Wars* (New York: Simon & Schuster, 2010). The White House's *National Strategy for Counterterrorism* (Washington, DC, 2011) lays out the considerations in a formal presentation, and President Obama gave several speeches on the issues at hand, including "Remarks by the President on National Security," delivered at the National Archives (Washington, DC, May 21, 2009); "Remarks by the President," delivered at the National Defense University (Washington, DC, May 23, 2013); "Remarks by the President on a New Strategy for Afghanistan and Pakistan," delivered at the Eisenhower Executive Office Building (Washington, DC, March 27, 2009); and "Remarks by the President in Address to the Nation on the Way Forward in Afghanistan and Pakistan" delivered at the U.S. Military Academy (West Point, December 1, 2009).

2 COMMANDER'S INTRODUCTION

1. Admiral Olson expressed the chapter's opening quote—"The public recognition is for our ability to put the habeas grabus on a terrorist in the middle of the night"—on our visit to MacDill. In addition, the commander used similar words in public remarks a few weeks later, at the Center for Strategic and International Studies (CSIS) in Washington, DC, on April 1, 2010, in the context of Coalition and partner forces in combat in Afghanistan: "It looks very much like the direct approach when they burst into a room in the middle of the night to put the habeas grabus on the bad guys, separate the good from the bad." Two years earlier, on March 3, 2008, in public remarks at the Center for New American Security in Washington, DC, speaking about the expertise of the force, the commander had remarked that "the breadth of what Special Operations provides and [is] really at both ends. There's still nobody better at surgical operations to put the habeas grabus on a terrorist in the middle of the night, but there's also nobody better in going out there and working one-on-one with the tribal leaders in order to encourage the kind of activity in the neighborhood that's helpful to them and to us."

2. Several publications provide overviews and analyses of U.S. Special Operations in this period. The Congressional Research Service reports by Andrew Feickert, titled *U.S. Special Operations Forces: Background and Issues for Congress*, appear with regularity, and outline current issues and recent trends. An important white paper on these challenges is by Michele L. Malvesti, *Time for Action: Redefining SOF Missions and Activities*

(Washington, DC: Center for a New American Security, 2009), and is expanded in the following year, in the publication by Michele L. Malvesti, *To Serve the Nation: U.S. Special Operations Forces in an Era of Persistent Conflict* (Washington, DC: Center for a New American Security, 2010). A number of publications by Linda Robinson are relevant, including "The Future of U.S. Special Operations Forces," Report No. 66 (New York: Council on Foreign Relations, 2013) and *One Hundred Victories: Special Ops and the Future of American Warfare* (New York: Public Affairs, 2013). The Center for Strategic and Budgetary Assessments (CSBA) provides related works, one by Jim Thomas and Chris Dougherty, *Beyond the Ramparts: The Future of U.S. Special Operations Forces* (Washington, DC: CSBA, 2013), and another by Robert C. Martinage, "Special Operations Forces: Future Challenges and Opportunities," in *Strategy for the Long Haul* (Washington, DC: CSBA, 2008). The extensive work of Christopher J. Lamb and David Tucker provides deep insights into U.S. Special Operations in a number of publications, including their book *U.S. Special Operations Forces* (New York: Columbia University Press, 2007) as well as their reports, notably "Restructuring Special Operations Forces for Emerging Threats," in *Strategic Forum* 219 (Washington, DC: Institute for National Strategic Studies, 2006): 1–6. For aspects of specific areas of U.S. Special Operations, see also Hy S. Rothstein and John Arquilla, eds., *Afghan Endgames: Strategy and Policy Choices for America's Longest War* (Washington, DC: Georgetown University Press, 2012); Christopher J. Lamb, *Review of Psychological Operations: Lessons Learned from Recent Operational Experience* (Washington, DC: National Defense University Press, 2005); Malcolm Brailey, *Not Many Jobs Take a Whole Army: Special Operations Forces and the Revolution in Military Affairs* (Singapore: Institute of Defence and Strategic Studies, March 2004); and Anna Simons and David Tucker, "United States Special Operations Forces and the War on Terrorism," *Small Wars and Insurgencies* 14:1 (Spring 2003): 77–91.

3. For discussion of the priorities of U.S. Special Operations before 2001, see the extensive research of John M. Collins, including *Special Operations Forces: An Assessment* (Washington, DC: National Defense University

Press, 1994); "Where Are the Special Operations Forces?" *Joint Forces Quarterly* 2 (Autumn 1993): 7–16; "Roles and Functions of U.S. Special Operations Forces," *Special Warfare* 6 (July 1993): 22–27; "Special Operations Forces in Peacetime," *Special Warfare* 13:1 (Winter 2000): 2–7; and *U.S. and Soviet Special Operations* (Washington, DC: Library of Congress, 1986); as well as his 2008 speech looking back on the making of these analyses, published as an article, "The Warlord on Special Operations Forces," *War on the Rocks,* warontherocks.com/2013/09/warlord-on-special-operations-forces/ (September 10, 2013). See also the U.S. Government Accounting Office reports, including *Special Operations Forces: Opportunities to Preclude Overuse and Misuse,* No. NSI-AD-97-85 (Washington, DC: Government Printing Office, May 1997); *Special Operations Forces: Force Structure and Readiness Issues: Report to the Chairman, Committee on Armed Services, House of Representatives* (Washington, DC: U.S. General Accounting Office, 1994); and *Defense Reorganization: DoD's Efforts to Streamline the Special Operations Command: Briefing Report to the Chairman, Subcommittee on Armed Services, House of Representatives* (Washington, DC, and Gaithersburg, MD: U.S. General Accounting Office, 1990). For in-depth treatments of the historical and strategic aspects of U.S. Special Operations, see Frank R. Barnett, Hugh B. Tovar, and Richard H. Shultz, Jr., eds., *Special Operations in U.S. Strategy* (Washington, DC: National Defense University Press, 1984); H. T. Hayden, *Shadow War: Special Operations and Low Intensity Conflict* (Vista, CA: Pacific Aero Press, 1992); Ross S. Kelly, *Special Operations and National Purpose* (Lexington, MA: Lexington Books, 1989); Linda Robinson, *Masters of Chaos: The Secret History of the Special Forces* (New York: Public Affairs, 2004); Richard H. Shultz, Jr., Robert L. Pfaltzgraff and W. Bradley Stock, eds., *Special Operations Forces: Roles and Missions in the Aftermath of the Cold War* (Collingdale, PA: Diane Publishing Company, 1996); John M. Collins, Frederick Hamerman, and James P. Seevers, *America's Small Wars: Lessons for the Future* (Washington, DC: Brassey's, 1991); and Loren B. Thompson, *Low-Intensity Conflict: The Pattern of Warfare in the Modern World* (Lexington, MA: Lexington Books, 1989). For books with historical depth, see John Arquilla, *From Troy to Entebbe: Special Operations in Ancient and Modern Times* (Lanham, MD: University Press of America, 1996);

Max Boot, *The Savage Wars of Peace: Small Wars and the Rise of American Power* (New York: Basic Books, 2003); Bruce Hoffman, *Commando Raids, 1946–1983* (Santa Monica: RAND Corporation, 1985); Bruce Hoffman, *Inside Terrorism* (New York: Columbia University Press, 2006); James D. Kiras, *Special Operations and Strategy: From World War II to the War on Terrorism* (New York: Routledge, 2006); Derek Leebaert, *To Dare and to Conquer: Special Operations and the Destiny of Nations, from Achilles to Al Qaeda* (New York: Little, Brown, 2006); Edward Luttwak et al., *A Systematic Review of "Commando" Special Operations, 1939–1980* (Potomac, MD: C & L Associates, 1982); William H. McRaven, *Spec Ops: Case Studies in Special Operations Warfare: Theory and Practice* (Novato, CA: Presidio, 1995); and John M. Mitchell, *Roles for Special Operations Forces in the 1990's* (Carlisle, PA: U.S. Army War College, 1993).

4. Dennis C. Blair, director of the Office of National Intelligence, and Ronald L. Burgess, Jr., director of the Defense Intelligence Agency, *Annual Threat Assessment of the U.S. Intelligence Community for the Senate Select Committee on Intelligence* (February 2, 2010).

5. Admiral Mike Mullen, then chairman of the Joint Chiefs of Staff, asserted that "the single biggest threat to our national security is our debt," while touring the Midwest on his Conversations with the Country Tour in August 2010, noting that the interest payments were equivalent to the annual budget of the U.S. Department of Defense. General Martin E. Dempsey followed him in that role, and soon after Dempsey emphasized the role of "the two heavyweights, that is Russia and China" in U.S. military policy and strategy. See his remarks at the Atlantic Council in Washington, DC, on May 14, 2014, and as further discussed in Martin E. Dempsey, *Chairman's Risk Assessment* (Washington, DC: U.S. Department of Defense, July 6, 2014). His successor, Joseph F. Dunford, Jr., in his nomination hearing before the U.S. Senate Armed Services Committee on July 9, 2015, testified about the reemergence of state threats: "If you want to talk about a nation that could pose an existential threat to the United States, I'd have to point to Russia. And if you look at their behavior, it's nothing short of alarming."

6. See Keith B. Richburg, *Out of America: A Black Man Confronts Africa* (New York: Basic Books, 1997), as well as his reporting for the *Washington*

Post throughout this period, including "Peace Effort in Somalia Meets Initial Failure. One Feuding Side Rebuffs U.N. Mediation" (January 4, 1992), in which he notes, "Somalia has ceased to exist . . . And right now, nobody cares"; and "In Somali Capital, Shrapnel Reigns; Civilians Pay Heavy Price in Artillery Duel for Power" (January 11, 1992), in which he writes, "People here talk of the shelling . . . like people elsewhere might discuss the rain: not too heavy today, but likely to pick up again tomorrow." Important articles by Richburg after the raids by U.S. Special Operations include "Aideed Exploited U.N.'s Failure to Prepare" (December 5, 1993) and "U.S. Envoy to Somalia Urged Policy Shift Before 18 GIs Died" (November 11, 1993).

7. See the *International Review of the Red Cross,* at that time published every two months, for updates on conditions in Somalia; Nos. 292–97 offer the complete set of briefings in 1993.

8. See Richburg (January 11, 1992).

9. See address to the nation by President George H. W. Bush on December 4, 1992, which followed U.N. Security Council Resolution 794, adopted unanimously on December 3, 1992. In President Bush's letter to U.N. Secretary General Boutros Boutros-Ghali, he wrote that the objective of sending forces forward was "to create security conditions which will permit the feeding of the Somali people." Bush publicly announced the U.S. intention of launching Operation Restore Hope in Somalia on Thanksgiving Day.

10. The Foreign Affairs Oral History Project of the Association for Diplomatic Studies and Training has extensive interviews of embassy personnel in Somalia. In particular, see the interview of Ambassador Smith Hempstone by Charles Stuart Kennedy on May 6, 1998, as well as Hempstone's memoir, *Rogue Ambassador: An African Memoir* (Sewanee, TN: University of the South Press, 1997). See also the interview of Ambassador Stevenson McIlvaine, on the ground in Mogadishu in 1993, by Charles Stuart Kennedy on September 23, 2003: "The logistics were daunting. This was a country in civil war. You couldn't find any airport. We managed to get some food in, but the frustrations built because the food kept being stolen by gunmen of various militia factions and you couldn't keep anybody on the ground safe without some sort of security. There was no security. You couldn't

make sure the food got to where it was supposed to get to. That frustration built. Working with the Pentagon, we organized a humanitarian relief effort, flying out of Mombasa, Kenya, C130s onto Somali airstrips to unload food. But here, too, as soon as the food was unloaded, the gunmen rode in on their technicals, which are jeeps with machine guns mounted in the back, and stole the food."

11. See interview of Stevenson McIlvaine by Charles Stuart Kennedy, The Foreign Affairs Oral History Project of the Association for Diplomatic Studies and Training (September 23, 2003).

12. See *United States Forces: After Action Report Somalia* and *Historical Overview: The United States Army in Somalia, 1992–1994* (Washington, DC: U.S. Army Center of Military History, 2003): "Coalition forces including large components from France, Italy, Belgium, Morocco, Australia, Pakistan, Malaysia, and Canada soon joined U.S. forces. During the course of RESTORE HOPE, some 38,000 soldiers from 23 different nations and representatives from 49 different humanitarian relief operations worked together to put food into the mouths of the starving people of Somalia."

13. See Matt Bryden and Jeremy Brickhill, "Disarming Somalia: Lessons in Stabilisation from a Collapsed State," *Conflict, Security and Development* 10:2 (2010): 239–62.

14. See U.N. Security Council, *Commission of Inquiry Report, Pursuant to Resolution 885* (1993) to investigate attacks on UNOSOM personnel, presented in New York on February 24, 1994; United Nations, Statement by the President of the Security Council on the Conditions for the Deployment and Renewal of Peacekeeping Operations, New York (May 3, 1994). For some analysis into conditions leading up to these events, see United Nations, *100-Day Action Programme for Accelerated Humanitarian Assistance for Somalia* (October 6, 1992) and Jonathan T. Dworken, "Restore Hope Coordinating Relief Operations," *Joint Forces Quarterly* 8 (Summer 1995): 14–20.

15. See Ann Wright, "Legal and Human Rights Aspects of UNOSOM Military Operations," Memorandum to the Special Representative of the Secretary General from UNOSOM Justice Division (July 13, 1993). See also Keith B. Richburg, "U.N. Helicopter Assault in Somalia Targeted Aideed's Top Commanders," *Washington Post* (July 16, 1993),

in which Howe explains, "We knew what we were hitting. It was well-planned." See Associated Press, "U.N. Raids Somali Clan's Base; Mob Kills at Least 2 Journalists," in which Major Leann Swieczkowski said that "damage was confined to the compound, where American infantrymen found radios, documents and small arms." See Robert F. Baumann and Lawrence A. Yates, with Versalle F. Washington, *My Clan Against the World: U.S. and Coalition Forces in Somalia, 1992–1994* (Fort Leavenworth, KS: Combat Studies Institute Press, 2003).

16. Donatella Lorch, "Four Friends," *New York Times* (August 22, 1993).

17. For shifting uses of military forces in conflict prevention and regional policing, see Robert M. Perito, *Where Is the Lone Ranger When We Need Him? America's Search for a Postconflict Stability Force* (Washington, DC: U.S. Institute of Peace Press, 2004), and Peter Andreas, *Policing the Globe: Criminalization and Crime Control in International Relations* (Oxford: Oxford University Press, 2006).

18. The official is quoted in Keith B. Richburg, "U.N.'s Somalia Quandary," *Washington Post* (August 8, 1993).

19. See Captain James O. Lechner, *A Monograph of Combat Operations in Mogadishu, Somalia, Conducted by Task Force Ranger* (Fort Benning, GA: U.S. Army, September 19, 1994).

20. See Paul Watson, *Where War Lives: A Journey into the Heart of War* (Toronto: McLelland and Stewart, 2007); his NPR *Fresh Air* interview on August 27, 2007; and his photojournalism for the *Toronto Star* in 1993.

21. See the Harmony Project of Combating Terrorism Center, West Point, for documents collected on the workings of al-Qaeda and affiliates, including primary source documents on Somalia, 1993 (e.g., the explanations of Saif al-Adel of their activities on the streets of Mogadishu), as well as analytical reports on these captured and covered materials that place this information in the overall context of the battlefield. See also Dominique Christian Mollard, "Somalia: A Reporter's Search for Al Qaeda," on PBS *Frontline* "Rough Cuts" series (February 16, 2007).

22. See interview with Michael J. Durant by John D. Gresham, in *The Year in Special Operations* (Tampa: Faircount Media, 2008).

23. Their operations have been covered in great detail, most prominently in Mark Bowden's reporting for the *Philadelphia Inquirer* and later as a

book, *Black Hawk Down: A Story of Modern War* (New York: Atlantic Monthly Press, 1999). For accounts of those months, see Michael J. Durant and Steven Hartov, *In the Company of Heroes* (New York: G. P. Putnam's Sons, 2003); Clifford E. Day, *Critical Analysis on the Defeat of Task Force Ranger* (Montgomery, AL: Air Command and Staff College, March 1997); Thomas DiTomasso, *Battle of the Black Sea: Bravo Company, 3rd Ranger Battalion, 75th Ranger Regiment, 3–4 October 1993* (Fort Benning, GA: U.S. Army, 1994); M. Eversmann and D. Schilling, eds., *The Battle of Mogadishu: Firsthand Accounts from the Men of Task Force Ranger* (New York: Presidio Press, 2006); James T. Faust, *Task Force Ranger in Somalia: Isaiah 6:8* (Carlisle, PA: U.S. Army War College, 1999); Charles P. Ferry, "Mogadishu, October 1993: Personal Account of a Rifle Company XO," *Infantry* (September/October, 1994): 23–31; Joe Frescura, *Mechanized Platoon and Company Operations in Somalia, October 1993 to March 1994* (Fort Benning, GA: U.S. Army, 1996); Elroy Garcia, "We Did Right That Night (Firefight in Somalia on 3–4 Oct 93)," *Soldiers* 49 (February 1994): 17–20; Mark A. B. Hollis, "Platoon Under Fire," *Infantry* 88:1 (January 1998): 27–34; Forrest L. Marion, "'Heroic Things': Air Force Special Tactics Personnel at Mogadishu, October 3–4, 1993," *Air Power History* 60:3 (Fall 2013): 32–43; Larry D. Perino, *Battle of the Black Sea* (Fort Benning, GA: U.S. Army, 1994); and L. A. Rysewyk, *Experiences of Executive Officer from Bravo Company, 3rd Battalion, 75th Ranger Regiment and Task Force Ranger during the Battle of the Black Sea on 3–4 October, 1993 in Mogadishu, Somalia* (Fort Benning, GA: U.S. Army Infantry School, May 1994). See also Tom Donnelly and Katherine McIntire, "Rangers in Somalia: Anatomy of a Firefight," *Army Times* (November 12, 1993): 14–16, 18; Marshall V. Ecklund, "Analysis of Operation Gothic Serpent: TF Ranger in Somalia," *Special Warfare* 16:4 (May 2004): 38; and USSOCOM History and Research Office, Naval Special Warfare Forces in Somalia, 1992–1995 (Tampa: U.S. Special Operations Command, 2001).

24. John L. Hirsch and Robert B. Oakley, *Somalia and Operation Restore Hope: Reflections on Peacemaking and Peacekeeping* (Washington, DC: U.S. Institute for Peace Press, 1995); and Robert B. Oakley, "An Envoy's Perspective," *Joint Forces Quarterly* 2 (Autumn 1993): 44–55.

25. For analysis of the Somalia aftermath, see Kenneth C. Allard, "Lessons Unlearned: Somalia and Joint Doctrine," *Joint Forces Quarterly* 9 (Autumn 1995): 105–9; Kenneth C. Allard, *Somalia Operations: Lessons Learned* (Washington, DC: National Defense University Press, 1995); John R. Bolton, "Wrong Turn in Somalia," *Foreign Affairs* 73:1 (January/February 1994): 56–67; Walter Clarke and Jeffrey Herbst, "Somalia and the Future of Humanitarian Intervention," *Foreign Affairs* 75:2 (March/April 1996): 70–85; Walter Clarke and Jeffrey Herbst, eds., *Learning from Somalia: The Lessons of Armed Humanitarian Intervention* (Boulder, CO: Westview, 1997); Christopher J. Lamb with Nicholas Moon, "Somalia: Did Leaders or the System Fail?" in *Case Studies,* Volume 1: *Project on National Security Reform* (Washington, DC, 2008); Robert Patman, *Strategic Shortfall: The Somalia Syndrome and the March to 9/11* (Santa Barbara: Praeger Security International, 2010); Jonathan Stevenson, *Losing Mogadishu: Testing U.S. Policy in Somalia* (Annapolis: Naval Institute Press, 1995); and Karin Von Hippel, *Democracy by Force: U.S. Military Intervention in the Post–Cold War World* (Cambridge: Cambridge University Press, 2000).

26. See President Bill Clinton's address to the nation on October 7, 1993 for the announcement and his "Message to the Congress Transmitting a Report on Somalia" on October 13, 1993, as well as Public Law 103-139 on November 11, 1993 for the update to U.S. combat operations in Somalia. Regarding "backing out of this mess," and the broader context of that assessment, see interview with M. A. Wright by Charles Stuart Kennedy, as part of the Foreign Affairs Oral History Project of the Association for Diplomatic Studies and Training (May 11, 2003). See John Warner and Carl Levin, "Review of the Circumstances Surrounding the Ranger Raid on October 3–4, 1993 in Mogadishu, Somalia," *U.S. Senate Armed Services Committee,* 104th Congress, First Session (September 29, 1995), which was an extensive inquiry, including hundreds of interviews with both U.S. and Somali forces.

27. See Anthony Zinni's PBS *Frontline* interview "Ambush in Mogadishu," discussing the period when he was director of operations for Unified Task Force, Somalia (UNITAF), from November 1992 until May 1993.

In October 1994, Zinni was the assistant to Ambassador Oakley, then the special envoy in Somalia, in the negotiations with Aidid for the release of captured pilot Michael Durant.

28. For analysis of these shifts in civilian decision-making, and the consequences of these changes, see Martin Binkin, *Who Will Fight the Next War? The Changing Face of the American Military* (Washington, DC: Brookings Institution, 1993); Rod Lenahan, *Crippled Eagle: A Historical Perspective of U.S. Special Operations, 1976–1996* (Charleston, SC: Narwhal Press, 1998); Eric V. Larson and Bogdan Savych, *American Public Support for U.S. Military Operations from Mogadishu to Baghdad* (Santa Monica: RAND Corporation, 2005); Gerard Prunier, *The Rwanda Crisis: History of a Genocide* (New York: Columbia University Press, 1995); and Philip Gourevitch, *We Wish to Inform You That Tomorrow We Will Be Killed with Our Families: Stories from Rwanda* (New York: Farrar, Straus and Giroux, 1998). For some historical context, see Andrew Feickert and Stephen Daggett, *A Historical Perspective on "Hollow Forces"* (Washington, DC: Congressional Research Service, January 13, 2012). For analysis of some operations that proceeded in the nineties, see Thomas K. Adams, *U.S. Special Operations Forces in Action: The Challenge of Unconventional Warfare* (London: Frank Cass, 1998); Daniel P. Bolger, *Savage Peace: Americans at War in the 1990s* (Novato, CA: Presidio, 1995); William J. Flavin, *Concept for the Strategic Use of Special Operations Forces in the 1990s and Beyond* (Carlisle, PA: U.S. Army War College, 1991); Leslie L. Fuller, *Role of United States Special Operations Forces in Peace Operations* (Carlisle, PA: U.S. Army War College, 1996); U.S. Special Operations Command, *Special Operations in Peace and War* (Tampa: U.S. Special Operations Command, 1996); and Carl E. Vuono, *A Strategic Force for the 1990s and Beyond* (Washington, DC: U.S. Department of the Army, January 1990). For regional and country-specific examples, see discussions of U.S. operations in the Gulf in Christopher P. Costa, "Changing Gears: Special Operations Intelligence Support to Operation Provide Comfort," *Military Intelligence* 18:4 (October/December 1992): 24–28; Lawrence Freedman and Efraim Karsh, *The Gulf Conflict, 1990–1991: Diplomacy and War in the New World Order* (Princeton: Princeton University Press,

1993); James N. Pruitt, *Desert Fury: Special Operations Command* (New York: Berkley Books, 1991); and Gordon W. Rudd, *Humanitarian Intervention: Assisting the Iraqi Kurds in Operation Provide Comfort, 1991* (Washington, DC: U.S. Department of the Army, 2004). In Haiti, see John R. Ballard, *Upholding Democracy: The United States Military Campaign in Haiti, 1994–1997* (Westport, CT: Praeger, 1998); and Bob Shacochis, *The Immaculate Invasion* (New York: Viking, 1999). In Colombia, see Mark Bowden, *Killing Pablo: The Hunt for the World's Greatest Outlaw* (New York: Atlantic Monthly Press, 2001); Janice Burton, "ARSOF in Colombia: 50 Years of Persistent Engagement," *Special Warfare Magazine* 25:4 (October/December 2012): 24–33; and Mark A. Haselton, *The Role of Special Operations Forces in Counter-Narcotic Operations* (Fort Leavenworth, KS: U.S. Army Command and General Staff College, 1990). In the Balkans, see Charles J. Dunlap, "Special Operations Forces After Kosovo," *Joint Forces Quarterly* 28 (Spring/Summer 2001): 7–12; Julian Borger, *The Butcher's Trail: How the Search for Balkan War Criminals Became the World's Most Successful Manhunt* (New York: Other Press, 2016), among others. For a comparison of the post-Somalia period to the previous decade, see analysis of U.S. Special Operations Forces in El Salvador, in Max G. Manwaring and Court Prisk, *El Salvador at War: An Oral History of Conflict from the 1979 Insurrection to the Present* (Washington, DC: National Defense University Press, 1988); and in the Gulf, see John W. Partin, *SOF in Operation Earnest Will: Prime Chance I* (Tampa: USSOCOM History & Research Office, 1998); and Harold Lee Wise, *Inside the Danger Zone: The U.S. Military in the Persian Gulf, 1987–1988* (Annapolis: Naval Institute Press, 2007).

29. Colin Powell, *My American Journey,* with Joseph E. Persico (New York: Random House, 1995).

30. Mark Bowden, "The Final Chapter: Freeing a Pilot, Ending a Mission," *Philadelphia Inquirer* (December 14, 1997), for interview of General Colin Powell: "No one expected a large number of soldiers to get killed. Is 18 a large number? People didn't start noticing in Vietnam until it was 500 a week." For background on special operations during the Vietnam War, see Robert M. Gillespie, *Black Ops, Vietnam: The*

Operational History of MACVSOG (Annapolis: Naval Institute Press, 2011); Charles Tustin Kamps, "Operation Kingpin: The Son Tay Raid," *Air & Space Power Journal* (February 2006); Harold G. Moore and Joseph L. Galloway, *We Were Soldiers Once . . . and Young: la Drang, the Battle That Changed the War in Vietnam* (New York: Random House, 1992); Benjamin F. Schemmer, *The Raid* (New York: Harper & Row, 1976); and Richard H. Shultz, Jr., *The Secret War Against Hanoi: Kennedy's and Johnson's Use of Spies, Saboteurs* and *Covert Warriors in North Vietnam* (New York: HarperCollins, 1999).

31. See quote by Walter Slocombe in Richard H. Shultz, Jr., "Showstoppers: Nine Reasons Why We Never Sent Our Special Operations Forces After al Qaeda Before 9/11," *Weekly Standard* 9:19 (January 26, 2004): 25–33.

32. For discussion, see William V. O'Brien, "Special Operations in the 1980s: American Moral, Legal, Political and Cultural Constraints," in *Special Operations in U.S. Strategy*, Frank R. Barnett, B. Hugh Tovar, and Richard H. Shultz, Jr., eds., (Washington, DC: National Defense University Press, 1984); Colin S. Gray, "Handfuls of Heroes on Desperate Ventures: When Do Special Operations Succeed?" *Parameters* 29 (Spring 1999): 2–24; Colin S. Gray, *Special Operations: What Succeeds and Why? Lessons of Experience, Phase I* (Fairfax, VA: National Institute for Public Policy, 1992); Henry L. T. Koren, Jr., "Congress Wades into Special Operations," *Parameters* 18 (December 1988): 62–74; and Michael McClintock, *Instruments of Statecraft: U.S. Guerrilla Warfare, Counterinsurgency and Counterterrorism, 1940–1990* (New York: Pantheon, 1992).

33. The quote by General George Decker appears in several monographs on counterinsurgency, including Douglas Porch, *Counterinsurgency: Exposing the Myths of the New Way of War* (Cambridge: Cambridge University Press, 2013), and is said to have been stated to President Kennedy in the context of fighting in Vietnam. Others, though, have pointed out that a U.S. special operator could also be thought of as akin to a SWAT team inside a police department, a specialized unit that is both apart from and part of a large force. For further context, see Christopher Andrew, *For the President's Eyes Only: Secret Intelligence*

and the American Presidency from Washington to Bush (New York: HarperCollins, 1995); Jack Goldsmith, *The Terror Presidency: Law and Judgment Inside the Bush Administration* (New York: W. W. Norton, 2007); Rhodri Jeffreys-Jones, *The CIA and American Democracy* (New Haven: Yale University Press, 1989); John Prados, *President's Secret Wars* (New York: Quill, 1988); and John Yoo, *War by Other Means: An Insider's Account of the War on Terror* (New York: Atlantic Monthly Press, 2006).

34. On some operations that impacted the use of these forces, see the fights over the *Mayaguez*, Grenada, and Panama. Regarding the *Mayaguez* incident (1975), see John Francis Guilmartin, *A Very Short War: The* Mayaguez *and the Battle of Koh Tang* (College Station, TX: Texas A&M University Press, 1995); Christopher J. Lamb, *Belief Systems and Decision-Making in the* Mayaguez *Crisis* (Gainesville, FL: University of Florida Press, 1989); Gregory D. Miller, "The *Mayaguez* Incident: A Model Case Study for PME," *Joint Forces Quarterly* 94 (Third Quarter 2019): 36–43; Roy Rowan, *The Four Days of* Mayaguez (New York: W. W. Norton, 1975); and Ralph Wetterhahn, *The Last Battle: The* Mayaguez *Incident and the End of the Vietnam War* (New York: Carroll & Graf, 2001). Regarding Grenada (1983), see Mark Adkin, *Urgent Fury: The Battle for Grenada,* Issues in Low-Intensity Conflict Series (Lexington, MA: Lexington Books, 1989); Daniel P. Bolger, "Special Operations and the Grenada Campaign," *Parameters* (December 1988): 49–61; Richard P. Cronin, *Grenada: Issues Concerning the Use of U.S. Forces,* Issue Brief No. IB83170 (Washington, DC: Congressional Research Service, 1983); Hugh O'Shaughnessy, *Grenada: An Eyewitness Account of the U.S. Invasion and the Caribbean History That Provoked It* (New York: Dodd, Mead, 1984); Bruce R. Pirnie, *Operation Urgent Fury: The United States Army in Joint Operations* (Washington, DC: U.S. Army Center of Military History, 1986); Edgar F. Raines, *The Rucksack War: U.S. Army Operational Logistics in Grenada, 1983* (Washington, DC: U.S. Army Center of Military History, 2010); and Paul Seabury and Walter A. McDougall, *The Grenada Papers* (San Francisco: Institute for Contemporary Studies, 1984). Regarding Panama (1989), see Center for Army Lessons Learned, *Operation Just Cause: Lessons Learned* (Fort Leavenworth, KS: U.S. Army Combined Arms Command, 1990); Ronald H. Cole, *Operation Just Cause: The Planning and Execution of Joint Operations in Panama, February 1988–January 1990* (Washington, DC: Joint History Office, Office of the Chairman of the Joint Chiefs of Staff, 1995); Ronald H. Cole, *Operation Urgent Fury: The Planning and Execution of Joint Operations in Grenada, October 12–November 2, 1983* (Washington, DC: U.S. Government Printing Office, 1997); Stacey Hagemeister and Jenny Solon, *Operation Just Cause: Lessons Learned*, Three Volumes (Fort Leavenworth, KS: Center for Army Lessons Learned, 1987–1990); Malcolm McConnell, *Just Cause: The Real Story of America's High-Tech Invasion of Panama* (New York: St. Martin's Press, 1991); Kurt Muse and John Gilstrap, *Six Minutes to Freedom* (New York: Citadel Press, 2007); Steven W. Senkovich, *From Port Salines to Panama City: The Evolution of Command and Control in Contingency Operations* (Fort Leavenworth, KS: U.S. Army Command and General Staff College, 1990); Jennifer M. Taw, *Operation Just Cause: Lessons for Operations Other Than War* (Santa Monica: RAND Corporation, 1996); and Lawrence A. Yates, *The U.S. Military Intervention in Panama: Origins, Planning* and *Crisis Management, June 1987–December 1989* (Washington, DC: U.S. Army Center of Military History, 2008).

35. Contemporary Operations Studies Team, *Interview with Jay E. Hines* (Fort Leavenworth, KS: Combat Studies Institute, January 11, 2006).

36. See Ivo H. Daalder and Michael E. O'Hanlon, *Winning Ugly: NATO's War to Save Kosovo* (Washington, DC: Brookings Institution Press, 2000); Tim Judah, *Kosovo: War and Revenge* (New Haven: Yale University Press, 2002); Alex Krongard, Linda Herlocker, and John W. Partin, *Operation Firm Response NEO in the Congo* (Tampa: U.S. Special Operations Command, 1997); Christopher J. Lamb, "Perspectives on Emerging SOF Roles and Missions," *Special Warfare* 8 (July 1995): 2–10; Benjamin S. Lambeth, *NATO's Air War for Kosovo: A Strategic and Operational Assessment* (Santa Monica: RAND Corporation, 2001); Steven Metz, *Disaster and Intervention in Sub-Saharan Africa: Learning from Rwanda* (Carlisle, PA: U.S. Army War College, 1994); Craig R.

Nation, *War in the Balkans, 1991–2002* (Carlisle, PA: U.S. Army War College, 2003); Sabrina P. Ramet, *Thinking About Yugoslavia: Scholarly Debates About the Yugoslav Breakup and the Wars in Bosnia and Kosovo* (Cambridge: Cambridge University Press, 2005); Richard H. Shultz, Jr., "Showstoppers: Nine Reasons Why We Never Sent Our Special Operations Forces After al Qaeda Before 9/11," *Weekly Standard* 9:19 (January 26, 2004): 25–33; Richard H. Shultz, Jr., "Preempting Terrorists Was Not an Option: The Non-Use of SOF CT Units in the 1990s," in Rowan Scarborough, *Rumsfeld's War: The Untold Story of America's Anti-Terror Commander* (Washington, DC: Regnery, 2004); Richard H. Shultz, Jr., Robert L. Pfaltzgraff, and Bradley W. Stock, *Special Operations Forces: Roles and Missions in the Aftermath of the Cold War* (Tampa: U.S. Special Operations Command, 1995); and Susan L. Woodward, *Balkan Tragedy: Chaos and Dissolution After the Cold War* (Washington, DC: Brookings Institution Press, 1995).

37. See Evan Thomas, "A Warrior Elite for the Dirty Jobs," *Time* (January 13, 1986): 17; and Eliot A. Cohen, *Commandos and Politicians: Elite Military Units in Modern Democracies* (Cambridge, MA: Harvard University Press, 1978).

38. For a comparison of the use of conventional and general purpose forces, in contrast to special operations forces, see Norman H. Schwarzkopf, *It Doesn't Take a Hero: The Autobiography of General H. Norman Schwarzkopf*, with Peter Petre (New York: Bantam, 1993).

39. See Jane Corbin, *Al-Qaeda: In Search of the Terror Network that Threatens the World* (New York: Nation Books, 2003). Corbin discusses bin Laden's first interview with a U.S. television network, when he described veterans of the 1980s war in Afghanistan ("They participated with their brothers in Somalia against the American occupation and killed large numbers of them") and with the Pakistani newspaper *Dawn:* "We believe that the United States is a great deal weaker than Russia. We have learned that from our brothers who fought in Somalia . . . They saw wonders about the weakness, feebleness, and cowardliness of the U.S. soldier. Hardly eighteen of them were killed, when they fled in the dark of the night, despite the uproar that was created worldwide about the New World Order."

40. For the fatwa to "fight and slay the pagans," see the World Islamic Front's statement, signed by five individuals including bin Laden, "Jihad Against Jews and Crusaders," February 23, 1998. It builds on bin Laden's earlier release, "Declaration of War Against the Americans Who Occupy the Land of the Two Holy Mosques," August 23, 1996. See also the grand jury's 238-count indictment of October 7, 1998, in the U.S. Southern District of New York, concerning the bombings of U.S. embassies in Kenya and Tanzania on August 7, 1998, which killed 224 people and wounded more than 4,000 people, as well as the training and material support of militants who attacked U.S. soldiers in Mogadishu in October 1993.

41. Billy Waugh, with Tim Keown, *Hunting the Jackal: A Special Forces and CIA Ground Soldier's Fifty-Year Career Hunting America's Enemies* (New York: HarperCollins, 2004). See Gina M. Bennett, "The Wandering Mujahidin: Armed and Dangerous," U.S. Department of State, Bureau of Intelligence and Research (August 21–22, 1993), declassified and released in full on November 23, 2007.

42. Excerpts from the 1998 intelligence community's assessment of al-Qaeda were discussed publicly in 2005, during congressional inquiries into lapses in counterterrorism in advance of the September 11, 2001 terrorist attacks on New York and Washington, DC. Those excerpts included CIA Director George J. Tenet's description of the seriousness of the threat posed by bin Laden and his organization, including "a dedicated al-Qa'ida cell, which met daily" before 9/11. This group was aware of al-Qaeda's "presence in at least 60 countries . . . that the UBL organization has extensively surveyed U.S. targets overseas for vulnerabilities to terrorist attack." Tenet's Memorandum of Notification in December 1998 stated starkly that "we are at war" with al-Qaeda.

43. *United States of America v. Usama bin Laden, et al.*, S(7) 98 Cr. 1023 (LBS), with decision date of November 4, 1998, regarding the bombings of the U.S. embassies in Africa.

44. CIA officer Barbara Sude, lead author of the August 6, 2001 memo, warned of bin Laden's efforts to attack the United States homeland, including "patterns of suspicious activity in this country consistent with preparations for a hijacking of U.S. aircraft." According to the

9/11 Commission report, the August 6 reference was the "36th PDB [Presidential Daily Briefing] item briefed so far that year that related to bin Ladin or al Qaeda, and the first devoted to the possibility of an attack in the United States."

45. Public Law 107-40, the Senate's Joint Resolution 23 and the House's Joint Resolution 64, passed on September 14, 2001. Four days later the president signed the legislation titled "To authorize the use of United States Armed Forces against those responsible for the recent attacks launched against the United States." However, Congress also kept in place the War Powers Resolution of 1973, notably to "insure that the collective judgment of both the Congress and the President will apply to the introduction of United States Armed Forces into hostilities."

46. On the coordination of the Central Intelligence Agency and U.S. Special Operations, among other military-intelligence activities at this time, see Richard C. Gross, *Different Worlds: Unacknowledged Special Operations and Covert Action* (Carlisle, PA: U.S. Army War College, 2009); Mark Mazzetti, *The Way of the Knife: The CIA, a Secret Army* and *a War at the Ends of the Earth* (New York: Penguin, 2013); Michael Morell, *The Great War of Our Time: The CIA's Fight Against Terrorism— From al Qa'ida to ISIS* (New York: Twelve, 2015); Timothy Naftali, *Blind Spot: The Secret History of American Counterterrorism* (New York: Basic Books, 2005); Colonel Kathryn Stone, *'All Necessary Means': Employing CIA Operatives in a Warfighting Role Alongside Special Operations Forces* (Carlisle, PA: U.S. Army War College, 2003); and Amy Zegart, *Spying Blind: The CIA, the FBI and the Origins of 9/11* (Princeton: Princeton University Press, 2007). These developments can be compared to arrangements as described in Jeffrey B. White, "A Different Kind of Threat: Some Thoughts on Irregular War," CIA Center for Intelligence Studies, *Studies in Intelligence* 39:5 (1996); Duane R. Clarridge, *A Spy for All Seasons: My Life in the CIA*, with Digby Diehl (New York: Scribner, 1997); and Bob Woodward, *Veil: The Secret Wars of the CIA, 1981–1987* (New York: Simon and Schuster, 1987), among other works. For on-the-ground reporting of this early fighting, see Jon Lee Anderson, *The Lion's Grave: Dispatches from Afghanistan* (New

York: Grove Press, 2002); Tim Judah, "The Center of the World," *New York Review of Books* (January 17, 2002); Syed Badrul Ashan, "The Afghanistan Story," *The Independent* (June 21, 2002); Kathy Gannon, "Afghanistan Unbound," *Foreign Affairs* 83:3 (May/June 2004): 35–46; and Eliza Grizwold, "Where the Taliban Roam," *Harper's* (September 2003): 57-65.

47. See the *Final Report of the National Commission on Terrorist Attacks upon the United States,* also known as the *9/11 Commission Report* (Washington, DC: Government Printing Office, 2004), and Chapter 10, "Wartime," page 332, which cites the source as a White House transcript of an interview of President Bush by Bob Woodward and Dan Balz on December 20, 2001.

48. See hearing of the U.S. House Armed Services Committee on June 29, 2006, *Assessing U.S. Special Operations Command's Missions and Roles,* as described by Mike Vickers, then director of strategic studies, Center for Strategic and Budgetary Assessments (CSBA). Vickers, a career special operator who had also served with the CIA, was named assistant secretary of defense for special operations, low-intensity conflict, and interdependent capabilities the following year, a position he held until 2011. His memoir, *By Any Means Necessary,* with Knopf, is anticipated in 2021.

49. See some of the shifting post-9/11 meanings applied to "war" in Jeh Johnson's address to the Oxford Union, "The Conflict Against Al Qaeda and Its Affiliates: How Will It End?" on November 30, 2012, when he was general counsel of the U.S. Department of Defense. Most notably, Johnson states that "'war' must be regarded as a finite, extraordinary and unnatural state of affairs. War permits one man—if he is a 'privileged belligerent,' consistent with the laws of war—to kill another. War violates the natural order of things . . . In its twelfth year, we must not accept the current conflict, and all that it entails, as the 'new normal.' Peace must be regarded as the norm toward which the human race continually strives."

50. As the seventh commander of SOCOM, General Bryan "Doug" Brown, put it: "To be the premier team of special warriors, thoroughly prepared, properly equipped, and highly motivated: at the right place,

at the right time, facing the right adversary, leading the Global War on Terrorism, accomplishing strategic objectives of the United States."

51. For discussion of these changes over time, including interpretations of Executive Order No. 12333 ("No person employed by or acting on behalf of the United States Government shall engage in, or conspire to engage in assassination") as excluding military targets during combat, see James E. Baker, *In the Common Defense: National Security Law for Perilous Times* (Cambridge: Cambridge University Press, 2007); Interview of Harold H. Koh, by James Traub, "'War on Terror,' an Insider's View," held at the Carnegie Council for Ethics in International Affairs, New York (February 25, 2014); Conrad C. Crane, "Special Commentary: The Lure of the Strike," *Parameters* 43:2 (Summer 2013): 5–12; Columbia University Law School, *Targeting Operations with Drone Technology: Humanitarian Law Implications* (New York: Human Rights Institute, Columbia University Law School, 2011); Edmund J. Hull, *High-Value Target: Countering al Qaeda in Yemen* (Washington, DC: Potomac Books, 2011); Brian Michael Jenkins, *International Terrorism: A Chronology, 1968–1974* (Santa Monica: RAND Corporation, March 1975); Brian Michael Jenkins, *Should Our Arsenal Against Terrorism Include Assassination?* (Santa Monica: RAND Corporation, 1987); Brian Michael Jenkins, *The Long Shadow of 9/11: America's Response to Terrorism* (Santa Monica: RAND Corporation, 2011); Daniel Klaidman, *Kill or Capture: The War on Terror and the Soul of the Obama Presidency* (New York: Houghton Mifflin Harcourt, 2012); Christopher J. Lamb and Evan Munsing, "Secret Weapon: High-Value Target Teams as an Organizational Innovation," in *Strategic Perspectives* (Washington, DC: National Defense University Press, 2011); Jonathan Masters, *Targeted Killings* (New York: Council on Foreign Relations, 2013); Abu Muqawama, "I Might Need You to Kill: Signatures, Patterns and Alternatives," Center for a New American Security (May 29, 2013); and Douglas T. Stuart, *Creating the National Security State: A History of the Law That Transformed America* (Princeton: Princeton University Press, 2008).

52. For analysis of the intersection of these raids and the increased use of drone strikes, see John B. Bellinger III, "Will Drone Strikes Become

Obama's Guantanamo?" *Washington Post* (October 2, 2011); Daniel Byman, "Why Drones Work: The Case for Washington's Weapon of Choice," *Foreign Affairs* 92:4 (July/August 2013): 32-43; Scott Hickie, Chris Abbott, and Raphaël Zaffran, *Trends in Remote-Control Warfare* (London: Open Briefing, October 2014); Jane Mayer, "The Predator War," *New Yorker* (October 26, 2009): 36–45; and Micah Zenko, *Reforming U.S. Drone Strike Policies,* Report No. 65 (New York: Council on Foreign Relations, 2013).

53. For further discussion, see William M. Thornberry, Jeff Miller, John Kline, et al., *House Committee on Armed Services, Subcommittee on Emerging Threats and Capabilities Holds a Hearing on the Future of Special Operations Forces,* September 22, 2011 (Washington, DC: Government Printing Office, 2011); Eric T. Olson, Keynote Address, Unrestricted Warfare Symposium Proceedings (Washington, DC, March 10, 2008); Eric T. Olson, Remarks at the National Security Leaders Forum (Washington, DC, March 3, 2008); Eric T. Olson, "Statement of Admiral Eric T. Olson to the House Armed Services Subcommittee on Terrorism and Unconventional Threats Regarding the Threats Posed by Al Qaida in the Arabian Peninsula and Other Regions and Special Operations Command's Efforts Against the Enduring Threat" (Washington, DC, January 20, 2010).

3 THE TOUR

1. The chapter's opening quote—"War is not composed of the tactics of targetry"—is from General James N. Mattis, "USJFCOM Commander's Guidance for Effects-Based Operations," *Parameters* (Autumn 2008): 18–25. Mattis further "places a premium on the importance of decentralized command and control as a means for resilient forces to prevail in chaos and degraded information environments."

2. See interview of General Bryan "Doug" Brown by Charles Oldham, in the *Year in Special Operations* (Tampa: Faircount Media, 2008).

3. *Report on Training Equipment Enhancements for the U.S. Special Operations Command* (Washington, DC: U.S. Department of Defense, 1996).

4. On some of these uses by U.S. Special Operations, see National Research Council, Standing Committee on Research Development

and Acquisition Options, *Sensing and Supporting Communications Capabilities for Special Operations Forces Abbreviated Vision* (Washington, DC: National Academies Press, 2009); Michael T. Flynn, Rich Juergens, and Thomas L. Cantrell, "Employing ISR: SOF (Special Operations Forces) Best Practices," *Joint Force Quarterly* 50 (Third Quarter 2010): 56–61; Patrick Tucker, "How Special Operators Are Taking Artificial Intelligence to War," *Defense One* (May 28, 2015); Patrick Tucker, "U.S. Special Forces Are Experimenting with Bug Drones," *Defense One* (May 28, 2015); C. M. Smith, *Detection of Special Operations Forces Using Night Vision Devices* (Oak Ridge, TN: Oak Ridge National Laboratory, September 2001); and Richard Whittle, "Predator's Big Safari," *Mitchell Institute for Airpower Studies*, Paper 7 (August 2011).

5. On the addition of Hellfire missiles to UAVs, see Walter Pincus, "U.S. Strike Kills Six in al-Qaeda," *Washington Post* (November 5, 2002). Lieutenant General James R. Clapper, Jr., described the objective of the unblinking eye, as it later came to be known: "The ultimate ideal here is to have a constant God's-eye view of the battlefield. Anywhere, anytime, all the time." In Steve Komarow, "'Lesser Conflicts': Big Defense Challenge," *USA Today* (November 1, 1994): 8.

6. For example, see Master Sergeant Steve Horton, "Predator Soars to Record Number of Sorties," Release of the 332nd Air Expeditionary Wing Public Affairs (August 9, 2007).

7. For the broader context, see P. W. Singer, *Wired for War: The Robotics Revolution and Conflict in the 21st Century* (New York: Penguin, 2009); and Christian Brose, *The Kill Chain: Defending America in the Future of High-Tech Warfare* (New York: Hachette, 2020). On U.S. Special Operations, more specifically, see U.S. Government Accountability Office and U.S. Congress Senate Committee on Armed Services, Subcommittee on Emerging Threats and Capabilities, *Defense Acquisitions: An Analysis of the Special Operations Command's Management of Weapon System Programs* (Washington, DC: U.S. Government Accountability Office, 2007); Anthony J. Davis, James Guerts, Adam Jay Harrison, et al., "Project Vulcan: Special Ops and the Tech Innovation End Game," *War on the Rocks*, warontherocks.com/2015/04/

project-vulcan-special-ops-and-the-tech-innovation-end-game (April 8, 2015); Rich Tuttle, "Equipping the Tip of the Spear: Entrepreneurial Companies Specialize in Off-the-Shelf Gear for Off-the-Hook Operations," *Defense Standard Quarterly* (Spring 2012): 56–61. On specific projects, examples include David Vergun, "Special Operations Command Seeks Prototypes for 'Iron Man Suit,'" U.S. Army News Service (October 18, 2013); and Patrick Tucker, "Special Operations Are Using Rapid DNA Readers," *Defense One* (May 20, 2015).

8. General Doug Brown noted that in the 9/11 wars, the "bottom line is that Special Operations Forces today are far more capable than ever in history, but not as capable as they will be as we continue to grow and focus on the global war on terror." See also Bryan "Doug" Brown, "U.S. Special Operations Command: Meeting the Challenges of the 21st Century," *Joint Forces Quarterly* 40 (First Quarter 2006): 38–43. For an in-depth analysis, see the U.S. Government Accountability Office, "Defense Acquisitions: An Analysis of Special Operations Command's Management of Weapon System Programs," a Report to the Subcommittee on Emerging Threats and Capabilities, Committee on Armed Services, U.S. Senate, No. GAO-07-620 (June 2007) and an update on the investments in John D. Gresham, "The Title 10 Budget Line: Sharpening the SOF Spear," *Defense Media Network* (May 3, 2010). By comparison, see the capabilities as discussed by his predecessors in the writings of Carl W. Stiner: "Large-Scale War to Forward Presence: USSOCOM's Wide-Ranging Area of Operations," *Army Magazine* 43 (April 1993): 30; "Special Operations Forces: Strategic Potential for the Future," *Special Warfare* 6 (May 1993): 2–9; "Special Ops: Unprecedented Risks, Opportunities Ahead," *Defense* 92 (May/June 1992): 29–38; "Strategic Employment of Special Operations Forces," *Military Review* 71 (June 1991): 2–13; "U.S. Special Operations Forces: A Strategic Perspective," *Parameters* 22 (Summer 1992): 2–13; *End of Tour Report: MacDill AFB, FL: U.S. Special Operations Command* (May 17, 1993); the writings of Lieutenant General Peter J. Schoomaker: "Special Operations: Shaping the Future Force," *Army* 47:4 (April 1997): 12–15; the writings of Henry H. Shelton: "Coming of Age: Theater Special Operations Command," *Joint Forces Quarterly*

14 (Winter 1997): 50–52; "Quality People: Selecting and Developing Members of U.S. SOF," *Special Warfare* 11:2 (Spring 1998): 2–6; *Without Hesitation: The Odyssey of an American Warrior,* with Ronald Levinson and Malcolm McConnell (New York: St. Martin's Press, 2010); the writings of Wayne A. Downing: "Joint Special Operations in Peace and War," *Joint Forces Quarterly* 8 (Summer 1995): 22–27; "Small Budget, Big Payoff: Interview with General Wayne A. Downing, CINC, U.S. Special Operations Command," *Armed Forces Journal International* 132 (August 1994): 44–45; "Special Operations Forces Evolve, Adapt to Change," *Defense Issues* 9:14 (1994): 1–7; "Special Operations Forces: Meeting Tomorrow's Challenges Today," *Special Warfare* 8 (January 1995): 2–10; and Dennis Steele, "'A Force of Great Utility That Cannot Be Mass-Produced,'" interview with Lieutenant General Wayne A. Downing, Commander of U.S. Army Special Operations Command," *Army Magazine* 42 (April 1992): 24. That can be further compared to the CENTCOM leadership perspective; for example, see Joseph P. Hoar, "A CINC's Perspective," *Joint Forces Quarterly* 2 (Autumn 1993): 56–63.

9. Representative Jim Saxton, Opening Statement to the Committee on Armed Services, U.S. House of Representatives, 109th Congress, Hearing on "Special Operations Command: Transforming for the Long War," March 8, 2006.

10. For the longue durée, see John Stanley Baumgartner, *The Lonely Warriors: Case for the Military-Industrial Complex* (Los Angeles: Nash, 1970); James Coates and Michael Killian, *Heavy Losses: The Dangerous Decline of American Defense* (New York: Penguin, 1985); James A. Donovan, *Militarism, USA* (New York: Scribner, 1970); John Kenneth Galbraith, *How to Control the Military* (Garden City, NY: Doubleday, 1969); Richard Halloran, *To Arm a Nation: Rebuilding America's Endangered Defenses* (New York: Macmillan, 1986); Sidney Lens, *The Military-Industrial Complex* (Philadelphia: Pilgrim Press, 1970); Victor Perlo, *Militarism and Industry: Arms Profiteering in the Missile Age* (New York: International Publishers, 1963); and J. A. Stockfish, *Plowshares into Swords: Managing the American Defense Establishment* (New York: Mason and Lipscomb, 1973).

11. William J. Lynn III, "The End of the Military-Industrial Complex: How the Pentagon Is Adapting to Globalization," *Foreign Affairs* 93:6 (November/December 2014): 104–10.

12. See Christian Davenport, "Robots, Swarming Drones and 'Iron Man': Welcome to the New Arms Race," *Washington Post* (June 17, 2016). Put a different way, as suggested by one operator's query: "Why am I building a new bomber when the electrical grid was just collapsed by hackers?" A further mismatch is offered by deputy head of strategy and planning of CENTCOM who offers a succinct example of the mismatch: "As an artillery officer I am not sure you want me to fire cannons at the internet."

13. See the unclassified administrative security manual, DoDM 5105.21, Volume 2, U.S. Department of Defense Sensitive Compartmented Information Administrative Security Manual, as well as open-source DoD Instruction 2000.12 and DoD Instruction 2000.16. The latter includes 10 US Code §2859, requiring the secretary of defense "to develop construction standards designed to reduce the vulnerability to terrorist attack and to improve the security of the occupants of those structures."

14. An unclassified explanation of Special Access Program (SAP)—"to apply extraordinary security measures to protect extremely sensitive information"—is presented in DoDD 0-5205.7 and DoDI 0-5205.11. In addition, the open-source DoD 5220.22–M describes three categories of SAPs: acquisition, intelligence, and operations and support. These unclassified SAP instructions do not apply to DoD instruct activities using Alternate Compensatory Control Measures (ACCMs), which are defined in DoD Manual 5200.01.

15. See Stephanie Sanok, *Theater Special Operations Command Strategic Review* (Washington, DC: Center for Strategic and International Studies, March 31, 2012).

16. Steven Meddaugh, "SOF Wargame Center Capabilities Overview and History," USSOCOM presentation (June 22, 2012).

17. See Carl H. Builder's *The Masks of War: American Military Styles in Strategy and Analysis* (Baltimore: Johns Hopkins University Press, 1989), a magisterial study that emerged from his work at RAND

Corporation. It provides a historical analysis of the institutions that comprise military planning and national security strategy, with an emphasis on how the differences among the military services have resulted in significant variety in analytic outcomes.

18. On the discussion of SOCOM potentially functioning as a sort of "fifth service" alongside the Army, Navy, Air Force, and Marine Corps, see Major Philip L. Mahla and Major Christopher N. Riga. "An Operational Concept for the Transformation of SOF into a Fifth Service" (Monterey, CA: Naval Postgraduate School, June 2003); and Austin Long and Colin Jackson, "The Fifth Service: The Rise of Special Operations Command," *U.S. Military Innovation since the Cold War: Creation Without Destruction,* Harvey Sapolsky, Benjamin Friedman, and Brendan Green, eds. (New York: Routledge, 2009). The U.S. Marine Corps has the most recent institutional history inside U.S. Special Operations Command, becoming a component command in 2006 as discussed in Mastin M. Robeson, "Forging Marine Special Operators," *Joint Forces Quarterly* 56 (First Quarter 2010): 85–88; and Dick Couch, *Always Faithful, Always Forward: The Forging of a Special Operations Marine* (New York: Random House, 2014). See also Dan Lamothe, "Growing MARSOC," *Marine Corps Times* (September 3, 2012). The U.S. Air Force became part of the SOCOM structure in 1990, as analyzed in Jerry L. Thigpen, *AFSOC: The Air Forces' Newest Command* (Carlisle, PA: U.S. Army War College, 1991); its development is covered in Donald C. Wurster, "Mastering the Art of the Possible: The Air Force Special Operations Command," *Joint Forces Quarterly* 56 (First Quarter 2010): 80–84; and Clark A. Murdock, *Special Operations Forces Aviation at the Crossroads* (Washington, DC: Center for Strategic and International Studies, September 2007). For historical analysis, see Michael E. Haas, *Apollo's Warriors: U.S. Air Force Special Operations During the Cold War* (Maxwell Air Force Base, AL: Air University Press, 1997) and Mike McKinney and Mike Ryan, *Chariots of the Damned: Helicopter Special Operations from Vietnam to Kosovo* (New York: St. Martin's Press, 2002). For more recent studies of certain components of U.S. Air Force Special Operations, see Steve Call, *Danger Close: Tactical Air Controllers in Afghanistan and Iraq* (College Station, TX:

Texas A&M University Press, 2007); and Michael Hirsh, *None Braver: U.S. Air Force Pararescuemen in the War on Terrorism* (New York: New American Library, 2003).

19. Regarding Naval Special Warfare, see the books of Dick Couch, including *The Finishing School: Earning the Navy SEAL Trident* (New York: Crown, 2004) and *The Warrior Elite: The Forging of SEAL Class 228* (New York: Crown, 2001). For historical analysis, see T. L. Bosiljevac, *SEALs: UDT/SEAL Operations in Vietnam* (Boulder, CO: Paladin Press, 1990). For analysis of U.S. Army components, see Alfred H. Paddock, *U.S. Army Special Warfare: Its Origins* (Lawrence, KS: University Press of Kansas, 2002); Richard W. Stewart, *SINE PARI: The Story of Army Special Operations* (Fort Bragg, NC: U.S. Army Special Operations Command, 1997). On the specific units within U.S. Army Special Operations, regarding Army Special Forces, see Tom Clancy and John Gresham, *Special Forces: A Guided Tour of U.S. Army Special Forces* (New York: Berkley Books, 2001); Anna Simons, *The Company They Keep: Life Inside the U.S. Army Special Forces* (New York: The Free Press, 1997); and Mark D. Boyatt, *Special Forces: A Unique National Asset, "Through, With, and By"* (Parker, CO: Outskirts Press, 2016). With regard to U.S. Army Rangers, see David W. Hogan, Jr., *Raiders or Elite Infantry? The Changing Role of the U.S. Army Rangers from Dieppe to Grenada* (Westport, CT: Greenwood Press, 1992); John D. Lock, *The Coveted Black and Gold: A Daily Journey through the U.S. Army Ranger School Experience* (Philadelphia: Xlibris, 2001). For analysis of U.S. Army Night Stalkers, see Michael J. Durant, Steven Hartov, and Robert L. Johnson, *The Night Stalkers: Top Secret Missions of the U.S. Army's Special Operations Aviation Regiment* (New York: G. P. Putnam's Sons, 2006); and Stephen Person and Fred J. Pushies, *Army Night Stalkers in Action* (New York: Bearport, 2014). For analysis of U.S. Army Special Operations Forces prior to the formation of SOCOM, see Aaron Bank, *From OSS to Green Berets: The Birth of Special Forces* (Novato, CA: Presidio, 1986); Geoffrey T. Barker, *A Concise History of U.S. Army Special Operations Forces* (Fayetteville, NC: Anglo-American, 1988); Richard Halloran, "Army's Special Forces Try to Rebuild Image by Linking Brains and Brawn," *New York Times* (August 21, 1982); Charles M. Simpson, *Inside*

the Green Berets: The First Thirty Years, A History of the U.S. Army Special Forces (New York: Presidio Press, 1983); and James Stejskal, *Special Forces Berlin: Clandestine Cold War Operations of the U.S. Army's Elite, 1956–1990* (Havertown, PA: Casemate, 2017). For historical analysis of U.S. Army components, see the journal *Veritas: Journal of Army Special Operations History* (Fort Bragg, NC: U.S. Army Special Operations Command).

20. On the role of private military contractors as they intersect with U.S. Special Operations Forces, see Allison Stanger, *One Nation Under Contract: The Outsourcing of American Power and the Future of Foreign Policy* (New Haven: Yale University Press, 2009) and Erik Prince, *Civilian Warriors: The Inside Story of Blackwater and the Unsung Heroes of the War on Terror* (New York: Penguin, 2013).

21. For historical analysis of force structure, missions, and functions, see John M. Collins, *Roles and Functions of U.S. Combat Forces: Past, Present, and Prospects,* Congressional Research Service Report for Congress No. 93-72 S (Washington, DC, January 1993); Office of the Joint Chiefs of Staff, *Report on Roles, Missions and Functions of the Armed Forces of the United States* (February 1993); and Congressional Research Service, *Military Roles and Missions: A Framework for Review,* CRS Report for Congress No. 95–517S (Washington, DC: Library of Congress, May 1, 1995).

22. In addition to the various official descriptions, see Lieutenant General Samuel V. Wilson, *Principles of Special Operations* (Archival Papers of Wilson, Hampden-Sydney College, undated).

23. For discussion of its development, see Stephen Graubard, *Command of Office: How War, Secrecy, and Deception Transformed the Presidency from Theodore Roosevelt to George W. Bush* (New York: Basic Books, 2004). For a discussion of the principal function of the command and its assigned missions at origination, see 10 U.S. Code Section 167—Unified combatant command for special operations forces.

24. On the role of the OSS, and the origins of the CIA and post–World War II U.S. Special Operations Forces, see Bradley F. Smith, *The Shadow Warriors: O.S.S. and the Origins of the C.I.A.* (New York: Basic Books, 1983); Michael Warner, "Central Intelligence: Origin and

Evolution," in Roger Z. George and Robert D. Kline, eds., *Intelligence and the National Security Strategist: Enduring Issues and Challenges* (Washington, DC: National Defense University Press, 2004); Russell Miller, *Behind the Lines: The Oral History of Special Operations in World War II* (New York: St. Martin's Press, 2002); Douglas C. Waller, *The Commandos: The Making of America's Secret Soldiers, from Training to Desert Storm* (New York: Simon & Schuster, 1994); and Douglas Waller, *Wild Bill Donovan: The Spymaster Who Created the OSS and Modern American Espionage* (New York: The Free Press, 2011). For a compelling memoir of a founding member of the OSS, with a four-decade career in U.S. Special Operations, see John K. Singlaub, with Malcolm McConnell, *Hazardous Duty: An American Soldier in the Twentieth Century* (New York: Simon & Schuster, 1991).

25. See testimony and prepared statement of Margaret Stock, attorney and lieutenant colonel, Military Police Corps, U.S. Army Reserve, "Immigration Needs of America's Fighting Men and Women," Hearing of the Committee on the Judiciary, U.S. House of Representatives, 110th Congress, 2nd Session (May 20, 2008): Volume 4.

26. See 10 USC Sec. 504 and 8 USC Sec. 1440 on the process for individuals to serve in the U.S. military and then apply for citizenship. Required lengths of service for military naturalization have varied along with the nation's willingness to waive requirements during hostilities, from one year of Union Army service during the Civil War to no minimum time stipulated by the end of World War I.

27. See T. E. Lawrence, "The Evolution of a Revolt," *Army Quarterly and Defence Journal* (October 1920) and *Seven Pillars of Wisdom: A Triumph* (London: Hodgson, 1926).

28. Lieutenant General David H. Petraeus, commander, U.S. Army Combined Arms Center, and James N. Mattis, commanding general, Marine Corps Combat Development Command, eds., *Counterinsurgency FM 3–24* (2006).

29. Lawrence, "The Evolution of a Revolt."

30. T. E. Lawrence, "Twenty-Seven Articles," *Arab Bulletin* (August 20, 1917).

31. This concept of direct and indirect approaches evolves from a book of military theory by Basil H. Liddell Hart, *Strategy* (London: Faber and Faber, 1954).

32. See Ori Brafman and Rod A. Beckstrom, *The Starfish and the Spider* (New York: Penguin, 2006).

33. See Martin J. Gorman and Alexander Krongard, "A Goldwater-Nichols Act for the U.S. Government: Institutionalizing the Interagency Process," *Joint Forces Quarterly* 39 (Fourth Quarter 2005): 51–58; Christopher J. Lamb and Edward Marks, *Chief of Mission Authority as a Model for National Security Integration* (Washington, DC: National Defense University Press, 2010); Christopher J. Lamb, "Redesigning White House and Interagency Structures," in Hans Binnendijk and Patrick M. Cronin, eds., *Civilian Surge: Key to Complex Operations* (Washington, DC: National Defense University Press, 2008): 33–64; and Gabriel Marcella, ed., *Affairs of State: The Interagency and National Security* (Carlisle, PA: U.S. Army War College, 2008).

4 MORE BOOTS YET TO COME

1. The opening quote—"Far more important. . . [are] those big ideas outside the wire under Kevlar, under body armor"—is part of General Petraeus's broader statement that "a lot of people would argue, and I certainly would, that it wasn't by any means just the surge of forces. In fact, far more important than the surge of 30,000 additional U.S. troops was the surge of ideas that helped us to employ those troops, and that surge of forces enabled the employment of the new ideas that were indeed the key to making the progress that has been achieved in Iraq over the course of the last three years. It was the team that took those big ideas outside the wire under Kevlar, under body armor . . . That was the key." This statement by General Petraeus was part of a larger discussion at the Institute for the Study of War on January 22, 2010, led by Kimberly Kagan.

2. For minds and hearts, see John Adams, letter to Hezekiah Niles on the American Revolution, February 13, 1818, Quincy, Massachusetts; Lyndon B. Johnson: "Remarks at a Dinner Meeting of the Texas Electric Cooperatives, Inc.," May 4, 1965: "So we must be ready to

fight in Vietnam, but the ultimate victory will depend upon the hearts and minds of the people who actually live out there." See the digital archives, *The American Presidency Project,* Gerhard Peters and John T. Woolley, eds., University of California, Santa Barbara, presidency. ucsb.edu; Sergio Miller, "Malaya: The Myth of Hearts and Minds," *Small Wars Journal* (April 16, 2012); and Elizabeth Dickinson, "A Bright Shining Slogan: How 'Hearts and Minds' Came to Be," *Foreign Policy* (August 22, 2009).

3. See Charles H. Briscoe et al., *Weapon of Choice: U.S. Army Special Operations Forces in Afghanistan* (Fort Leavenworth, KS: Combat Studies Institute Press, 2003); *All Roads Lead to Baghdad: Army Special Operation Forces in Iraq* (Fort Bragg, NC: U.S. Army Special Operations Command History Office, 2006); and *U.S. Army Special Operations in Afghanistan* (Boulder, CO: Paladin Press, 2006). See also David J. Kilcullen, "New Paradigms for 21st Century Conflict," *Small Wars Journal* (June 2007); *The Accidental Guerrilla: Fighting Small Wars in the Midst of a Big One* (Oxford: Oxford University Press, 2009); and *Counterinsurgency* (Oxford: Oxford University Press, 2010).

4. For aspects of that evolution in military strategy, see Terry M. Neal, "Bush Backs into Nation Building," *Washington Post* (February 26, 2003); Christopher J. Lamb and Martin Cinnamond, "Unity of Effort: Key to Success in Afghanistan," *Strategic Forum* 248, Institute for National Strategic Studies, National Defense University (October 2009): 1-12; Steve Bowman and Catherine Dale, "War in Afghanistan: Strategy, Military Operations, and Issues for Congress" (Washington, DC: Congressional Research Service, December 3, 2009); Jennifer Taw, *Mission Revolution: The U.S. Military and Stability Operations* (New York: Columbia University Press, 2012); Christopher Paul, Brian J. Gordon, et al., *A Building Partner Capacity Assessment Framework* (Santa Monica: RAND Corporation, 2015); and Dominic Tierney, "The Backlash Against Nation-Building," *Prism* 5:3 (April 2016): 13–27.

5. See report by Michael D. Becker, *Operational Art in Counterinsurgency Campaign Planning* (Newport: U.S. Naval War College, June 17, 1994).

6. See Sergio Miller, "Building a Hollow ANSF—Vietnam Revisited," *Journal of Military Operations* 1:1 (Summer 2012): 4–7.

7. For analysis of U.S. military strategy in Afghanistan after 2001, see Stephen Biddle, *Afghanistan and the Future of Warfare: Implications for Army and Defense Policy* (Carlisle, PA: U.S. Army War College, November 2002); Mary Anne Weaver, *Pakistan: In the Shadow of Jihad and Afghanistan* (New York: Farrar, Straus and Giroux, 2003); Sarah Chayes, *The Punishment of Virtue: Inside Afghanistan After the Taliban* (New York: Penguin, 2006); Hy S. Rothstein, *Afghanistan and the Troubled Future of Unconventional Warfare* (Annapolis: Naval Institute Press, 2006); James Dobbins, *After the Taliban: Nation-Building in Afghanistan* (Dulles, VA: Potomac Books, 2008); Seth G. Jones, *Counterinsurgency in Afghanistan* (Santa Monica: RAND Corporation, 2008); Seth G. Jones, *In the Graveyard of Empires: America's War in Afghanistan* (New York: W. W. Norton, 2009); Jim Michaels, *A Chance in Hell: The Men Who Triumphed over Iraq's Deadliest City and Turned the Tide of War* (New York: St. Martin's Press, 2010); Sarah Sewall and Larry Lewis, *Reducing and Mitigating Civilian Casualties, Afghanistan and Beyond, Joint Civilian Casualty Final Report* (Suffolk, VA: Joint and Coalition Operation Analysis, August 31, 2010); Basil Catanzaro and Kirk Windmueller, "Taking a Stand: Village Stability Operations and the Afghan Local Police," *Special Warfare Magazine* 24:3 (July/September 2011): 32–34; Stephen N. Rust, "The Nuts and Bolts of Village Stability Operations," *Special Warfare* 24:3 (July/September 2011): 28–31; Austin G. Long, *Locals Rule: Historical Lessons for Creating Local Defense Forces for Afghanistan and Beyond* (Santa Monica: RAND Corporation, 2012); Kevin Maurer, *Gentlemen Bastards: On the Ground in Afghanistan with America's Elite Special Forces* (New York: Berkley Books, 2012); Bing West, *The Wrong War: Grit, Strategy, and the Way Out of Afghanistan* (New York: Random House, 2012); and Peter Tomsen, "The Good War? What Went Wrong in Afghanistan—and How to Make It Right," *Foreign Affairs* 93:6 (November/December 2014): 47–54.

8. For the evolution of U.S. military strategy in Iraq, see George Packer, *The Assassins' Gate: America in Iraq* (New York: Farrar, Straus and Giroux, 2005); Rajiv Chandrasekaran, *Imperial Life in the Emerald City: Inside Iraq's Green Zone* (New York: Alfred A. Knopf, 2006); Michael R. Gordon and Bernard E. Trainor, *Cobra 2: The Inside Story of the Invasion*

and Occupation of Iraq (New York: Pantheon Books, 2006); Thomas E. Ricks, *Fiasco: The American Military Adventure in Iraq* (New York: Penguin, 2006); Ali Allawi, *The Occupation of Iraq: Winning the War, Losing the Peace* (New Haven: Yale University Press, 2007); Peter R. Mansoor, *Baghdad at Sunrise: A Brigade Commander's War in Iraq* (New Haven: Yale University Press, 2008); Bing West, *The Strongest Tribe: War, Politics, and the Endgame in Iraq* (New York: Random House, 2008); Mark Moyar, *A Question of Command: Counterinsurgency from the Civil War to Iraq* (New Haven: Yale University Press, 2009); Thomas E. Ricks, *The Gamble: General David Petraeus and the American Military Adventure in Iraq, 2006–2008* (New York: Penguin, 2009); and David E. Johnson, M. Wade Markel, and Brian Shannon, *The 2008 Battle of Sadr City* (Santa Monica: RAND Corporation, 2011).

9. For the changing terror, antiterror, and counterterror approaches, see John Arquilla and David Ronfeldt, eds., *Networks and Netwars: The Future of Terror, Crime, and Militancy* (Santa Monica: RAND Corporation, 2001); Ahmed Rashid, *Taliban: Militant Islam, Oil and Fundamentalism in Central Asia* (New Haven: Yale University Press, 2000); Ahmed Rashid, *Jihad: The Rise of Militant Islam in Central Asia* (New York: Penguin, 2002); Marc Sageman, *Understanding Terror Networks* (Philadelphia: University of Pennsylvania Press, 2004); Ahmed Rashid, *Descent into Chaos: The United States and the Failure of Nation Building in Pakistan, Afghanistan, and Central Asia* (New York: Viking, 2008); Assaf Moghadam, *The Globalization of Martyrdom* (Baltimore: Johns Hopkins University Press, 2008); Syed Saleem Shahzad, *Inside Al-Qaeda and the Taliban: Beyond Bin Laden and 9/11* (New York: Palgrave Macmillan, 2011); Daniel Benjamin and Steven Simon, *The Age of Sacred Terror* (New York: Random House, 2002); Marc Sageman, *Leaderless Jihad: Terror Networks in the Twenty-First Century* (Philadelphia: University of Pennsylvania Press, 2008); Bruce Riedel, *The Search for Al Qaeda* (Washington, DC: Brookings Institution Press, 2010); Bruce Riedel, *Deadly Embrace: Pakistan, America, and the Future of the Global Jihad* (Washington, DC: Brookings Institution Press, 2011); Ali H. Soufan, *The Black Banners: The Inside Story of 9/11 and the War Against Al-Qaeda,* with Daniel Freedman (New York:

W. W. Norton, 2011); and Seth G. Jones, *Hunting in the Shadows: The Pursuit of Al Qa'ida since 9/11* (New York: W. W. Norton, 2012).

10. See the evolution in Dana Priest, *The Mission: Waging War and Keeping Peace with America's Military* (New York: W. W. Norton, 2003); Robert D. Kaplan, *Imperial Grunts: The American Military on the Ground* (New York: Random House, 2005); Kimberly Kagan, *The Surge: A Military History* (New York: Encounter Books, 2008); Linda Robinson, *Tell Me How This Ends: General David Petraeus and the Search for a Way out of Iraq* (New York: Public Affairs, 2008); and Fred M. Kaplan, *The Insurgents: David Petraeus and the Plot to Change the American Way of War* (New York: Simon & Schuster, 2013).

11. Regarding the evolution of counterinsurgency, see John Nagl, *Learning to Eat Soup with a Knife: Counterinsurgency Lessons from Malaya and Vietnam* (Westport, CT: Praeger, 2002); Jim Gant, *One Tribe at a Time: A Strategy for Success in Afghanistan* (Los Angeles: Nine Sisters Imports, 2009); Kalev I. Sepp, "Best Practices in Counterinsurgency," *Military Review* (May/June 2005): 8–12; Ken Tovo, *From the Ashes of the Phoenix: Lessons for Contemporary Counterinsurgency Operations* (Carlisle, PA: U.S. Army War College, 2005); Jonathan Morgenstein, "The Global Counter Insurgency: America's New National Security and Foreign Policy Paradigm," *Small Wars Journal* (January 1, 2008); Ralph Wipfli and Steven Metz, *COIN of the Realm: U.S. Counterinsurgency Strategy* (Carlisle, PA: U.S. Army War College, 2008); Christopher Paul, Colin P. Clarke, and Beth Grill, *Victory Has a Thousand Fathers: Sources of Success in Counterinsurgency* (Santa Monica: RAND Corporation, 2010); and Austin G. Long, *Partners or Proxies? U.S. and Host Nation Cooperation in Counterterrorism Operations* (West Point: Combating Terrorism Center, 2011).

12. David Howell Petraeus, "The American Military and the Lessons of Vietnam: A Study of Military Influence and the Use of Force in the Post-Vietnam Era" (Ph.D. diss., Princeton University, 1987).

13. See "How Technology Won Sadr City Battle: U.S. Military Gives Rare Access to *60 Minutes* in Discussing Aerial Footage and Weaponry," *CBSNews.com* (October 12, 2008); Leslie Stahl, "The Battle of Sadr City," *60 Minutes* (October 12, 2008); and David E. Johnson, M. Wade Markel, and Brian Shannon, *The 2008 Battle of Sadr City* (Santa Monica: RAND Corporation, 2011).

14. See interview of H. R. McMaster in Elisabeth Bumiller, "We Have Met the Enemy and He Is Powerpoint," *New York Times* (April 27, 2010) and related discussion in David W. Barno, "The Army's Next Enemy? Peace," *Washington Post* (July 13, 2014).

15. U.S. Secretary of Defense Robert M. Gates, "Remarks at the United States Military Academy" (West Point, February 25, 2011).

16. For the context of this remark by General Stanley McChrystal, see the article by Julian Borger, "Afghanistan: The PowerPoint Solution," *Guardian* (April 27, 2010). For further strategic discussion, see Stanley McChrystal, *My Share of the Task* (New York: Penguin, 2013).

17. See General David Petraeus, statement as commander, International Security Assistance Force, U.S. Senate Armed Services Committee "Hearing on the Situation in Afghanistan" (March 15, 2011).

5 AMERICA'S SUPERHEROES

1. This chapter's opening quote—"Wandering Mujahidin. Armed and Dangerous."—is the title of an important intelligence report in 1993 that raised concern about bin Laden, noting that "Among private donors to the new generation, Usama bin Laden is particularly famous for his religious zeal and financial largess." See Gina Bennett, *The Wandering Mujahidin: Armed and Dangerous* (U.S. Department of State, Bureau of Intelligence and Research, August 21–22, 1993), declassified and released in full on November 23, 2007. For a discussion of the range of public responses, see Larisa Epatko, "World Reaction to Bin Laden Death Ranges from Caution to Glee," PBS *NewsHour* (May 2, 2011).

2. The real-time witness account is offered by Sohaib Athar, an information technology consultant, then living in Abbottabad, on his Twitter account @ReallyVirtual.

3. See Catherine Scott-Clark and Adrian Levy, *The Exile: The Stunning Inside Story of Osama bin Laden and Al Qaeda in Flight* (New York: Bloomsbury, 2018), for a detailed family tree. See Declan Walsh, "Pakistan Arrests Five Men for Helping CIA Spy on Bin Laden House," *Guardian* (June 15, 2001), on efforts to establish a pattern of life at the compound, which did not culminate in conclusive evidence identifying bin Laden as a resident.

4. See, for example, one letter that Hamza bin Laden wrote from detention in Iran, dated July 2009, which reached his father at the Abbottabad compound: "I was 13 years old . . . My beloved father, I could not imagine the length of this bitter separation, when you left me, my brother Khalid, and my brother Bakr at the foot of the mountains . . . Eight consecutive years. My eyes still remember the last time they saw you, when you were under the olive tree and you gave every one of us a misbaha . . . then you bid us farewell." This document is one of several hundred found at the Abbottabad compound, which were subsequently reviewed, translated, and released in May 2015 by the Office of the Director of National Intelligence.

5. See the Abbottabad Commission Report, an examination of the circumstances of the Abbottabad raid. The Commission members, led by Justice Javoud Iqbal, were appointed by the Prime Minister of Pakistan in June 2011. The Abbottabad Commission Report was delivered to the Prime Minister in January 2013, and released to Al Jazeera in July 2013 which broadly circulated it. See also Scott-Clark and Levy, *The Exile* (2018), regarding the journey of the third wife, Khairiah, her one child, Hamza, and some of Najwa's children and grandchildren. The wives of bin Laden gave extensive interviews after his death. Najwa, for example, described their peripatetic life: "Fleeing from country to country under assumed names and fake passports," she explained, became the norm of their family life. Bin Laden's fourth wife, Siham, in a later interview, offered marriage and childbirth details to illustrate another change. Back when the family was still living in Jeddah, in 1988, Siham went into labor prematurely, prompting Usama to drive "his gold Mercedes at breakneck speed to the city's most exclusive private clinic." Their second daughter, Miriam, survived. Siham's first daughter, Khadija, though, had a very different experience: Married to a Saudi fighter at age thirteen at Tarnak Qila, a concrete hanger and huts in a remote section of Kandahar, Afghanistan, she died in childbirth in their post-9/11 safe house in Waziristan, Pakistan.

6. See Nicholas Schmidle, "Getting Bin Laden," *New Yorker* (August 8, 2011), for the first detailed print account of the raid as told by a journalist.

7. See Commander (ret.) Jamal Hussain, Pakistani Air Force, "The Phantom Raid," *Combating Terrorism Exchange (CTX) Journal* (September 2011), which describes the timeline of May 1–2, 2011 from the vantage point of these forces, including that they launched from Mushaf Air Base, in Sargodha, headquarters of Pakistan Central Air Command, about 240 kilometers away, only to find that U.S. forces had already exited Pakistani airspace. An interview with Brigadier Khalil Dar, as presented in the Abbottabad Commission Report (pages 126–27), describes what they found, including an emphasis on the U.S. helicopter left behind: "Most of the wreckage was completely burnt. However, the tail rotor section was partially intact and lay outside the boundary wall. The tail rotor blades were not damaged. The tail rotor shaft drive was extended over the wall. While the power train was identical to a Black Hawk, a new kind of tail rotor section coupled with a honey comb encased body gave the helicopter a very different aerodynamic shape."

8. See public remarks by Secretary of State Hillary Clinton made during her visit to Pakistan in July 2010, about "elements in the government" knowing the hiding location of bin Laden in their country. See also the news coverage of Clinton's statement offered by Eric Zimmerman in *The Hill* (July 20, 2010) and by Fawaz Gerges for CNN (August 15, 2010), among others.

9. See Scott-Clark and Levy, *The Exile* (2018), for discussion of bin Laden's commemorative video tapes. For the broader context, see Peter L. Bergen, *The Osama bin Laden I Know: An Oral History of al Qaeda's Leader* (New York: Free Press, 2006); Steve Coll, *Ghost Wars: The Secret History of the CIA, Afghanistan and Bin Laden, from the Soviet Invasion to September 10, 2001* (New York: Penguin, 2004); Zahid Hussain, *Frontline Pakistan: The Struggle with Militant Islam* (New York: Columbia University Press, 2007); and Nigel Inkster, "9/11/11: A Decade of Intelligence," *Survival: Global Politics and Strategy* 53:6 (2001): 5–13.

10. See further discussion in *The Abbottabad Commission Report* (2013); Scott-Clark and Levy, *The Exile* (2018); Bergen, *Manhunt* (2012); and Mark Bowden, "The Hunt for 'Geronimo,'" *Vanity Fair* (November 2012): 144–50, among others.

11. See Scott-Clark and Levy, *The Exile* (2018), for discussion of the shipping container as listening post near Margalla Hills in August 2010, as confirmed by Jamal Ismail, a journalist in Islamabad.

12. On General Petraeus's travels to Pakistan the year prior, February 22–24, 2010, to meet Pakistani Army counterparts at the Academy, Abbottabad was one of the stops.

13. See Stuart L. Farris, "Joint Special Operations Task Force—Philippines: A Monograph" (Fort Leavenworth, KS: School of Advanced Military Studies, 2009) and Maria Ressa, *Seeds of Terror: An Eyewitness Account of Al-Qaeda's Newest Center of Operations in Southeast Asia* (New York: The Free Press, 2003) for aspects of combating terrorism in the Philippines.

14. For a discussion of the scenario planning, see Mark Bowden, *The Finish: The Killing of Osama Bin Laden* (New York: Atlantic Monthly Press, 2012) and Bergen, *Manhunt* (2012).

15. See the CIA's unclassified biographical sketch "Usama Bin Laden: Islamic Extremist Financier" (1996), which described, among other construction projects in Afghanistan, his aim to build "roads, tunnels, hospitals, and storage depots through Afghanistan's mountainous terrain to move and shelter fighters and supplies." See Scott-Clark and Levy, *The Exile* (2018), for details of bin Laden's construction in Pakistan, notably the completion of the family compound in 2005, designed by an architectural firm in Abbottabad and built on land purchased from a local doctor.

16. See Justice Javaid Iqbal and the *Abbottabad Commission Report* (2013) for a discussion of these perimeter changes and the perceptions of neighbors. While the final report was not published, an early draft appeared on Al Jazeera, www.aljazeera.com/indepth/spotlight/binladenfiles/. See Al Jazeera Investigation Unit, "Document: Pakistan's Bin Laden Dossier" (July 8, 2013).

17. See Najwa bin Laden and Omar bin Laden, *Growing Up Bin Laden: Osama's Wife and Son Take Us Inside Their Secret World*, with Jean Sasson (New York: St. Martin's Press, 2009).

18. See Michael R. Gordon and Bernard E. Trainor, *The Generals' War: The Inside Story of the Conflict in the Gulf* (Boston: Little, Brown, 1995).

19. See Robert Fisk, "Anti-Soviet Warrior Puts His Army on the Road to Peace," *The Independent* (December 6, 1993), in which bin Laden, when asked about training soldiers for jihad wars in Algeria, Egypt, and Tunisia, among others, replies, "The rubbish of the media and the embassies . . . I am a construction engineer and an agriculturalist. If I had training camps here in Sudan, I couldn't possibly do this job." Four years later, in March 1997, in a television interview with Peter Arnett of CNN, when asked, "What are your future plans?," bin Laden replies, "You'll see them and hear about them in the media, God willing." See also Bruce Lawrence, *Messages to the World: The Statements of Osama bin Laden* (New York: Verso, 2005) and Flagg Miller, *The Audacious Ascetic: What the Bin Laden Tapes Reveal about Al-Qa'ida* (Oxford: Oxford University Press, 2015).

20. See Najwa bin Laden and Omar bin Laden, *Growing Up Bin Laden: Osama's Wife and Son Take Us Inside Their Secret World,* with Jean Sasson (New York: St. Martin's Press, 2009), chapter 20.

21. For the comment regarding the Sheraton, see Abdel Bari Atwan, *The Secret History of Al Qaeda* (Berkeley: University of California Press, 2006), which includes details about Atwan's travels to Tora Bora in 1996 to interview bin Laden. See also Atwan's article "Inside Osama's Mountain Lair," in the *Guardian* (November 11, 2001). In Scott-Clark and Levy, *The Exile* (2018), the site is described as a "dun-colored fort . . . surrounded by four-meter-high mud walls and crowned with guard towers . . . [which] Osama had grandiosely named . . . Jalalabad fort Najm al-Jihad, the Star of the Holy War . . . Saad bin Laden, his third son . . . had dubbed it 'Star Wars.'" A *New York Times* series titled "A Nation Challenged," special reporting after September 11, described the progression of some of these caves, from natural-forming caves and karezi, or irrigation tunnels, to more elaborate and fortified areas. A geologist from the University of Nebraska, who prepared a national atlas of Afghanistan, described some as "multi-level, dogleg tunnels. They have air vents and escape hatches out the back." One account described "forty-one caves in all," adding that "it had everything then: a bakery, a hotel with overstuffed furniture, a hospital with an ultrasound machine, a library, a mosque, weapons of every

imaginable stripe; a service bay with a World War II–era Soviet tank inside, in perfect running order." *Time* (December 11, 2001) offered a view as well, "Inside the Tora Bora Caves," by Matthew Forney, who described "signs of habitation. It contained two empty white boxes decorated with palm trees and the words, 'Sherjah Dates.' Scattered on the floor were a few green metal boxes of ammunition with Russian writing on them, and a canister about the size of an unexploded cluster bomb but the wrong color—red instead of yellow. Another cave next to it was about the same size and filled with ammunition, mostly bullets for Kalashnikovs and rocket-propelled grenades." See also PBS *Frontline*, "Campaign Against Terror" (September 8, 2002), which broadcast interviews with U.S. soldiers on the ground in Tora Bora in November and December 2001, part of Operational Detachment Alpha (ODA) 572.

22. See Scott-Clark and Levy, *The Exile* (2018), chapter on Tora Bora (December 3, 2001). The pursuit of bin Laden that month has been extensively analyzed. See, among others, U.S. Senate Committee on Foreign Relations, John F. Kerry, Chairman, *Tora Bora Revisited: How We Failed to Get Bin Laden and Why It Matters Today* (November 30, 2009); Peter Krause, "The Last Good Chance: A Reassessment of U.S. Operations at Tora Bora," *Security Studies* 17:4 (Winter 2008): 644–84; Sharon LaFraniere, "Bombing of Enclave Intensifies; Several Thousand Hold Out in Taliban's Northern Stronghold," *Washington Post* (November 19, 2001); and Mary Anne Weaver, "Lost at Tora Bora," *New York Times Magazine* (September 11, 2005).

23. See Najwa bin Laden and Omar bin Laden (2009).

24. See Nasser al-Bahri and Georges Malbrunot, *Dans l'ombre de bin Laden: Révélations de son garde du corps* (Paris: Michel Lafon, 2010) and Scott-Clark and Levy, *The Exile* (2018), regarding bin Laden's statement about Holy Tuesday, the planes-into-bombs operation, "an epoch that begins today."

25. For further descriptions from inside bin Laden's circle, see Nasser al-Bahri, *Guarding Bin Laden: My Life in al-Qaeda*, with Georges Malbrunot, trans. Susan de Muth (London: Thin Man Press, 2013); Omar Nasiri, *Inside the Jihad: My Life with Al Qaeda* (New York: Basic

Books, 2006); Abu Walid al-Masri, "The Story of the Arab Afghans from the Time of Their Arrival in Afghanistan until Their Departure with the Taliban," *Al Sharq al-Awsat* (December 8–14, 2004); Report of the Foreign Broadcast Information Service, *Compilation of Usama bin Laden Statements, 1994–2004* (January 2004); Anonymous (later named as Michael Scheuer), *Through Our Enemies' Eyes: Osama bin Laden, Radical Islam, and the Future of America* (Lincoln: University of Nebraska Press, 2003); Michael Scheuer, *Osama bin Laden* (Oxford: Oxford University Press, 2011); and West Point's collections of al-Qaeda documents, translated by Nelly Lahoud et al., at the Combating Terrorism Center.

26. Simon Sinek, *The Infinite Game* (New York: Penguin Portfolio, 2019). For further analysis of this period, see Peter L. Bergen, *The Longest War: The Enduring Conflict Between America and Al-Qaeda* (New York: The Free Press, 2011); Owen Bennett-Jones, *Pakistan: Eye of the Storm* (New Haven: Yale University Press, 2002); Anand Gopal, *No Good Men Among the Living: America, the Taliban, and the War through Afghan Eyes* (New York: Picador, 2015); Rohan Gunaratna, *Inside Al Qaeda: Global Network of Terror* (New York: Columbia University Press, 2002); Gilles Kepel, *The War for Muslim Minds: Islam and the West* (Cambridge, MA: Harvard University Press, 2004); Gilles Kepel and Jean-Pierre Milelli, *Al-Qaeda in Its Own Words* (Cambridge, MA: Harvard University Press, 2008); and Lawrence *Wright, The Looming Tower: Al-Qaeda and the Road to 9/11* (New York: Random House, 2006).

27. Stephen Robinson, "Washington's Waiting Game: Two Insider Accounts of the Tension-Packed Hours Leading up to the Raid to Kill Osama Bin Laden," London *Sunday Times* (October 21, 2012).

28. One policymaker described it as "thirty-eight of the most intense minutes," watching the grainy imagery from Washington. Another senior official, watching it in a conference room at the CIA, described the effect as an odd kind of voyeurism, with cookies being served on plates, and far too many nonessential personnel included in observation of the raid. The outcome of the operation was soon publicly announced: Office of the Press Secretary, the White House, "Press Briefing by Senior Administration Officials on the Killing of Osama

bin Laden," May 2, 2011. On aspects of these military operations, before and after the Abbottabad raid, see David E. Sanger's two books: *The Inheritance: The World Obama Confronts and the Challenges to American Power* (New York: Crown, 2009) and *Confront and Conceal: Obama's Secret Wars and Surprising Use of American Power* (New York: Crown, 2012).

29. The fiftieth anniversary of the Atlantic Council at Washington's Ritz-Carlton Hotel on May 3, 2011, which was described by Tony Harnden, "Joe Biden Opens His Mouth about U.S. Navy SEALs," *Telegraph* (May 4, 2011), among other journalists.

30. See the interview of CIA Director Leon Panetta by Jim Lehrer, on PBS *NewsHour* (May 3, 2011). For further analysis by Panetta, see Leon Panetta, *Worthy Fights: A Memoir of Leadership in War and Peace*, with Jim Newton (New York: Penguin, 2015).

31. The Command arrangements for the operation were unusual, a derivative of what has been referred to as "Title 60," a part of the U.S. Code that does not exist formally, but rather refers to instances when Title 10 and Title 50 authorities are both drawn upon. According to two U.S. special operators directly involved in both the planning and execution of the raid, the decision to run the operation through the CIA rather than the infrastructure of U.S. Special Operations did have a material impact on air and ground operations. For discussion of "Title 60" aspects, see Richard A. Best, Jr. and Andrew Feickert, *Special Operations Forces (SOF) and CIA Paramilitary Operations: Issues for Congress* (Washington, DC: Congressional Research Service, 2005); Robert Chesney, "Military-Intelligence Convergence and the Law of the Title 10/Title 50 Debate," *Journal of National Security Law & Policy* 5:2 (July 2012): 539–629; Jeff Mustin and Harvey Rishikoff, "Projecting Force in the 21st Century—Legitimacy and the Rule of Law: Title 50, Title 10, Title 18 and Article 75," *Rutgers Law Review* 63:4 (January 1, 2011): 1235–51; Andru E. Wall, "Demystifying the Title 10-Title 50 Debate: Distinguishing Military Operations, Intelligence Activities & Covert Action," *Harvard National Security Journal* 3:1 (September 2011): 85–142; Joseph B. Berger, "Covert Action Title 10, Title 50 and the Chain of Command,"

· *Joint Forces Quarterly* 67 (Fourth Quarter 2012): 32–39; and Philip Zelikow, "Codes of Conduct for a Twilight War," *Houston Law Review* 49:1 (April 2012): 1–52. For the evolution and historical antecedents of such arrangements, see James Bamford, *Body of Secrets: Anatomy of the Ultra-Secret National Security Agency: From the Cold War through the Dawn of a New Century* (New York: Doubleday, 2001); James Bamford, *The Puzzle Palace: A Report on America's Most Secret Agency* (New York: Penguin, 1983); William J. Daugherty, *Executive Secrets: Covert Action and the Presidency* (Lexington, KY: University Press of Kentucky, 2004); Loch K. Johnson, *America's Secret Power: The CIA in a Democratic Society* (Oxford: Oxford University Press, 1989); Loch K. Johnson, *Secret Agencies: U.S. Intelligence in a Hostile World* (New Haven: Yale University Press, 1998); John Prados, *Presidents' Secret Wars: CIA and Pentagon Covert Operations since World War II* (New York: Morrow, 1986); John Prados, *Safe for Democracy: The Secret Wars of the CIA* (Chicago: Dee, 2006); and Gregory F. Treverton, *Covert Action: The Limits of Intervention in the Postwar World* (New York: Basic Books, 1987).

32. For further discussion of Joint Special Operations Command, see Marc Ambinder and D. B. Grady, *The Command: Deep Inside the President's Secret Army* (New York: John Wiley & Sons, 2012); Jennifer D. Kibbe, "The Rise of the Shadow Warriors," *Foreign Affairs* 83:2 (2004): 102–15; and Eric Schmitt and Thom Shanker, *Counterstrike: The Untold Story of America's Secret Campaign Against Al Qaeda* (New York: Times Books, 2011).

33. See Mark Boal, *Zero Dark Thirty: An Original Screenplay* (Sony Pictures, October 3, 2011). Directed by Kathryn Bigelow, the film premiered in 2012 and grossed more than $100 million. More major Hollywood films about U.S. Special Operations followed, including *Lone Survivor* (2013), *Captain Phillips* (2013), and *American Sniper* (2014). Further discussion of this trend can be found in Belinda Luscombe, "Read the Full Interview with American Sniper Chris Kyle That Didn't Make It to Press," *Time* (January 20, 2015) and Jordan Zakarin, "'Act of Valor' and the Military's Long Hollywood Mission," *Huffington Post* (February 17, 2012).

34. Buck McKeon, U.S. representative from California and then chair of the House Armed Services Committee, included this in remarks to a SOCOM Conference at the Ronald Reagan Building, Washington, DC, in June 2011.

6 FOURTEEN MINUTES OF FAME

1. The chapter's opening quote—"These days, the sun never sets on America's special-operations forces"—appeared in the *Wall Street Journal* on April 24, 2015, and is part of a broader style of reporting that emphasizes the activities of U.S. special operators in the 9/11 wars, generally underscoring the activities of U.S. special operators more than other U.S. military and intelligence units.

2. The event was held on July 25, 2012, at the Aspen Institute campus in Aspen, Colorado. This was the second year in a row that the Aspen Institute kicked off its Security Forum with the SOCOM commander as its keynote speaker. See the Archives of the Aspen Institute for a full transcript of the McRaven-Blitzer interview.

3. Other similar responses to that same question included: "Nothing. I'm not going to address that . . . I'm not going to answer it . . . Don't want to talk about other places . . . Yes, I'm not going to get into that . . . You know, that's a great question and I'm not going to answer it."

4. McRaven's further remarks on the topic include: "The force was frayed and I think that was exactly the right term . . . we're not crumbling . . . we're not destroyed, but we are clearly fraying . . . I think that fraying is getting a little worse . . . our suicide rate. It is as high as it has been." A SOCOM report later that year included among the military's concerns "an increase in domestic and family relational and behavioral problems, substance abuse and self-medication problems, risk-taking behavior, post-traumatic stress and suicide." The quote "a culture of anything goes" appeared in a 2013 *Business Insider* article. For further context, see Charles D. Allen, "The Impact of a Decade at War," *Armed Forces Journal* (May 2011): 14–36; Caroline Alexander, "The Invisible War on the Brain," *National Geographic Magazine* (February 2015): 33-52; Howard Altman, "Rising Suicide in Special Operations Forces Prompts Call for Review," *Tampa Tribune* (April 29,

2014); Committee on the Assessment of Ongoing Efforts in the Treatment of Post-Traumatic Stress Disorder, *Treatment for Post-Traumatic Stress Disorder in Military and Veteran Populations: Final Assessment* (Washington, DC: National Academies Press, 2012); Robert Emmet Meagher, "Wounded Warriors, Wounded Nation," *Cicero Magazine* (April 14, 2015); Nancy Sherman, *Afterwar* (Oxford: Oxford University Press, 2015); Warren Strobel, "U.S. Special Forces Struggle with Record Suicides," *Reuters* (April 17, 2014); and U.S. Government Accountability Office, *Special Operations Forces: Several Human Capital Challenges Must Be Addressed to Meet Expanded Role* (Washington, DC: U.S. Government Accountability Office, 2006).

5. For further context, Admiral McRaven offers, "When you start getting down into the specifics of who did it, that becomes a red line for us because it is really about protecting the individual and the—and their families . . . we go to great lengths to protect our national security, that's very great lengths . . . So all of that we guard very carefully. Unfortunately, not everybody guards that very carefully." See also the Archives of the Woodrow Wilson International Center for Scholars, Washington, DC, for a transcript of "U.S. Special Operations 2020," the discussion between William McRaven and Jane Harman at the center on May 3, 2013, on these and related topics.

6. For a more extended analysis of raids and other special operations by William H. McRaven, see "The Theory of Special Operations," Master's thesis (Naval Postgraduate School, 1993) and *Spec Ops: Case Studies in Special Operations Warfare: Theory and Practice* (Novato, CA: Presidio, 1995). For how he presented some of those concerns at this time, see "Written Statement of Admiral William H. McRaven, USN Commander, United States Special Operations Command Before the 113th Congress Senate Armed Services Committee Emerging Threats and Capabilities Subcommittee" (April 9, 2013).

7. Mark Owen, *No Easy Day: The Autobiography of a Navy SEAL: The Firsthand Account of the Mission That Killed Osama Bin Laden*, with Kevin Maurer (New York: Dutton, 2012) is one of the highest-profile books written about U.S. Special Operations, but it is by no means the first written by an operator. Other prominent examples include Charlie A.

Beckwith, *Delta Force*, with Donald Knox (San Diego: Harcourt Brace Jovanovich, 1983); Pete Blaber, *The Mission, the Men and Me: Lessons from a Former Delta Force Commander* (New York: Berkley Caliber, 2008); Jerry Boykin, *Never Surrender: A Soldier's Journey to the Crossroads of Faith and Freedom*, with Lynn Vincent (New York: Faith Words, 2008); Tom Clancy and Carl Stiner, *Shadow Warriors: Inside the Special Forces*, with Tony Koltz (New York: G. P. Putnam's Sons, 2002); Dalton Fury (pseud.), *Kill Bin Laden: A Delta Force Commander's Account of the Hunt for the World's Most Wanted Man* (New York: St. Martin's Press, 2008); Eric L. Haney, *Inside Delta Force: The Story of America's Elite Counterterrorist Unit* (New York: Delacorte Press, 2002); Chris Kyle, *American Sniper: The Autobiography of the Most Lethal Sniper in U.S. Military History*, with Jim DeFelice and Scott McEwen (New York: Morrow, 2013); Marcus Luttrell, *Service: A Navy SEAL at War*, with James D. Hornfischer (New York: Little, Brown, 2012); Marcus Luttrell, *Lone Survivor: The Eyewitness Account of Operation Redwing and the Lost Heroes of SEAL Team 10*, with Patrick Robinson (New York: Little, Brown, 2007); Don Mann, *Inside SEAL Team Six: My Life and Missions with America's Elite Warriors*, with Ralph Pezzullo (New York: Little, Brown, 2011); Richard Marcinko, *Rogue Warrior*, with John Weisman (New York: Pocket Books, 1992); Chuck Pfarrer, *Warrior Soul: The Memoir of a Navy SEAL* (New York: Random House, 2004); Howard E. Wasdin, *SEAL Team Six: Memoirs of an Elite Navy SEAL Sniper*, with Stephen Templin (New York: St. Martin's Press, 2011); Billy Waugh, *Hunting the Jackal: A Special Forces and CIA Ground Soldier's Fifty-Year Career Hunting America's Enemies*, with Tim Keown (New York: Morrow, 2004); and Brandon Webb, *The Red Circle: My Life in the Navy SEAL Sniper Corps and How I Trained America's Deadliest Marksmen*, with John David Mann (New York: St. Martin's Press, 2012).

8. A year after *No Easy Day* was published, Robert O'Neill provided his own first-hand account in an interview with Phil Bronstein, "The Shooter," *Esquire* (March 2013) and in an interview with Toby Harnden, "I Fired Twice and Bin Laden Crumpled," London *Sunday Times* (February 8, 2015). O'Neill later described the raid in a book,

The Operator: Firing the Shots that Killed Osama bin Laden and My Years as a SEAL Team Warrior (New York: Scribner, 2017), becoming the second operator to do so. Analysis of the national security leadership, including command structure and intelligence principals, is found in Mark Bowden, *The Finish: The Killing of Osama Bin Laden* (New York: Atlantic Monthly Press, 2012). Further accounts include Seymour M. Hersh, *The Killing of Osama Bin Laden* (London: Verso Books, 2016) and Chuck Pfarrer, *SEAL Target Geronimo: The Inside Story of the Mission to Kill Osama Bin Laden* (New York: St. Martin's Press, 2011).

9. The full quote of the U.S. Naval Special Warfare leader, Rear Admiral Sean Pybus, in a letter to the community (October 13, 2014), is: "I am disappointed, embarrassed and concerned. Most of us have always thought that the privilege of working with some of our nation's toughest warriors on challenging missions would be enough to be proud of, with no further compensation or celebrity required. Today, we find former SEALs headlining positions in a presidential campaign; hawking details about a mission against Enemy Number 1; and generally selling other aspects of NSW training and operations. For an elite force that should be humble and disciplined for life, we are certainly not appearing to be so. We owe our chain of command much better than this." For analysis, see Barbara Starr, "Scathing Message Sent to Navy SEALs on Discussing Secret Work," *Fox News* (September 5, 2012).

10. Coverage and reviews of *No Easy Day* are extensive, including Peter Bergen, in conversation with Neal Conan, "'Manhunt' Author Reviews Navy SEAL's 'No Easy Day,'" NPR *Talk of the Nation* (August 30, 2012); Dexter Filkins, "Taking Bin Laden," *New York Times Book Review* (October 21, 2012); Janet Maslin, "A SEAL's Own Story, Bin Laden and All," *New York Times* (September 2, 2012); Tony Perry, "Bringing Down Osama bin Laden," *Los Angeles Times Book Review* (September 5, 2012); Eric Schmitt, "Book on Bin Laden Killing Contradicts U.S. Account," *New York Times* (August 30, 2012); Joby Warrick, "For Bin Laden, a Passive End: Former SEAL's Book Depicts Osama bin Laden as Passive During Raid," *Washington Post* (August 30, 2012); and Bing West, "Former SEAL Writes a Book; Cue Indignation;

'No Easy Day,' About the Bin Laden Raid, Joins a Multimedia Tradition," *Wall Street Journal* (August 29, 2012).

11. "An essential piece of modern history," as the publisher called it, is described by Julie Bosman in "Bin Laden Book Release Moved Up," *New York Times* (August 29, 2012); she also writes about the operation's potential impact on the 2012 U.S. presidential campaign. The fast pace of the book's inception—from the time of the operation to hitting the bookstores—is described by Kevin Maurer, a reporter in North Carolina who had covered Camp LeJeune and Fort Bragg for the Associated Press and U.S. forces deployed to Afghanistan, and who also assisted in the writing of *No Easy Day*. In that same year, his book cowritten with Mitch Weiss also came out: *No Way Out: A Story of Valor in the Mountains of Afghanistan* (New York: Berkley Caliber, 2012).

12. See Owen (2012).

13. See Maurer (2012).

14. See Scott Pelley, "SEAL's First-Hand Account of Bin Laden Killing," CBS *60 Minutes*, September 9, 2012; transcript posted online September 24, 2012, cbsnews.com/news/seals-first-hand-account-of-bin-laden-killing.

15. Mark Bowden has written extensively on U.S. Special Operations, as a reporter for the *Philadelphia Inquirer, The Atlantic*, and *Vanity Fair*, among others, and in books, including *Black Hawk Down: A Story of Modern War* (New York: Atlantic Monthly Press, 1999); *Killing Pablo: The Hunt for the World's Greatest Outlaw* (New York: Atlantic Monthly Press, 2001); *Guests of the Ayatollah: The Iran Hostage Crisis: The First Battle in America's War with Militant Islam* (New York: Grove Press, 2006); and *The Finish: The Killing of Osama Bin Laden* (New York: Atlantic Monthly Press, 2012).

16. Department of Defense spokesman Lieutenant Colonel Todd Breasseale stated that the Pentagon and CIA were "shocked" to learn that more than a half-million copies of *No Easy Day* had already been printed, as described in Sharon Churcher, "How I Killed Bin Laden," London *Daily Mail* (September 2, 2012). The legal consequences for the author, who had not followed the prepublication review process

of the U.S. Department of Defense, are further analyzed in Mark Hosenball, "Pentagon Escalates Case that Former Navy SEAL Broke Secrecy Pledge," *Reuters* (September 7, 2012).

17. See Krishnadev Calamur, "Pentagon May Take Legal Action Against SEAL Author," *NPR* (August 30, 2012); and Howard Altman, "Battle Lines Drawn Over Book on Bin Laden Killing," *Tampa Tribune* (September 3, 2012).

18. See Andy Lewis, "Controversial Navy SEAL Book Displaces 'Fifty Shades' as Amazon's No. 1," *Hollywood Reporter* (August 27, 2012).

19. See *TV by the Numbers,* September 11, 2012, which reported an audience of 12.32 million viewers based on Nielsen ratings for Sunday, September 9, 2012. For analysis of these high ratings, see Marisa Guthrie, "The Secret World Behind '60 Minutes,'" *Hollywood Reporter* (April 10, 2013). Guthrie described the decision to devote the entire broadcast to the book as an "exception," but quoted Jeff Fager, the show's executive producer, as saying that it was "newsworthy on a number of fronts, including the fact that he was even talking about [the mission] and writing a book about it."

20. Jeremy Herb, "Pentagon: Secrets Divulged in SEAL's Book on Bin Laden Raid," *The Hill* (September 4, 2012), noting that it contained "sensitive and classified" information.

21. See letter from Robert D. Luskin of Patton Boggs LLP to the Honorable Charles Jeh Johnson, general counsel, U.S. Department of Defense, on August 31, 2012: "Mr. Owen takes seriously his obligations to the United States and to his former colleagues. They are as important to him as any mission he undertook while on active duty. Mr. Owen sought legal advice about his responsibilities before agreeing to publish his book and scrupulously reviewed the work to ensure that it did not disclose any material that would breach his agreements or put his former comrades at risk. He remains confident that he has faithfully fulfilled his duty. As you are well aware, the Classified Information Non-Disclosure Agreement, which you attached to your letter, invites, but by no means requires Mr. Owen to submit materials for pre-publication review. Although the Sensitive Compartmented

Information Nondisclosure Statement does require pre-publication security review under certain circumstances, that obligation is expressly limited to specifically identified Special Access Programs. That agreement was executed in January 2007, and the Special Access Programs to which it applies were identified on that date. Accordingly, it is difficult to understand how the matter that is the subject of Mr. Owen's book could conceivably be encompassed by the non-disclosure agreement that you have identified." This is further analyzed in Jeremy Herb, "Navy SEAL Says He Did Not Reveal Classified Info in Bin Laden Book," *The Hill* (August 31, 2012) and John Hudson, "Navy SEAL Author Rejects the Pentagon's Legal Threat," *The Atlantic* (August 31, 2012).

22. See Dan Lamothe, "Navy SEAL Who Wrote bin Laden Raid Book Must Pay Government at Least $6.8 Million," *Washington Post* (August 19, 2016); and *Reuters* (August 20, 2016), "Ex-U.S. Navy Seal Author Agrees to Pay $6.8 Million to Government," which reported his statement as: "I accept responsibility for failing to submit the book for review and apologize sincerely for my oversight."

23. See Dave Maxwell, "A Recommendation for Quiet Professionals," *Small Wars Journal* (May 2011) for an analysis of the culture. For a discussion of monetization that went beyond the personal memoir, see Dan Lamothe, "Want to Shoot Machine Gun with Navy SEAL Who Killed Osama Bin Laden? That'll Be $50,000, Please," *Washington Post* (April 24, 2015). See also Mark Owen, *No Hero: The Evolution of a Navy SEAL* (New York: Dutton, 2014), for the sequel that presented his reflections on the postpublication circumstances of *No Easy Day*.

24. Owen (2012): chapter 16.

25. SOF Week, an annual gathering of the U.S. Special Operations community, held in Tampa each May, and organized by the Special Operations Forces Industry Conference, happened to fall on the calendar three weeks after the Abbottabad raid. For journalists' perspectives on the public discussions at the conference, see Sharon Weinberger, "How Osama bin Laden's Death Reverberates through the Defense Sector," *Popular Mechanics* (May 19, 2011); David Crane,

"Atlantic Signal," *Defense Review* (May 15, 2011); and Jim Fallon, "US Special Operations Forces: The Quiet Warriors of USSOCOM," *Microwave Journal* (June 14, 2011). In subsequent years, a number of publications addressed these questions, including the working paper of Christopher P. Costa, "Post–Bin Laden SOF Operations, Strategy and Reflections on Future Threats"; Jeffrey Kaplan and Christopher P. Costa, "The Islamic State and the New Tribalism," *Terrorism and Political Violence* 27:5 (2015): 926–69; Nate Rawlings, "Two Years After bin Laden Raid, the Future of Special Operations," *Time* (May 2, 2013); Fabius Maximus, "Expanding the Size and Scope of Our Special Operations Forces, an Alternative to Learning from Our Failed Wars," *Fabius Maximus Website* (November 3, 2013); Nick Turse, "Washington Puts Its Money on Proxy War," *The Nation* (August 9, 2012); Nick Turse, "The U.S. Carried Out 674 Military Operations in Africa Last Year. Did You Hear About Any of Them?" *The Nation* (April 14, 2015); and Jeremy Scahill, *Dirty Wars: The World Is a Battlefield* (New York: Nation Books, 2013).

7 FALLEN ANGEL

1. The opening quote—"You want Pashtun boys to shoot their cousins—this is a strategy?"—is from Ann Jones, "Ballots and Bullets for Afghanistan," *Nation* (August 18, 2009), which appeared at the time of national elections amid widespread violence. For reporting on the Tangi Valley and surrounding region, see Deb Riechmann and Lolita C. Baldor, "The War in Afghanistan: Focus Shifts to Special Ops, Crash Shows Increasing Use of Night Missions and Its Dangers," *Associated Press* (August 9, 2011) and Deb Riechmann, "August Deadliest Month for U.S. in Afghan War," *Associated Press* (August 31, 2011). On the broader conflicts and fights inside Afghanistan, see Ewan W. Anderson and Nancy Hatch Dupree, eds., *The Cultural Basis of Afghan Nationalism* (London: Pinter, 1990); Robert D. Crews and Amin Tarzi, *The Taliban and the Crisis of Afghanistan* (Cambridge, MA: Harvard University Press, 2008); Gilles Dorronsoro, *Revolution Unending: Afghanistan, 1979 to the Present* (New York: Columbia University Press, 2005); and Mohammad Yousaf and

Mark Adkin, *The Bear Trap: Afghanistan's Untold Story* (London: Cooper, 1992).

2. For on-the-ground reporting of this time and place, see Anand Gopal, "US Troops in Afghanistan Face Tough Battle: Making 'Clear, Hold, and Build' Work," *Christian Science Monitor* (July 8, 2009) and "In Afghanistan Surge, Soldiers Negotiate a Complex Web of Local Loyalties," *Christian Science Monitor* (July 7, 2009). The latter is the source for the quote from First Lieutenant Christopher Wallgren, 3rd Brigade, 10th Mountain Division, about COP Tangi. See "Meet the Bomb Hunters," *Taranaki Daily News* (October 20, 2009), for the quote about "getting kissed by the devil," from Lieutenant Christopher George.

3. Agence France-Presse, "Afghanistan's Bamiyan on Frontline of War Zone Tourism," (July 27, 2015); Karin Brulliard, "Garish 'Poppy Palaces' Lure Affluent Afghans," *Washington Post* (June 06, 2010).

4. For the "three-cups-of-tea" strategy, see Greg Mortenson and David Oliver Relin, *Three Cups of Tea: One Man's Mission to Promote Peace . . . One School at a Time* (New York: Penguin, 2007).

5. Regarding experiences at FOB Shank in this period, see "Three Kalispell Members of the Montana Army National Guard's Detachment 3," *Daily Inter Lake* (January 6, 2011), quoting one engineer as describing an "occasional incoming mortar round . . . that base had attacks three or four times a month." Two years later, a doctor in the U.S. Army Reserves described a continuation of the attacks in an interview with Georgetown University, "Doctor Operates on Soldiers with Wartime Trauma Injuries While Under Constant Threat of Enemy Attacks," *medstargeorgetown.edu* (February 20, 2014).

6. See Ejaz Haider, "We Have a Wicked Problem," *Pakistan Today* (August 12, 2011) for a description of local governance: "Thousands of miles away from Afghanistan, in April, Abdullah said to me with matter-of-fact grimness on the sidelines of a Brookings conference that the venture was doomed . . . We have not been able to reach out to the people and we have failed to provide them good governance . . . He noted then that President Hamid Karzai's ministers could not go to their own provinces which are de facto ruled by

the Taliban . . . [including] Maydan, Wardak and Logar, among others."

7. Ismatullah is quoted in Jason Burke, "War in Afghanistan: Taliban Win Over Locals at the Gates of Kabul," London *Observer* (August 24, 2008). See also Julius Cavendish, "Losing the Battle for Afghan Hearts and Minds," *Sunday Herald* (January 4, 2009).

8. Deb Riechmann and Lolita C. Baldor, "Deadly Crash Highlights Role of U.S. Elite Forces," *Associated Press* (August 7, 2011) reported: "Ali Ahmad Khashai, deputy governor of Wardak province, said Taliban insurgents frequently moved through the Tangi Valley. 'This area concerns us because many attacks in Wardak are organised and planned in Tangi,' he said. 'The enemy is active and the [military] operations have not been effective, unfortunately, because it is between three provinces that no one is taking responsibility for.'"

9. See M. Hassan Kakar, *Afghanistan: The Soviet Invasion and the Afghan Response, 1979–1982* (Berkeley: University of California Press, 1995), in which he remembers: "My diary entry for 21 November [1980] reads: 'The actual number of the casualties is unknown . . . In many places dead bodies lay here and there. No one dared to bury them' . . . [and for] 14 May 1981 that the Soviets 'showed no mercy to any human being.'" See the writings of Edward Girardet, a journalist with the *Christian Science Monitor,* who took five trips to the region during 1979–1982 and described "a deliberate policy by the Soviet government to chase the [Afghan] people into exile, thereby ridding the resistance groups of any possibility of support." An article in the *New York Times* provides further details, including a description from Michael Barry, a monitor who worked for an investigating tribunal and photographed a massacre by Soviet soldiers in the Tangi Valley on September 13, 1982. See Richard Bernstein, "Afghans, in New York, Tell of a Massacre by Russians," *New York Times* (January 28, 1983). According to Barry, local villagers hid in a canal, into which the soldiers poured flammable chemicals, killing all: "We found the canal; we have seen that the underground irrigation channel, which is essentially a damp, mud tunnel several kilometers long, for several score yards is completely scorched and uniformly coated with soot." See also the

declassified report from the CIA, Special Report 104, on Afghanistan, 1983. Secretary of State George Shultz stated publicly, "Our suspicions that mycotoxins have been used [by Soviet and Afghan government forces] in Afghanistan have now been confirmed . . . reports during 1980 and 1981 described a yellow-brown mist being delivered in attacks which caused blistering, vomiting and other symptoms similar to those described by 'yellow rain' victims in Southeast Asia."

10. See Jerry Laber and Barnet Rubin, eds., *A Report from Helsinki Watch, 1979–1984* (New York: U.S. Helsinki Watch Committee, 1984).

11. Mohammad Rahim, Tangi Valley resident, quoted in "Helicopter Crash Highlights Instability Near Kabul," *Times of Oman* (August 14, 2011).

12. See Ann Jones, "Women and Warlords: Letters from Afghanistan," *Nation* (May 22, 2006); Pamela Constable, "Many Afghans Lost to Hazards of Childbirth," *Washington Post* (June 6, 2006); and Griff Witte, "Afghanistan's Chance to Heal," *Washington Post* (December 18, 2005). See also Jonathan S. Landay and Hashim Shukoor, "Afghans in Valley Support Insurgents," *Spokesman Review* (August 8, 2011), which includes a description by Roshanak Wardak: "'They are coming to our houses at night.' The raids occur 'every night. We are very much miserable,' said Roshanak Wardak." A second doctor, speaking on condition of anonymity, said, "There are night raids every day or every other day."

13. See Deb Riechmann, "Afghan Witnesses Describe Deadly Chinook Crash," *Associated Press* (August 10, 2011) for quote by Alam Gul, chief of the local council in the Sayd Abad District: "The foreigners are guests, but what has changed in 10 years? . . . [and] Yes, you are our guests, but you have done a lot of bad things."

14. See Ray Rivera, Alissa J. Rubin, and Thom Shanker, "Copter Downed by Taliban Fire: Elite U.S. Unit Among Dead," *New York Times* (August 6, 2011), which quotes the commander of 10th Mountain Division's Task Force Warrior: "As we lose U.S. personnel, we have to concentrate on the greater populations . . . We are going to continue to hunt insurgents in Tangi and prevent them from having a safe haven."

15. The definitive history of Extortion 17 is Ed Darack, *The Final Mission of Extortion 17: Special Ops, Helicopter Support, SEAL Team Six, and the*

Deadliest Day of the U.S. War in Afghanistan (Washington, DC: Smithsonian Books, 2017). See also his article "The Final Flight of Extortion 17," *Smithsonian Air & Space Magazine* (March 2015).

16. See Riechmann, "Afghan Witnesses," for the account of Farhad.

17. A U.S. Marine F/A-18D weapons and sensors operator explains the "To Whom It May Concern" phenomenon.

18. See Deb Riechmann, "New Targets in War Against Taliban," *Associated Press* (August 10, 2011), who quoted Zabiullah Mujahid as saying that the fighters had a general sense of the target's significance, but not its exact details: "We didn't know exactly that it was that Navy SEAL unit, but we know whenever they have the night raids and they plan to attack mujahideen [holy warriors] somewhere, they always use their special forces so we knew they were very important."

19. See the *Australian* (August 12, 2011) for the Taliban's counterstatement: "The Taliban insisted last night that the fighters who shot down a US helicopter killing 38 troops in Afghanistan are still alive, despite a US announcement they had been killed." Shortly thereafter, the Pentagon released a statement on August 10, 2011, that included a quote from General John R. Allen, then leading the International Security Assistance Force (ISAF), that "Coalition forces killed the Taliban insurgents responsible for this attack."

20. They filmed their entrance into the abandoned U.S. military outpost and posted it to YouTube. Badri, the local Taliban commander, stated, "Even the barbed wire we gave away to cemeteries, madrassas and mosques."

21. Kevin Sieff, "Afghan Soldiers Enter a Taliban Nest—Without U.S. Troops by Their Side," *Washington Post* (April 7, 2013) described the makeshift bomb that detonated when Afghan forces reached the outcrop and went to take the Taliban flag from its peak. Sieff goes on to report that, in just four days, "more than 40 makeshift bombs had detonated" in their move through the Valley. Colonel Sami Badakshani, executive officer of the Afghan Army's Fourth Brigade explained, "Terrorists own the Tangi . . . The American military left. The Afghan government left."

22. See Schmidle (August 8, 2011).

23. Will McCants, *The ISIS Apocalypse: The History, Strategy, and Doomsday Vision of the Islamic State* (New York: St. Martin's, 2015); Jacob N. Shapiro, *The Terrorist's Dilemma: Managing Violent Covert Organizations* (Princeton: Princeton University Press, 2013); Joby Warrick, *Black Flags: The Rise of ISIS* (New York: Random House, 2015). See also Jonathan Masters, *Al-Qaeda in the Islamic Maghreb* (New York: Council on Foreign Relations, 2015).

24. Thomas Joscelyn, "U.S.-Backed Forces Declare End to Islamic State's Physical Caliphate," *Long War Journal* (March 23, 2019).

25. Al-Baghdadi audio message on September 16, 2019, distributed by Al Furqan Establishment for Media Production and discussed in the *Long War Journal* by Thomas Joscelyn, "Abu Bakr al-Baghdadi Praises the Islamic State's Global Operations" (September 17, 2019).

26. See Combating Terrorism Center, U.S. Military Academy, *Sentinel* 12:10 (November 2019), for this issue that analyzes the death of al-Baghdadi and expected leadership succession.

27. Tony Capaccio, "Inside the Drone Strike that Killed Qasem Soleimani," *Bloomberg News* (January 7, 2020).

28. See Capaccio, "Inside the Drone Strike" (2020) which reports that "[a] U.S. official told reporters in Washington on Friday . . . that Soleimani was a 'target of opportunity.'" See also interview of Ambassador Ryan Crocker by Deborah Amos, "Global Reactions to Soleimani Killing," NPR *All Things Considered* (January 4, 2020); John B. Bellinger III, "Does the U.S. Strike on Soleimani Break Legal Norms?" in *Brief,* Council on Foreign Relations (January 6, 2020); Peter Baker, Ronen Bergman, David D. Kirkpatrick, Julian E. Barnes, and Alissa J. Rubin, "Seven Days in January: How Trump Pushed U.S. and Iran to the Brink of War," *New York Times* (January 11, 2020); and Combating Terrorism Center, U.S. Military Academy, *Sentinel* 13:2 (February 2020), for this issue that analyzes the killing of Soleimani and expected Iranian retaliations.

8 USE OF THE GOLDEN SPEAR

1. The opening quote—"Thus the long war, from everlasting waged"— from the first century B.C., appears in Lucretius's *De rerum natura,* or *On the Nature of Things* (Oxford: Clarendon Press, 1910). At the MacDill

runway, Senior Airman Adam R. Shanks, of the 6th Air Mobility Wing, described the training squadrons making use of the facilities, including the T-45C Goshawk, F/A-18F Super Hornet, and EA-18G Growler, in statement by 6th Air Mobility Wing (Tampa: MacDill Air Force Base, November 7, 2018). They meet the needs of any aircraft, including "bombers, fighters and other specialized jets." See also the MacDill Air Force Base, *Installation Facility Standards, Pre-Draft* (June 4, 2018), for the comprehensive planning for base facilities and future developments.

2. See base assessments, including MacDill Air Force Base, *Environmental Assessment for SOCCENT Operations Facility, Draft* (March 2018); U.S. Department of the Air Force, *Environmental Assessment, Construction of an Additional Warehouse Complex, MacDill Air Force Base, Florida, Draft* (June 2016); MacDill Air Force Base, *Environmental Assessment of Installation Development, Final* (March 2013); Air Mobility Command, *Environmental Assessment of Installation Development at MacDill Air Force Base, Florida* (January 2007); and U.S. General Accounting Office, *Defense Management: Issues in Contracting for Lodging and Temporary Office Space at MacDill Air Force Base GAO-04-296* (January 2004).

3. Olga Oliker, Richard Kauzlarich, James Dobbins, et al., *Aid During Conflict: Interaction Between Military and Civilian Assistance Providers in Afghanistan, September 2001–June 2002* (Santa Monica: RAND Corporation, 2004) for discussion of the initial establishment of the Coalition Coordination Center. Established at MacDill at the beginning of Operation Enduring Freedom (OEF) to work with Coalition partners, the center also included liaison representatives from the U.S. Department of State, the U.S. Agency for International Development, and the U.N. High Commissioner for Refugees, among others. For its initial development, see Betty Liu, "Coalition Village Unites Troops for War on Terrorism," *Financial Times* (March 2, 2002); George Coryell, "Coalition Village Raises a War," *Tampa Tribune* (November 16, 2001); and Roger Roy, "America: Attacking Terrorism," *Orlando Sentinel* (November 28, 2001). It was a kind of Coalition effort that MacDill had previously led during the 1991 Persian Gulf War—thirty-eight nations joined forces then—but this was a different kind of command arrangement. See Nora Bensahel, *The Counterterror Coalitions:*

Cooperation with Europe, NATO, and the European Union (Santa Monica: RAND Corporation, 2003) on shifting multilateral military and intelligence capabilities in this period.

4. President George W. Bush to a Joint Session of Congress on September 20, 2001: "We ask every nation to join us . . . The United States is grateful that many nations and many international organizations have already responded with sympathy and with support—nations from Latin America to Asia to Africa to Europe to the Islamic world. Perhaps the NATO charter reflects best the attitude of the world: An attack on one is an attack on all. The civilized world is rallying to America's side . . . Every nation, in every region, now has a decision to make. Either you are with us, or you are with the terrorists. From this day forward, any nation that continues to harbor or support terrorism will be regarded by the United States as a hostile regime. Our nation has been put on notice, we're not immune from attack."

5. See Contemporary Operations Studies Team, *Interview with Mr. Jay E. Hines* (Fort Leavenworth, KS: Combat Studies Institute, January 11, 2006), in which Hines described how a parking lot was "turned into a trailer park. There are about 60 trailers and each country has its own trailer . . . That's the coalition village. That was for Afghanistan, and then for Iraq we had to create another coalition village because we couldn't co-mingle the two missions. We had some countries which still support us 100 percent on Afghanistan, but they balked at OIF." See Paul de la Garza and Dong-Phuong Nguyen, "MacDill's New 'Village' Helps Coordinate Globe," *St. Petersburg Times* (October 27, 2001) and Paul de La Garza, "MacDill's Coalition Village," *St. Petersburg Times* (October 30, 2001) for a discussion of its setup: "described by eyewitnesses as a whole city, [the Village] is going up on a parking lot on the south side of the headquarters of the Central Command, or CENTCOM," to meet the needs of military, intelligence, and other personnel arriving from around the world, a Coalition warfare team to combat global terrorism.

6. Roy Eccleston, "Our Top Brass Warns of SAS Casualty Risk," *Weekend Australian* (December 8, 2001).

7. See President Bush's news conference on October 11, 2001, from the White House's East Room, where he gave an update to the American people on the global war on terror one month after the homeland attacks: "One month ago today, innocent citizens from more than 80 nations were attacked and killed without warning or provocation in an act that horrified not only every American, but every person of every faith and every nation who values human life. The attack took place on American soil, but it was an attack on the heart and soul of the civilized world. And the world has come together to fight a new and different war, the first, and we hope the only one, of the 21st century; a war against all those who seek to export terror and a war against those governments that support or shelter them. We've accomplished a great deal in one month. Our staunch friends, Great Britain, our neighbors Canada and Mexico, our NATO allies, our allies in Asia, Russia and nations from every continent on the Earth have offered help of one kind or of another, from military assistance to intelligence information to crack down on terrorist financial networks. This week, 56 Islamic nations issued a statement strongly condemning the savage acts of terror and emphasizing that those acts contradict the peaceful teachings of Islam. All is strong and united on the diplomatic front." He then took questions from the press corps. On the context of these early months, see *The 9/11 Commission Report: Final Report of the National Commission on Terrorist Attacks Upon the United States* (Washington, DC: U.S. Government Printing Office, 2004) and Office of the President, *The National Security Strategy of the United States* (Washington, DC: Government Printing Office, 2002). See also Bob Woodward, *The War Within* (New York: Simon & Schuster, 2008); Donald Rumsfeld, *Known and Unknown: A Memoir* (New York: Sentinel, 2011); George Tenet, *At the Center of the Storm: My Years at the CIA* (New York: HarperCollins, 2007); Richard A. Clarke, *Against All Enemies: Inside America's War on Terror* (New York: The Free Press, 2004); and Douglas J. Feith, *Decision: Inside the Pentagon at the Dawn of the War on Terrorism* (New York: HarperCollins, 2008).

8. On new types of attacks and new use of force, see Jennifer K. Elsea and Matthew C. Weed, *Declarations of War and Authorizations for the Use*

of Military Force: Historical Background and Legal Implications (Washington, DC: Congressional Research Service, April 18, 2014); Norman Friedman, *Terrorism, Afghanistan, and America's New Way of War* (Annapolis: U.S. Naval Institute Press, 2003); Frank G. Hoffman, *Conflict in the 21st Century: The Rise of Hybrid Wars* (Arlington, VA: Potomac Institute for Policy Studies, 2007) and *Decisive Force: The New American Way of War* (Westport, CT: Praeger, 1996); James F. Hoge, Jr. and Gideon Rose, eds., *How Did This Happen? Terrorism and the New War* (Washington, DC: Public Affairs, 2001); and John Prados, *America Confronts Terrorism: Understanding the Danger and How to Think About It: A Documentary Record* (Chicago: Ivan R. Dee, 2002). In comparison, see Barbara Salazar Torrean and Sofia Plagakis, *Instances of Use of United States Armed Forces Abroad, 1798–2020* (Washington, DC: Congressional Research Service, July 20, 2020). On the early developments of the 9/11 wars, on the ground in Afghanistan and Pakistan, see Gary Berntsen and Ralph Pezzullo, *Jawbreaker: The Attack on Bin Laden and Al Qaeda: A Personal Account by the CIA's Key Field Commander* (New York: Crown, 2005); Gary C. Schroen, *First In: An Insider's Account of How the CIA Spearheaded the War on Terror in Afghanistan* (New York: Random House, 2005); Robert Grenier, *88 Days to Kandahar: A CIA Diary* (New York: Simon & Schuster, 2015); Robert Baer, *See No Evil: The True Story of a Ground Soldier in the CIA's War on Terrorism* (New York: Crown, 2002); Henry A. Crumpton, "Intelligence and War: Afghanistan 2001–2002," in *Transforming U.S. Intelligence,* in Jennifer E. Sims and Burton Gerber, eds., (Washington, DC: Georgetown University Press, 2005); Henry A. Crumpton, *The Art of Intelligence: Lessons from a Life in the CIA's Clandestine Service* (New York: Penguin, 2012); and Michael Allen, *Blinking Red: Crisis and Compromise in American Intelligence After 9/11* (Dulles, VA: Potomac Books, 2013).

9. On CENTCOM immediately after 9/11, see Tommy Franks, *American Soldier,* with Malcolm McConnell (New York: HarperCollins, 2004) and Ron Martz, "From Tampa, Franks on Top of the War," *Atlanta Journal* (April 18, 2002). Franks explained, "Technology allows [me] to sit in a small room adjacent to [my] office on the third floor of Central Command HQ and closely monitor the war 9 1/2 time zones

away . . . [there are] maps that are updated every one-sixteenth of a second with the positions of every coalition military unit, ship, and aircraft involved in the war effort . . . and [we can] call up live video from unmanned aerial vehicles scouting Afghanistan . . . radar images and video from J-STARS aircraft." See also Christopher Buchanan, "Campaign Against Terror," transcript of interview with General Tommy Franks, PBS *Frontline* (June 12, 2002). For SOCOM, see Edward F. Bruner, Christopher Bolkum, and Ronald O'Rourke, *Special Operations Forces in Operation Enduring Freedom: Background and Issues for Congress* (Washington, DC: Congressional Research Service, October 15, 2001); Renee Montagne, Steve Inskeep, and Jeremy Scahill, "After September 11, Special Ops Were 'Injected with Steroids,'" *NPR* (November 5, 2013); and U.S. Special Operations Command, *Posture Statement, 2003–2004: Transforming the Force at the Forefront of the War on Terrorism* (Washington, DC: Government Printing Office, 2003). For initial appraisals of Operation Enduring Freedom, see Carl Conetta, *Strange Victory: A Critical Appraisal of Operation Enduring Freedom and the Afghanistan War* (Washington, DC: Project on Defense Alternatives, 2002); Anthony H. Cordesman, *The Lessons of Afghanistan: War Fighting, Intelligence* and *Force Transformation* (Washington, DC: Center for Strategic and International Studies, 2002); and U.S. Army, *A Different Kind of War: U.S. Army in Operation Enduring Freedom, October 2001– September 2005* (Fort Leavenworth, KS: Combat Studies Institute Press, 2009).

10. See Alec Russell, "Philosophy of Fighting al-Qaeda," *Daily Telegraph* (April 10, 2006) for the long-term nature of the campaign, as described by CENTCOM's deputy head of strategy and planning: "We will not roll up our sleeping bags or untie our tents after we capture or kill bin Laden." For the early days of the fight, see Personnel of the 3rd Battalion, 5th Special Forces Group, "The Liberation of Mazar-e Sharif: 5th Special Forces Group Conducts Unconventional Warfare in Afghanistan," *Special Warfare* 15:2 (June 2002): 34–41; Doug Stanton, *Horse Soldiers: The Extraordinary Story of a Band of U.S. Soldiers Who Rode to Victory in Afghanistan* (New York: Scribner, 2009); and Sean Naylor, *Not a Good Day to Die: The Untold Story of Operation Anaconda* (New York:

Berkley Books, 2005). On the use of airpower, see Rebecca Grant, *Airpower in Afghanistan* (Portland, ME: Mitchell Institute for Airpower Studies, 2009); Benjamin S. Lambeth, *Air Power Against Terror: America's Conduct of Operation Enduring Freedom* (Santa Monica: RAND Corporation, 2005); and Walter L. Perry and David Kassing, *Topping the Taliban: Air-Ground Operations in Afghanistan, October 2001–June 2002* (Santa Monica: RAND Corporation, 2015).

11. See de la Garza and Dong-Phuong, "MacDill's New 'Village' Helps Coordinate Globe" (2001).

12. On the evolution of Coalition warfare, see Daniel Byman, "Remaking Alliances for the War on Terrorism," *Journal of Strategic Studies* 29:5 (October 2006): 767–811; Naureen Chowdhury Fink, "Meeting the Challenge: A Guide to United Nations Counterterrorism Activities" (International Peace Institute, June 27, 2012); David C. Gompert and Raymond C. Smith, "Creating a NATO Special Operations Force," *Defense Horizons* 52 (March 2006): 1–8; James L. Jones, "Transforming NATO Special Operations," *Joint Forces Quarterly* 45 (Second Quarter 2007): 36–40; Thomas S. Szayna and William Welser, *Developing and Assessing Options for the Global SOF Network* (Santa Monica: RAND Corporation, 2013); and Paul de B. J. Taillon, "Coalition Special Operations Forces," *Military Technology* 33 (2009): 12–17. On the contributions of special operators from particular nations, see James Adams, *Secret Armies: The Full Story of the SAS, Delta Force and Spetsnaz* (New York: Pan Books, 1988); Paul de B. J. Taillon, *The Evolution of Special Forces in Counter-Terrorism: The British and American Experiences* (Westport, CT: Praeger, 2001); Simon Dunstan, *Israel's Lightning Strike: The Raid on Entebbe, 1976* (Oxford and New York: Osprey, 2009); Michael Eisenstadt, "Israel's Approach to Special Operations," *Special Warfare* 7 (January 1994): 22–29; Thomas H. Henriksen, *The Israeli Approach to Irregular Warfare and Implications for the United States* (Hurlburt Field, FL: Joint Special Operations University, 2007); Robert Macklin, *Warrior Elite: Australia's Special Forces—From Z Force and the SAS to the Wars of the Future* (Sydney: Hachette Australia, 2015); D. M. Horner, *SAS: Phantoms of War: A History of Australian Special Air Service* (New South Wales: Allen & Unwin, 2002); Piet Nortje, *32 Battalion:*

The Inside Story of South Africa's Elite Fighting Unit (Cape Town: Zebra Press, 2003); Piet Nortje, *The Terrible Ones: A Complete History of 32 Battalion*, Two Volumes (Cape Town: Zebra Press, 2012); Eric Micheletti, *French Special Forces: Special Operations Command* (Paris: Histoire & Collections, 1999); Bernd Horn and Tony Balasevicius, *Casting Light on the Shadows: Canadian Perspectives on Special Operations Forces* (Kingston, ON: Canadian Defense Academy Press, 2007); Bernd Horn, *More Than Meets the Eye: The Invisible Hand of SOF in Afghanistan* (Kingston, ON: Canadian Defense Academy Press, 2011); Bernd Horn, *No Lack of Courage: Operation Medusa, Afghanistan* (Toronto: Dundurn Press, 2010); Mike Rouleau, *Between Faith and Reality: A Pragmatic Sociological Examination of Canadian Special Operations Forces Command's Future Prospects* (Kingston, ON: Canadian Defense Academy Press, 2012); Emily Spencer, *Special Operations Forces: A National Capability* (Kingston, ON: Canadian Defense Academy Press, 2011); Emily Spencer, *Special Operations Forces: Building Global Partnerships* (Kingston, ON: Canadian Defense Academy Press, 2012); and Alvaro de Souza Pinheiro, *Knowing Your Partner: The Evolution of Brazilian Special Operations Forces* (Tampa: Joint Special Operations University, MacDill Air Force Base, August 2012).

13. See Paul de la Garza, "Officers Quietly Forge Coalition," *St. Petersburg Times* (April 7, 2003) and Robert Schlesinger, "US, Allies Can Fight on Several Fronts, Says Top General," *Boston Globe* (February 4, 2003).

14. On President Bush's visit to MacDill Air Force Base on June 16, 2004, he drew attention to the international partnership of Coalition Village: "Here at CENTCOM, the Coalition Village flies the flags of 65 nations that are doing their part in the war on terror. On behalf of our country, I thank all of [our] friends and allies for serving with America in the cause of freedom." He also paid tribute to the weighty mission of CENTCOM and its historical context: "The Command was activated in the 1980s. Back then, America needed CENTCOM to help protect our allies from aggression and to support Afghan freedom fighters. Now, at the start of a new century, the men and women of CENTCOM have liberated two nations, and have rescued more than 50 million people from tyranny. Today your nation is counting on you to ensure the

defeat of terrorists, to secure America, and to advance freedom throughout the Middle East. That's our mission." He also briefly shone the spotlight on SOCOM: "MacDill is also the headquarters for our quiet warriors, the United States Special Operations Command. It is the nature of Special Ops that many of your victories are unseen and must remain secret—but I know about them. Our Special Operations Forces are the worst nightmare of America's worst enemies, and you're making us proud."

15. Three years later, on May 1, 2007, President Bush returned and addressed the CENTCOM Coalition Conference, underscoring its unifying role: "CENTCOM's Coalition Village is a welcome reminder that in the fight against radicals and extremists and murderers of the innocent, we stand as one. We appreciate your country's contributions to this enormous challenge in the 21st century. I appreciate the fact that your work has helped to liberate millions of people . . . helped keep millions of people safe. And so I thank you for defending the security of the civilized world . . . the mission is vital."

16. President Barack Obama, "Remarks," MacDill Air Force Base, Tampa, FL (September 17, 2014).

17. President Barack Obama, "Administration's Approach to Counterterrorism," MacDill Air Force Base, Tampa, FL (December 6, 2016).

18. Brigadier General Jens Praestegaard, Coalition chairman and senior national representative of Denmark, is quoted in "Coalition of Nations Supporting the War," *MacDill Thunderbolt* (May 24, 2012). See Stephen M. Saideman and David P. Auerswald, "Comparing Caveats: Understanding the Sources of National Restrictions Upon NATO's Mission in Afghanistan," *International Studies Quarterly* 56:1 (March 2012): 67–84 for a discussion of the constraints on the International Security Assistance Force (ISAF) in operationalizing coalition warfare in Afghanistan.

19. With regards to the physical marker, see John Hendren, "Response to Terror," *Los Angeles Times* (December 17, 2001): "Coalition Village, a makeshift military version of the United Nations where nearly two dozen new flags flutter above no-frills tan-and-brown trailers in what

was once CENTCOM's main parking lot. Looming highest, above an American trailer designated for coordination with coalition members, is the American flag." For a discussion of challenges in coalition military training and joint security force assistance, see Nina M. Serafino, *Global Security Contingency Fund: Summary and Issue Overview* (Washington, DC: Congressional Research Service, April 4, 2014); Nina M. Serafino, *Security Assistance Reform: "Section 1206" Background and Issues for Congress* (Washington, DC: Congressional Research Service, December 8, 2014); Nina M. Serafino, *The Department of Defense Role in Foreign Assistance: Background, Major Issues* and *Options for Congress* (Washington, DC: Congressional Research Service, December 9, 2008); and David Maxwell, "Considerations for Organizing and Preparing for Security Force Assistance Operations," *Small Wars Journal* (July 1, 2009).

20. Secretary of Defense James N. Mattis, "Resignation Letter," December 20, 2018.

21. For the longue durée, see Andrew J. Bacevich, ed., *The Long War: A New History of U.S. National Security Policy since World War II* (New York: Columbia University Press, 2007); Philip Bobbitt, *The Shield of Achilles: War, Peace, and the Course of History* (New York: Knopf, 2002); Fred J. Cook, *The Warfare State* (New York: Macmillan, 1962); Aaron L. Friedberg, *In the Shadow of the Garrison State: America's Anti-Statism and Its Cold War Grand Strategy* (Princeton: Princeton University Press, 2000); Edward Luttwak, *Strategy: The Logic of War and Peace* (Cambridge, MA: Harvard University Press, 2001); Thomas Schelling, *Arms and Influence* (New Haven: Yale University Press, 1966); Thomas Schelling, *The Strategy of Conflict* (Cambridge, MA: Harvard University Press, 1960); and Kenneth Waltz, *Man, the State* and *War* (New York: Columbia University Press, 1959).

22. U.S. Congress, House of Representatives and Senate, 107th Congress, *Authorization of the Use of Military Force, S.J. Res. 23* (Washington, DC: Government Printing Office, 2001).

23. On the financial costs of the 9/11 wars, see Amy Belasco, *The Cost of Iraq, Afghanistan and Other Global War on Terror Operations since 9/11* (Washington, DC: Congressional Research Service, 2011), and updates

to this report in other years; Linda J. Bilmes, "The Financial Legacy of Iraq and Afghanistan: How Wartime Spending Decisions Will Cancel Out the Peace Dividend," *The Economics of Peace and Security Journal* 9:1 (2014): 5–18; Stephen Daggett, *Costs of Major U.S. Wars* (Washington, DC: Congressional Research Service, June 29, 2010); Stephen Daggett, *Military Operations: Precedents for Funding Contingency Operations in Regular or in Supplemental Appropriations Bills* (Washington, DC: Congressional Research Service, June 13, 2006); Aaron L. Martin, *Paying for War: Funding U.S. Military Operations since 2001* (Santa Monica: RAND Corporation, 2011); Dinah Walker, *Trends in U.S. Military Spending* (New York: Council on Foreign Relations, 2012); and *Cost of Activities Related to the Military Operations Taking Place in and around Afghanistan* (Washington, DC: Congressional Budget Office, 2002). As a baseline for analysis immediately before September 11, see George C. Wilson, *This War Really Matters: Inside the Fight for Defense Dollars* (Washington, DC: CQ Press, 2000). On the specific budgets of U.S. Special Operations, see David E. Hill, Jr., *The Shaft of the Spear: U.S. Special Operations Command, Funding Authority and the Global War on Terrorism* (Carlisle, PA: U.S. Army War College, 2006).

24. The Annual Congressional Statements by the commanders of U.S. Special Operations Command—Charles R. Holland (2000–2003); Bryan D. Brown (2003–2007); Eric T. Olson (2007–2011); William H. McRaven (2011–2014); Joseph L. Votel (2014–2016); Raymond A. Thomas III (2016–2019); and Richard D. Clarke (2019–present)— show the evolution of these numbers since 9/11. Regarding funding through Overseas Contingency Operations (OCO) budgets specifically, see David R. O'Leary, *The United States' Overseas Contingency Operations / Global War on Terror: A Military Revolution* (Fort Leavenworth, KS: U.S. Army Command and General Staff College, 2014).

25. See the chairman of the Joint Chiefs of Staff, *Manual on Special Operations JP 1-02* (2003), with the emphasis on the use of U.S. Special Operations when there is "no broad conventional force requirement." For a discussion of the broader trade-offs between conventional and nonconventional forces, see Stephen J. Hadley, William J. Perry, et al., *The QDR in Perspective: Meeting America's National Security*

Needs in the 21st Century (Washington, DC: U.S. Institute of Peace, 2010). For a discussion of some of the benefits and limits of light footprints and irregular warfare, see Fernando Lujan, *Light Footprints: The Future of American Military Intervention* (Washington, DC: Center for a New American Security, 2013); Stephen Watts, "The Foreign Policy Essay: The Limits of Small Footprints," *RAND* (March 31, 2014); and Mark Grdovic, "Ramping Up to Face the Challenge of Irregular Warfare," *Special Warfare* 22 (September/October 2009): 15–18.

26. See the important framework presented by Jeh C. Johnson, "The Conflict Against Al Qaeda and Its Affiliates: How Will It End?," speech at the Oxford Union (November 30, 2012). The endless nature of the 9/11 wars is a focus of Dexter Filkins's *Forever War* (New York: Knopf, 2008). For broader statements on war, peace, and security in the twenty-first century, see Rupert Smith, *The Utility of Force: The Art of War in the Modern World* (New York: Vintage, 2008); Richard N. Haass, *War of Necessity, War of Choice* (New York: Simon & Schuster, 2009); and Loch K. Johnson, *The Threat on the Horizon: An Inside Account of America's Search for Security After the Cold War* (Oxford: Oxford University Press, 2011).

27. For substantive rejections of the false dichotomy of war and peace, see Rosa Brooks, "There's No Such Thing as Peacetime," *Foreign Policy* (March 13, 2015); Antonia Chayes, *Borderless Wars: Civil Military Disorder and Legal Uncertainty* (Cambridge: Cambridge University Press, 2015); Janine Davidson, *Lifting the Fog of Peace: How Americans Learned to Fight Modern War* (Ann Arbor: University of Michigan Press, 2010); and Charles T. Cleveland, *The American Way of Irregular War: An Analytical Memoir*, with Daniel Egel (Santa Monica: RAND Corporation, 2020). For a discussion of the quick fix, see George Withers, "The Special Operations Command: Our Clandestine International Quick-Fixers?," *WOLA Commentary* (June 29, 2012). For the uses of U.S. Special Operations Forces after the first decade of the 9/11 wars, see Joseph L. Votel, Charles T. Cleveland, Charles T. Connett, and Will Irwin, "Unconventional Warfare in the Gray Zone," *Joint Forces Quarterly* 80 (First Quarter 2016): 101–9; Paul R. Pillar, "Special Forces," *New York Times* (October 11, 2013); and Matthew

Rosenberg, "U.S. Is Escalating a Secretive War in Afghanistan," *New York Times* (February 12, 2015).

28. U.S. Secretary of Defense Robert M. Gates, "Remarks at the United States Military Academy" (West Point, February 25, 2011).

29. The public release clearance of this publication by the Department of Defense does not imply Department of Defense endorsement or factual accuracy of the material. The views expressed in this publication are those of the author and do not necessarily reflect the official policy and position of the Department of Defense or the U.S. government.

ACKNOWLEDGMENTS

A lot is missing from this book—deliberately.

This is not the place to find out who first shot bin Laden or how that night ended in the Benghazi annex. This narrative does not peel apart the stories of *American Sniper* or *Lone Survivor.* It is neither an airbrush nor a whitewash. This book is not an exposé.

Instead, this book is intended for readers who seek a deeper understanding of U.S. Special Operations and the forces at the center of America's 21st-century wars. Violence on behalf of the nation by sacred trust, sums up one military leader. Rings of sorrow, paraphrases another. While fighting matters evoke raw sentiment—and rightly so—the focus here is on the everyday reality of national security, not the extremes.

I set out—and received authorization—to conduct this research across the interagency. Throughout, I adhere strictly to the classifications of national security and to the core values of academia to respect confidential sources and sensitive information. Upon completion, this book was reviewed in its entirety by the U.S. Department of Defense, Office of Prepublication and Security Review, and by other governmental agencies.

I wish to express gratitude to Yale University and Columbia University for a deep culture of interdisciplinary scholarship, and to Annapolis and West Point for a strong community of leaders. I am deeply appreciative of the University of Chicago, Columbia University, Harvard University, and Yale University for funding this work. I offer many thanks to Yale University Press for being a rigorous and exceptional publisher at every stage of this project.

INDEX

Abbottabad: bin Laden in, 131–32; compound in, 128–31, 132–33, 134, 135; earthquake in, 133–34; Iqbal in, 129–31; U.S. awareness of, 128–31. *See also* bin Laden raid

ACCMs (Alternate Compensatory Control Measures), 78

Adams, John, 102

Afghanistan: bin Laden family in, 261–62n21; bin Laden in, 136, 138–41; bin Laden manhunt in, 140–41; CENTCOM's mission in, 102–3; COP Tangi, 167–71, 172, 180, 185; counterinsurgency efforts in, 113, 114; duration of operations in, 92, 93, 173; Farah airstrike, 179; FOB Shank, 171; focus on, 114; genocide in, 174–76, 275–76n9; hostages in, 11, 16–18, 219n18; Islamic revolutionary action in, 16–18; Kabul, 168, 169; local governance, 274–75n6; mujahideen, 136, 174, 176; objectives in, 170, 171–72; opposition to U.S. forces in, 179–80; proxy fights in, 18 (*see also* Cold War); raids in, 179–80; refugees from, 175; skepticism about objectives in, 172–73; socioeconomic operations in, 102–3; Soviet occupation of, 10, 131, 136, 174–76, 275–76n9; surviving in, 169; Tangi Valley, 166, 170; U.S. forces in, 28, 171, 180–84; war on terror and, 61, 200, 203. *See also* Extortion 17; Taliban

Agha, Gul, 179

Ahmed, Abrar, 119, 122, 126, 129, 132, 133

Ahmed, Bushra, 119, 122, 127, 129

Ahmed, Ibrahim, 119, 122, 126, 127, 128, 129

Ahmed, Maryam, 119, 121, 122, 125, 127, 129

Aidid, Mohamed Farrah, 41, 42–43, 44, 46, 47, 48, 49, 52. *See also* Operation Gothic Serpent; Somalia

Alaskan Command, 7, 8. *See also* combatant commands

al-Baghdadi, Abu Bakr, 188–89, 190, 191. *See also* Da'esh

al-Baghdadi, Abu Omar, 104

al-Bashir, Omar, 137

Algiers Accords, 26

al-Jazeera, 58, 128

Allen, John R., 184

al-Libi, Abu Faraj, 132

al-Masri, Abu Ayyub, 104

al-Muhandis, Abu Mahdi, 192

al-Qaeda: attacks on U.S. embassies in Kenya and Tanzania, 58, 59; bin Laden's death and, 165; intelligence community's assessment of, 239n42; leaders of, 104; objective of, 57; resources of, 141; support of Aidid's forces, 48–49; U.N. on, 199. *See also* bin Laden, Usama

al-Sadr, Muqtada, 113

Alternate Compensatory Control Measures (ACCMs), 78

al Uteybi, Juhayman, 22, 23

ammunition, 72–73

Annual Threat Assessment, 33–34

Article V, 198

Aspen Institute, 146–47, 153, 266n2

Aspin, Les, 47, 53

Athar, Sohaib (@ReallyVirtual), 117–20, 123, 127

Atlantic Command, 7. *See also* combatant commands

Atlantic Council, 143

Authorization for the Use of Military Force, 60, 208, 240n45

Awale, Abdi Hasan, 45–46

Azad, Umaidullah, 169

Baqizoi, Abdul Kayum, 185

Bazargan, Mehdi, 19

Bennett, Gina M., 58, 115, 257n1

Biden, Joe, 143

bin Laden, Amal, 119, 121, 122, 123, 125, 126, 133

bin Laden, Hamza, 123, 124, 125, 257–58n4, 258n5

bin Laden, Khairiah, 119, 123, 125, 127, 130, 258n5

bin Laden, Khalid, 122, 126

bin Laden, Najwa, 135, 258n5

bin Laden, Omar, 138–39, 140

bin Laden, Sa'ad, 139

bin Laden, Siham, 119, 127, 133, 258n5

bin Laden, Sumayya, 122

bin Laden, Usama, 131; in Afghanistan, 136, 138–41; death of (*see* bin Laden raid); exile from Saudi Arabia, 137; fading focus on, 114; on foreign tactics, 23; goals of, 57–59; hunt for (*see* bin Laden manhunt); indictment against, 59; investigations pertaining to, 59; lessons from Somalia, 57, 238n39; media and, 128, 238n39, 261n19; operation against, 29 (*see also* bin Laden manhunt; bin Laden raid); outlook of, 139–40; resources of, 141; response to call for his capture/kill, 128; spelling of name, 220–21n27; in Sudan, 137–38; support of Afghans, 131–32; surveillance of, 138; Taliban and, 140; turn to jihad, 136; U.N. on, 199; U.S. National Security community's perspective on, 59. *See also* al-Qaeda

bin Laden compound, 128–31, 132–33, 134, 135

bin Laden family: in Afghanistan, 261–62n21; construction projects in Mecca, 23; in detention in Iran, 125; in hiding, 124–25, 133, 258n5, 261–62n21; Iran and, 125

bin Laden manhunt, 105, 124–25; in Afghanistan, 140–41; after 9/11, 59; downgrading of, 134–35; Iqbal's role in, 129–31; Pakistan blamed for delays in, 128; surveillance during, 128–31; Waugh and, 58

bin Laden raid, 115–17, 187; aftermath of, 125–27; anonymity of participants, 267n5; appraisal of, 164–65; books about, 268–69n8 (see also *No Easy Day* [Owen]);

command arrangements for, 264n31; decision to launch, 148; description of, 116–23; discussion of, 269n9; effects of, 164–65; film about, 144, 265n33; McRaven's interview about, 147–53, 266nn3, 266nn4, 267n5; media coverage of, 187; movie about, 144–45; observation of, 263n28; participants in, 144–45, 149–50, 151–52, 153–54; planning of, 131; in public eye, 144–45, 147; reaction to, 142–44; tweets about (*see* Athar, Sohaib [@ReallyVirtual])

Black, Cofer, 61

Black Hawk Down, 35, 54, 158. *See also* Operation Gothic Serpent; Somalia

Blitzer, Wolf, 147–53

Bowden, Mark, 49, 157, 157–58, 221n28, 222n29, 230–31n23, 234nn28, 234nn30, 259n10, 260n14, 269n8, 270n15

Boykin, William G., 213n2, 268n7

Brown, Bryan "Doug," 66, 71, 241–42n50, 245n8

Brzezinski, Zbigniew, 9

budget, SOF's, 71–72, 75–76

Bush, George H. W., 38

Bush, George W., v, 39, 60; formal declaration of war on terror, 60; on hunt for bin Laden, 105; mobilization effort after 9/11, 197, 280n4; on SOF, 202; visit to

Bush, George W. (*continued*)
    MacDill, 202, 285–86n14,
    286n15; on war on terror, 199,
    281n7

Caliphate, 189. *See also* Da'esh
Cambodia, 10, 176
Cameroon, in war on terror, 203
capability building, 102. *See also*
    counterinsurgency
capture/kill operations, 64, 95, 96.
    See also bin Laden manhunt; bin
    Laden raid; manhunts; raids
Caribbean Command, 7. *See also*
    combatant commands
Carter, Jimmy, 9, 12, 24, 25, 26,
    218–19n16
Castor, Kathy, 101
CENTCOM (Central Command).
    See combatant commands;
    MacDill Air Force Base
Central Intelligence Agency (CIA),
    14, 20, 24, 54, 58, 59, 61, 86,
    131, 142, 144, 160, 162
Chad, in war on terror, 203
Cheney, Dick, 105
China, 10, 34, 227n5
CIA (Central Intelligence Agency),
    14, 20, 24, 54, 58, 59, 61, 86,
    131, 142, 144, 160, 162
citizenship, of SOF personnel, 87–90
Clinton, Hillary, 128
Cold War, 10, 216n10; Article V
    and, 198; focus of, 32; proxy
    fights, 18, 32, 136; Soviet

occupation of Afghanistan, 10,
    131, 136, 174–76, 275–76n9;
    special operations in, 85; war
    plans in, 32. *See also* Soviet Union
combatant commands, 2; big-
    picture issues, 32; Bush on,
    284–85n14; characteristics of
    grey wars, 29; culture of, 28, 29;
    decision-making processes, 81;
    establishment of, 213n2, 218n15;
    geographic scope of, 88; priorities
    of, 28, 32–33; responsibilities of,
    6; revised plan for, 9; shift to,
    7–9; strategic outlook of, 32–33.
    See also National Security, U.S.
commercial actors, willingness to
    work with military, 73–75
conventional forces/warfare. *See*
    Forces, General Purpose
Council on Foreign Relations, 2
counterinsurgency, 85, 103; in
    Afghanistan, 113, 114; conflict
    in, 105–6; inclusion in, 103; in
    Iraq, 104, 111–12, 114; personal
    accounts of, 107–11; pillars of,
    101; principles of, 103; skeptics
    of, 103–4; social constructivist
    model of, 96; strategies of, 103–
    4; success in, 113–14; whole-of-
    government approach to, 112
counterinsurgency manual, 91–92,
    93
counterproliferation, 85
counterterrorism, 2, 85; approach-
    es to, 94–96; change in meaning,

62; focus on, 35; investment in, 217–18n14; need for capabilities in, 223n31; personnel for, 108; as priority, 9, 61, 62; U.S. investments in, 27; as war, 62. *See also* war on terror

counterterrorism command: designation of, 12. *See also* combatant commands

Crocker, Ryan, 192

Cronkite, Walter, 21, 26

Da'esh, 188–92, 204, 206

debt, 34, 227n5

decision-making processes, 81

Decker, George, 55

Defense Acquisition University, 73

defense corporations, 74–75

Defense Intelligence Agency, 34

Dempsey, Martin E., 34, 227n5

Department of Defense, U.S. (DoD): counterterrorism as priority in, 62; objections to *NED*, 160–63; reorganization of, 216n8; SOF in, 61–62

deployments, 166, 170–71, 208–9. *See also* personnel, SOF

direct approach/action, 94, 224n1. *See also* capture/kill operations

director of national intelligence, 34

disinformation, during Cold War, 85

Doctors Without Borders, 174

DoD (Department of Defense, U.S.). *See* Department of Defense, U.S. (DoD)

Donovan, William J., 31, 86

drones, 67, 69, 179

Dubs, Spike, 16, 27, 219n18

Dunford, Joseph F., Jr., 34, 227n5

Dutton, 154–56, 161

Eisenhower, Dwight D., 7, 74, 216n8

equipment, SOF's, 66–73, 75–76

European Command, 7. *See also* combatant commands

Evolution of a Revolt, The (Lawrence), 91

Extortion 17, 167, 181–84, 185–88; Taliban response to, 277n19. *See also* Afghanistan

Farah airstrike, 179

Far East Command, 7. *See also* combatant commands

Federal Acquisition Regulation, 73

fighters. *See* personnel, SOF

Flatin, Bruce A., 219n18

Forces, General Purpose, 49, 54–56, 61, 82, 84, 85, 112–13, 180, 288n25

Ford, Gerald, 8

Foucault, Michel, 13

Franks, Tommy, 200

Gates, Robert M., 1, 54, 110, 211, 213n1

General Purpose Forces, 49, 54–56, 61, 82, 84, 85, 112–13, 180, 288n25

genocide, in Afghanistan, 174–76

Global War on Terror. *See* war on terror

guerrilla principles, 91

Habr Gidr, 44

Hakimi, Ehssabullah, 177

Hempstone, Smith, 39–40

Hoar, Joseph P., 47

hostage-rescue capabilities, need for, 11–12

hostages: in Afghanistan, 11, 16–18, 27, 219n18; high-profile, 27; hostage-rescue capabilities, 217–18n14, 223n31; in Iran, 11, 14, 16, 20, 21, 23, 24–26, 35, 54, 167, 188, 223n31; in Mecca, 21–22, 23, 27, 135

Howe, Jonathan T., 43, 44, 47

ideologically-driven violence, 87, 102, 112

immigrants, in military, 87–90

inclusion, in counterinsurgency, 94, 103. *See also* Lawrence, T. E.

Independent (newspaper), 128

indirect approach/action, 95–96, 97

industrial power centers, 32

information, security of, 78–79

information operations, 112. *See also* counterinsurgency

insurgency, 92. *See also* counterinsurgency

Inter-Services Intelligence (ISI), 126

Iqbal, Saeed, 129–31

Iran: Afghan refugees in, 175; bin Laden family detained in, 124–25; government crackdowns in, 12–14; hostages in, 11, 14, 16, 20, 21, 23, 24–26, 35, 54, 167, 188, 223n31; Islamic revolutionary action in, 15–16; Khomeini in, 15, 21, 22, 27; lack of emphasis on, 103; shah, 12–15, 19–20, 21, 219n16, 220n20; threats from, 210; U.S. embassy in, 14, 18–19, 219–20n20; U.S. stance on, 12–13, 14, 19–20, 218–19n16, 220n20

Iraq: CENTCOM's mission in, 102–3; conventional military operations in, 113; counterinsurgency efforts in, 104, 111–12; duration of operations in, 93; in fight against Da'esh, 204; focus on, 114; socioeconomic operations in, 102–3; in war on terror, 203. *See also* Da'esh

Ishaqzai, Amanullah, 177

ISI (Inter-Services Intelligence), 126

ISIL. *See* Da'esh

ISIS. *See* Da'esh

Islamic Emirate of Afghanistan, 176. *See also* Taliban

Islamic revolutions, 12, 15–18, 135. *See also* Iran

Islamic State. *See* Da'esh

Ismatullah (village elder), 173

jihad, bin Laden's turn to, 136

jihadists, effect of bin Laden's death on, 165

Johnson, Jeh, 160, 241n49

Johnson, Lyndon B., 8, 102, 216n10

Joint Chiefs of Staff, 34

Joint Operations Center (JOC), 76–79. *See also* MacDill Air Force Base

Joint Special Operations Command (JSOC), 144, 265n32. *See also* combatant commands; counter-terrorism command

Kakar, Hassan, 174, 175

Karzai, Hamid, 180

Kennedy, John, 8, 216n9

Kenya, attacks on U.S. embassies in, 58, 59

Khan, Shamraiz, 130

Khashai, Ali Ahmad, 173

Khomeini, Grand Ayatollah Ruhollah, 15, 21, 22, 27

Kissinger, Henry, 9, 10

Kuwait, 196

Laingen, L. Bruce, 219n20

Laos, 176

Lawrence, T. E., 90–92, 93–94

Lehrer, Jim, 144

Libya, 203, 210

MacDill Air Force Base, 12, 101; Afghan operations overseen at, 200; blank spaces at, 207; Bush's visit to, 285–86n14, 286n15; Coalition Village, 196–97, 201–6, 280n5, 285n14, 286n15 (*see also* war on terror); construction of CENTCOM facilities, 100; descriptions of, 1–6, 66–71, 99–100; infrastructure projects, 195–96; Joint Operations Center, 76–79; mission of, 205; purpose of, 6; SOCCENT, 196

Major Force Program 11 (MFP-11), 72

Mali, in war on terror, 203

manhunts: for al-Baghdadi, 191; avoidance of SOF for, 53–56; for Persons Indicted for War Crimes, 56. *See also* Aidid, Mohamed Farrah; bin Laden manhunt

Mattis, James N., 91, 92, 206, 243n1

MAVNI (Military Accessions Vital to the National Interest), 87–90

McChrystal, Stanley A., v, 110–11

McIlvaine, Stevenson, 40, 228n10

McKenzie, Jr., Kenneth F., 191

McNamara, Robert, 8

McRaven, William H., 144, 147–53, 266nn3, 266nn4, 267n5, 288n24

Mecca, hostages in, 21–22, 23, 27, 135

Médecins sans Frontières, 174

MFP-11 (Major Force Program 11), 72

military, U.S.: immigrants in, 87–90; shifts in priorities, 35; shift to combatant commands, 7–9 (*see also* combatant commands)

Military Accessions Vital to the National Interest (MAVNI), 87–90

military-industrial complex, 73–75

Mogadishu, Somalia. *See* Operation Gothic Serpent; Somalia

Mohammad, Nazar, 125

Mojatba, Gholam, 172

Mujahid, Zabiullah, 184

mujahideen, 136, 174, 176. *See also* Afghanistan

Mullen, Mike, 34, 227n5

Musharraf, Pervez, 132

mycotoxins, 176, 275–76n9

National Command Authority, 85

National Defense Appropriations Act, 53

National Security, U.S.: counterinsurgency operations and, 103, 104; counterterrorism as priority in, 62; SOF and, 210–11; threats to, 33–35, 210, 227n5. *See also* combatant commands

National Security Act of 1947, 7

NATO, 198, 206, 280n4

Navy SEALs, 143, 148–49, 153, 181–84, 269; discussion of operations by, 269n9 (see also *No Easy Day* [Owen]); establishment of, 216n9. *See also* bin Laden raid; personnel, SOF

NED (Owen). See *No Easy Day* (Owen)

Niger, in war on terror, 203

Nigeria, in war on terror, 203

Night Stalkers, 50, 120

9/11: changes after, 60; global response to, 197–99, 281n7; initial response to, 60–61; military planning and, 35; mobilization effort after, 197, 280n4; plans for, 140

9/11 wars. *See* war on terror

No Easy Day (Owen), 154–64; legal dispute over, 160–63, 271–72n21; objections to, 160–63; reaction to, 155, 270nn11, 270nn16; sales of, 162. *See also* bin Laden raid

No Hero: Evolution of a SEAL (Owen), 164

Noori, Habibullah, 177

North American Aerospace Defense Command (NORAD), 10–11. *See also* combatant commands

Northeast Command, 7. *See also* combatant commands

North Korea, threats from, 210

nuclear alert system, 10–11

nuclear command, 10. *See also* combatant commands

Oakley, Robert B., 46, 52
Obama, Barack, v; death of bin Laden and, 115, 142; at MacDill, 203, 204–5
Office of Strategic Services (OSS), 31, 86
Olson, Eric, 30, 35, 63, 87, 88, 89, 91, 94, 97, 224n1, 288n24
O'Neill, Robert, 268–69n8
Operation Desert Storm, 56–57
Operation Eagle Assist, 198
Operation Eagle Claw, 24–26, 35, 54, 167, 188, 223n31
Operation Gothic Serpent, 35, 49–52, 54, 167, 188
operations: books about, 267–68n7 (see also *No Easy Day* [Owen]); discussion of by participants, 269n9; failed, 26, 167, 187–88 (*see also* Extortion 17; Operation Eagle Claw; Operation Gothic Serpent); films about, 265n33. *See also* raids
operators. *See* personnel, SOF
OSS (Office of Strategic Services), 31, 86
overwhelming force, doctrine of, 94
Owen, Mark, 157–64, 271–72n21. *See also* bin Laden raid

Pacific Command, 7, 8. *See also* combatant commands

Pahlavi, Shah Mohammad Reza, 12–15, 19–20, 21, 219n16, 220n20
Pakistan: Afghanistan and, 136–37; Afghan refugees in, 175; attack on U.S. embassy in, 22–23; blamed for delays in bin Laden manhunt, 128; CENTCOM's mission in, 102–3; lack of emphasis on, 103; reaction to bin Laden raid, 126–27. *See also* Abbottabad; bin Laden compound; bin Laden raid
Panetta, Leon, 144
Patek, Umar, 130
Patterson, Robert P., 7
peace, 193, 241n49
Persian Gulf region, 9. *See also individual countries*
Persian Gulf War, 56–57, 136
personnel, SOF, 79–84, 107; anonymity of raid participants, 149–50, 151–52, 153–54, 267n5; deployments of, 166, 170–71, 208–9; descriptions of, 84–85; discussion of operations by, 269n9; emulation of Lawrence, 90–92; expectations of, 83–84; intersection with equipment, 86; language/cultural skills of, 87–90; number of, 83; personal accounts of counterinsurgency, 107–11; problems of, 150–51; selection of, 82; service centrality and, 82. *See also* Navy SEALs

Persons Indicted for War Crimes (PIFWCs), 56

Petraeus, David, 91, 92, 101, 252n1; in Abbottabad, 129; office of, 111; perception of, 108–9; on whole-of-government approach, 112

Powell, Colin, 47, 53

Project Lawrence, 90

public affairs campaigns, 112. *See also* counterinsurgency

Pybus, Sean, 269n9

Qatar, 196

Rahim, Mohammad, 177–78

raids: in Afghanistan, 179–80; al-Baghdadi's death in, 191; anonymity of participants, 149–50, 151–52, 153–54, 267n5; avoidance of SOF for, 53–56; books about, 267–68n7 (see also *No Easy Day* [Owen]); discussion of by participants, 269n9; failed, 26, 167, 187–88 (*see also* Extortion 17; Operation Eagle Claw; Operation Gothic Serpent); overreliance on, 63–64; uncertainty in, 54; in war on terror, 62–63, 208–9. *See also* bin Laden raid; capture/kill operations

Reagan, Ronald, 26, 218n16

@ReallyVirtual (Sohaib Athar), 117–20, 123, 127

refugees: Afghan, 175; fleeing fight against Da'esh, 204

remotely piloted vehicle. *See* drones

Richburg, Keith B., 36, 37, 45, 46

Rove, Karl, 163

Rumsfeld, Donald, 8–9, 60

Russia, 34, 210, 227n5. *See also* Soviet Union

SAP (Special Access Program), 78, 247n14

Saudi Arabia: Afghanistan and, 136; bin Laden's exile from, 137; hostages in Mecca, 21–22, 23, 27

Saxton, Jim, 72

Schlesinger, James, 8

security. *See* National Security, U.S.

Sensitive Compartmented Information Facility (SCIF), 77

September 11, 2001. *See* 9/11; war on terror

service operators. *See* personnel, SOF

Seven Pillars of Wisdom (Lawrence), 91–92

75th Ranger Regiment, 181. *See also* Extortion 17

Shultz, George, 176, 222n31, 276n9

socioeconomic operations, 102–3. *See also* counterinsurgency

SOCOM (Special Operations Command). *See* combatant commands; counterterrorism; MacDill Air Force Base

Soleimani, Qasem, 191–92
Somalia, 35–53; Abdi House
    assault, 45–46; al-Qaeda's sup-
    port of Aidid's forces, 48–49;
    American media in, 38–39; con-
    ditions in, 228–29n10, 229n12;
    death of journalists in, 45–46;
    exit strategy in, 53; in media,
    36–38; miscasting of mission,
    45–46; Operation Gothic
    Serpent, 49–52; reversal of U.S.
    policy in, 52–53; targeting of
    U.S. helicopters, 47–49; United
    Nations in, 40–45; U.S. forces in,
    38, 39–40, 42, 43–45; in war on
    terror, 203. See also Aidid,
    Mohamed Farrah; Operation
    Gothic Serpent
Southern Command, 8. See also
    combatant commands
Soviet Union, 34; in Afghanistan,
    10, 131, 136, 174–76, 275–76n9;
    Article V and, 198; readiness for
    confrontation with, 32. See also
    Cold War; Russia
Special Access Program (SAP), 78,
    247n14
Special Operations Command
    (SOCOM). See combatant com-
    mands; counterterrorism;
    MacDill Air Force Base
Sri Lanka, mass attacks in, 190
Stirrup, G. E., 201
Strategic Air Command, 7. See also
    combatant commands

Sudan, bin Laden in, 137–38
Sude, Barbara, 59
Swift, Elizabeth Ann, 220n20
Syria: in fight against Da'esh, 204;
    lack of emphasis on, 103; in war
    on terror, 203. See also Da'esh

Tahir, Qari, 181. See also Extortion
    17
Taliban, 113; bin Laden and, 140;
    elites targeted by, 177–79; oppo-
    sition to, 177–79; rise of, 176;
    security provided by, 176–77;
    takedown of COP Tangi, 185;
    U.N. on, 199. See also
    Afghanistan; Extortion 17
Tanzania, attacks on U.S. embas-
    sies in, 58, 59
technology, SOF's, 66–73, 75–76
Tehran. See Iran
Tenet, George J., 60, 239n42
terrorism, 188. See also
    counterterrorism; Da'esh; war
    on terror
Thomas, Tony, v, 190, 288n24
threat-based logic, 110
threats to national security, 33–35,
    210, 227n5
Toronto Star, 48
trichothecene toxin, 176
Truman, Harry S., 7

Ukraine, 210
United Nations: response to 9/11,
    198, 199; in Somalia, 40–45

Vickers, Mike, 61
Vietnam, 10
Vietnam War, 85, 102
Voice of America, 22
Votel, Joseph L., v, 288n24

Wall Street Journal, The (newspaper), 146, 266n1
Wardak, Abdullah, 172, 173
Wardak, Roshanak, 166, 178–79
warfare, conventional, 49, 54–56, 61, 82, 84, 85, 112–13, 180, 288n25
warfare, unconventional, 2, 6, 8, 56, 61, 85, 91, 210
war on terror, 207; Afghanistan in, 200; as American endeavor, 206; bin Laden's death as end of, 164; briefings on, 2 (*see also* MacDill Air Force Base); broadened mission of, 209; calls for end of, 209; as central to U.S. military's mission, 209; Coalition Village, 196–97, 201–6, 280n5, 285n14, 286n15; countries in, 199, 201, 281n7; deployments in, 208–9; end of, 164, 165; enemy in, 165; formal declaration of, 60; geographic focus of, 203; inside work, 208; local

partners in, 203; MacDill and, 200; military priorities and, 35; raids in, 62–63, 208–9; SOF's focus on, 60–62; timelines and durations of, 92–93; uncertainty of, 207. *See also* counterterrorism
War Powers Resolution of 1973, 240n45
Washington Post (newspaper): on combatant commands, 6; on Somalia, 35–38
waste, classified, 77–78
Watson, Paul, 48, 51
Waugh, Billy, 58
White, Mary Jo, 59
White House Correspondents' Dinner, 141–42
World Islamic Front, 57, 221n27, 239n40
World War II, special operations in, 85

Yemen, 103, 203
Young, Bill, 101

Zero Dark Thirty (film), 144, 265n33
zero defect, 107
Zinni, Anthony, 53